The Tory Islanders

The Tory Islanders

A people of the Celtic fringe

ROBIN FOX

Professor of Anthropology
Rutgers University

CAMBRIDGE UNIVERSITY PRESS

CAMBRIDGE

LONDON   NEW YORK   MELBOURNE

Published by the Syndics of the Cambridge University Press
The Pitt Building, Trumpington Street, Cambridge CB2 1RP
Bentley House, 200 Euston Road, London NW1 2DB
32 East 57th Street, New York, NY 10022, USA
296 Beaconsfield Parade, Middle Park, Melbourne 3206, Australia

© Cambridge University Press 1978

First published 1978

Printed in the United States of America
Typeset by Lexigraphics, Inc., New York, NY
Printed and bound by Vail-Ballou Press, Inc., Binghamton, NY
Library of Congress Cataloging in Publication Data
Fox, Robin, 1934–
The Tory Islanders.
Bibliography: p.
1. Tory Island, Ire.–Social life and customs.
2. Ethnology–Ireland–Tory Island.   I.   Title.
DA990.T6F69   301.29′416′93   77–83992
ISBN 0 521 21870 5 in hard covers
ISBN 0 521 29298 0 as a paperback

Do mhuintir an oileáin

Contents

Preface

I do not attempt, in this book, a complete ethnographic account of Tory Island. What I have done is to take several features of the social order – genealogy, kinship, inheritance of land, recruitment of boat crews, marriage and household – and tried to analyze their internal structures, and their relationships to each other. There is another volume that could be added, for example, on beliefs, ideas, values, attitudes, folklore, language, ethnoscience, etc. In a sense that is perhaps a little old-fashioned now in anthropology, I have confined myself to "social structure" rather than to "culture." There is still another volume that could have been written on "history and legend." I have confined this to the first chapter, and what I have attempted there is more a kind of evocation than an analysis: It is dependent on the scholarship, but is not itself scholarly. To have ignored its history however, would have been to lose much of the spirit of the place. There is danger enough of losing this in the dry business of analysis anyway, so I have let it stand by way of introduction.

Again, although various themes concerning the ecology, economy, and material culture of the island run, inevitably, through these pages, they are not the point of departure. They too require their own study.

The reader will find, however, that although the analysis is avowedly "anthropological," in that only an anthropologist would have written it this way, it is also redolent of recent history; that is, the history of the last 200 years. This is not a result of any principle or deliberate theoretical stance on my part. Anthropologists are usually spared the embarrassment of dealing with the dimension of absolute time because their subjects have no written history of their own and not much written about them. For Tory, however, at least as far as land is concerned, records do exist. One is therefore led to history simply because it is there. For me, and I hope for the reader, part of the sheer enjoyment of this analysis lies in the reconciling of "anthropological" and "historical" materials and methods, in a way that illustrates their mutually supportive roles.

But this applies not only to materials and methods; it applies also to interpretation. Many things about Tory social structure appear peculiar until viewed historically, and, as I hope to demonstrate, much of the history is illuminated when looked at anthropologically. Not only historians, but in particular social geographers – who often cover identical ground to mine – should find that this confluence of methods and interpretations is useful to them. Students of peasant society, be they historically, ecologically, anthropologically, or sociologically minded, should find here a little case history in method, as well as a collection of absorbing facts about a society that is, although unique, yet uniquely representative.

For, in a strange sense, Tory is semifossilized history. It is not that Tory has not changed – indeed change is the theme of the book – but that external pressures (largely the English) have impinged relatively less on this island than on the rest of Ireland. Even the Irish themselves are somewhat coy about Tory (for reasons that will become apparent), and hustle aspiring anthropologists off to the Aran Islands or the well-trodden turf of County Clare if they get half a chance. The sheer inaccessibility of the place has meant that patterns almost gone from Ireland – or from peasant Europe generally – survive. Patterns of inheritance, kinship, marriage, belief, landholding, classification, etc., have lingered on here. Some drastic intrusions occurred and I note them duly in their place. But Tory was able to ride them out, and either adapt or ignore in ways that the mainland Irish could not ignore plantations and legislation, or that the peasants of Europe could not sidestep easily the impact of the Napoleonic Code. (For example, the Code's effect on something so intimate to the community as the sharp rise in incidence of cousin marriages following the abolition of primogeniture. See W. F. Bodmer and L. L. Cavalli-Sforza, *Genetics, Evolution and Man;* San Francisco: Freeman, 1976, pp. 364–6).

Despite the changes, in some sense we can read Tory back into history better than most other places, because a less contaminated version exists there. Thus, while not hoping to settle the issue, I have tried to show how the Tory material can help us to understand the functioning of the ancient "rundale" system of landholding: joint holding by groups of kin on the open-field system. Also, patterns of inheritance that are clearly prefamine persist on Tory – particularly the partible inheritance of land and the consequent lack of dowries – because neither land acts nor landlords totally destroyed them, despite some curious inroads.

Here lies, I think, this book's contribution to sheer ethnography (the description of the society and culture of particular peoples). This has three aspects: the purely Irish, the European, and the universal. (To European one might add "Indo-European" – but here we go beyond my amateur competence.) In each case, it enables us to ask crucial questions about ready generalizations that have been made. Again, these questions are only hinted at here, largely for the sake of students and general readers, because my aim has been an internal description, not a comparative analysis. The interested specialists will spot them for themselves, and perhaps find some I have overlooked.

At the purely Irish level, the Tory example corrects the one-sided view of "the Irish" that comes from having as the prototype the relatively prosperous farmers of County Clare. Any ethnographer of Ireland is fortunate in having as a standard reference the brilliant *Family and Community in Ireland,* by C. M. Arensberg and S. T. Kimball, a book that has justifiably joined the ranks of the classics of functional anthropology. (First edition, Cambridge, Mass.: Harvard University Press, 1940. Second edition, with additional material, 1968.) My analysis runs as an almost conscious counterpoint to theirs. Although at first glance Tory presents certain decidedly "Irish" themes, it offers its own seemingly idiosyncratic solutions. But, I suspect, these solutions were much more common in many parts of Ireland – particularly the north – before the famine and the land acts of the late nineteenth century. What Arensberg and Kimball – and later Robert Creswell in his excellent ecological study, again of County Clare – describe, can almost be seen as consequences of these. *(Une Communauté Rurale de l'Irlande;* Paris: Institut d'Ethnologie, Musée de l'Homme, 1969.) I am cautious here, because North–South differences did precede the famine in any case, but were accentuated after it.

Thus Tory represents variations on pan-Irish themes – late marriage and nonmarriage, land fragmentation, migration, etc. – that are different because of its isolation and island ecology. But it also represents the last gasp of a tradition that is different altogether from that of County Clare: the complex surrounding the open-field and common-ownership traditions – the ancient alternatives to the single-family farm.

Of late, more studies in other parts of Ireland have helped redress the balance (see the excellent review by Elliott Leyton, "Studies in Irish Social Organization: The State of the Art," Unpublished Ms., Memorial Univ., Newfoundland), but so far no one has come up with quite the same depth of material as exists on Tory – the contrasts otherwise tend to be minimal. I was simply lucky in my choice, I suppose.

This brings us to the European relevance, because the two alternatives I have spoken of pervade the peasant land-tenure systems of that continent, especially in Scandinavia, Italy, France, and Spain – together with the equally ancient patriarchal joint-family traditions of the Slavs,

Greeks, and Teutons, which take us back to our Indo-European roots. We understand well enough both the single-family farm system with its stress on primogeniture and the problem of younger sons and dowried daughters, and that of the joint family with its stress on impartible inheritance and the males as a corporation. We have understood their importance since Sir Henry Maine, and Greece and Yugoslavia still provide us with examples of the joint-family pattern, with its male corporate group and again the dowried daughters. But the "common ownership" by the village cluster is less well understood for the simple reason that it was usually the solution of the very lowest peasantry and therefore got the least recognition from the historians and chroniclers.

Its great problem was land fragmentation. What the Tory example shows is how such a system could work to minimize such a problem, even within a subsistence framework. Part of the secret lies in the sea; the mixed economy making accommodations possible that were not open to Alpine peasants, for example. But it lies also in the dynamics of the Tory inheritance and ownership system itself. In any case, "peasantologists" of the European persuasion will find much to ponder here, especially that subtype of Atlantic-fringe "crofter" communities. The best general study of comparative European land tenure that I know is *Family and Inheritance,* edited by Jack Goody, Joan Thirsk, and E. P. Thompson (New York: Cambridge University Press, 1976), but, like many others, this deals mostly with differing legal and customary rules; we have little idea how, historically, these systems worked out "on the ground."

The universal aspects of this contribution are primarily anthropological: That is, they pertain to problems in anthropological theory and information that cross national, continental, and cultural boundaries. Tory becomes, for example, an addition to the literature on cognatic kinship systems, which is one reason I have presented the genealogies in such detail, and shown how they articulate with the mode of reckoning kin and the system of personal names. In the aftermath of anthropology's initial love affair with unilineal descent groups, we are gradually learning to understand that cognatic systems are not some kind of deficient alternative, but quite respectable and worthy of analysis in their own right. Tory can only increase our respect and add, I hope not insignificantly, to the analysis. The system of land tenure and the mechanisms of inheritance that are the centerpiece of the book, and that themselves articulate with the genealogical structure, are not just of European interest, but serve to illustrate how a nonunilineal system can handle these issues. In particular, the household system on Tory can add sophistication to the analysis of domestic cycles – source of a continuing set of problems in social anthropology ever since the idea of static "rules of residence" was abandoned. The tracks taken by the Tory households are perhaps unique, but the principle of the cycle is firmly established. Finally, and perhaps most startling, is the Tory pattern of separate residence for husband and wife – once predominant and even now prominent. As I note in the text, this has been found in such places as West Africa and Southwest India, and has given rise to various theories linking it to matrilineal descent or polyandry. That it occurs, in the absence of either, as part of the Tory domestic cycle raises the Tory case to the level of a crucial experiment in theory. It also will give pause to theorists of the "nuclear family," and should interest sociologists of this phenomenon, at once so seemingly solid and so infuriatingly elusive.

Also, at the universal level, we can look at Tory as an island ecosystem and a beautiful example of adaptive processes over time. The rhythm of "boats and land" and the shifting emphasis between the two, with the changes resulting from technology and migration, make this a case study of a declining island population with a history of carefully balanced adaptive strategies.

At the very highest universal level, Tory represents a hymn to the human spirit – and again I hope this is not lost in the prosaic detail of the analysis. Humanity consists here not only in heroism – although there is that – but in many little things that collectively make a viable way of life in the teeth of the odds. And this is how it has been for 99 percent of human existence, for 99 percent of human beings. Tory survives: no small thing given the battering it has taken from man and nature. This is also a case study, then, in human survival and social creativity. Of course, in a sense, all ethnography is that, but anthropologists rarely say so: It is not "scientific" and casts doubt on their detachment and disinterestedness. I am not detached about Tory – which does not mean I cannot both see its blemishes and analyze its social structure objectively. What it does mean is that I cannot detach my scientific curiosity from a sense of wonder at the brilliance and fragility of the human spirit that is revealed by it, and which is manifested in the collective, the social wisdom, not in individual genius (although there is that, too).

I have already written (in *Encounter with Anthropology*) of the same sense of wonderment at the unconscious feat of social engineering that I found in the social structure of an American Indian tribe. Ultimately, this is a fraction of the wonderment one feels at the whole process of evolution and adaptation, natural and cultural. Thus, to me, this book is as much an epic as an analysis. Like any responsible epic it is stuffed with myth, genealogy, place names, and lists of boats and heroes. For what

can a bard – a man of learning – offer to his people, in the Celtic
tradition at least, other than the preservation of their achievements in a
massive form that will preserve their memories for future generations? I
would never claim the high status of a *seanchaí*, but, as a wondering
outsider, I offer such tribute as I am able.

I stress this because the islanders are likely to be offended by parts of
the book. They are touchy on points of honor, and I could not have
escaped injuring some sensibilities. But many of them will know how
much more I knew, about which I have kept silent – even to the detri-
ment of analysis. This is always a tricky problem for any ethnographer. I
hope I have betrayed no trusts, and I have tried to stay with "public"
knowledge: that which would have been available to any diligent observer who was not entrusted with secrets.

This leads me to say a few words about my personal involvement with
Tory. I hate to call it "fieldwork" in the pompous professional sense. It
was a constant and hilarious pleasure despite the trivial physical discom-
forts. There is another book to be written about this – but it must wait,
perhaps forever. I never meant to go to Tory. As I have explained in my
introduction to the section on the island in *Encounter with Anthropology*, I was in Donegal thinking about studying bilingualism. I hopped
aboard a boat simply because it was going, and Tory, like Everest, was
there. That was in 1960. I went back every year for five years at varying
seasons, but mostly, of necessity, in the spring and summer. I visited
islanders in Scotland and London, and got to know the immediate sur-
roundings (Northwest Donegal) fairly well. I gradually improved my
Gaelic until it was passable in conversation and song – very important. I
lived with the same family each time, and took part in all activities from
wakes to lobster fishing. Once it was clear that I was not a spy but a
scholar, people were open and cooperative. I had several marvelous
guides to Tory customs in the older men, and to ongoing events among
the younger. I was able to keep out of serious quarrels, and when involved could always invoke my "outsider" position as a peacemaker. My
non-Catholic status bothered no one (the islanders are notably tolerant
in all such matters), but I went to Mass each Sunday anyway and kept the
observances. The two men who were the curates when I was there,
Fathers Sweeney and O Colm, were friendly and interested. The island
was well used to Gaelic scholars, so such interests as mine were seen,
rightly, as extensions of theirs. Once some of the more literate and
traveled of the people realized the scope of my inquiry, they became
invaluable companions in research. I made many dear friends. Some,

unfortunately, I have lost, and have had to wake them alone and in silence.

When I refer to "today" in the following pages, the reader should understand "1960–5." Some data I "froze" in 1963 for convenience. The book has been long in the making because many other things have intervened, and I was not sure there was a book there in all those notes; not one I wanted to write, anyway. But it gradually emerged and took shape of its own accord. It "thought itself out through me," as Lévi-Strauss has said of myth, and I offer it to my friends as the best that I can do. They deserve much more. As of now (1977) they are still there, so the story is not yet over. Plans for their removal are mooted annually. But, as the islanders say, "sin a' dóigh" – which we can translate, à la Vonnegut, as "so it goes."

A word to the Gaelic scholar and his opposite. The former will find much of what I have to write about the language (although I keep it to a minimum) either obvious or inaccurate. But the latter is my real problem. Gaelic is a written language and in using it I have to abide by its spellings and cannot retreat into phonetics or some awful "imitated pronunciation," as anthropologists manage to do with the unwritten tongues that are their normal beat. With the names, therefore, which are the main problem, I have just had to plough ahead, occasionally trying to indicate pronunciation in some of the more bizarre cases, or repeatedly giving the English equivalents. There is simply no easy way around this, and, in any case, the reader does not have to be able to pronounce the names to get the point. It is a minor difficulty, but I have avoided using Gaelic for its own sake, and can only ask for forbearance in this, and in all matters where detail or technique come between the reader (as opposed to the specialist) and the story.

And, finally, I cannot resist a word to those of my colleagues who, knowing that my interests over the last ten years (or more) have been in the evolution of behavior, ethology, sociobiology, etc., express surprise that I should be writing this at all, and not a piece on "primatology." To these innocents I can only reply that this *is* a piece on primatology, and that if they would only grasp that, then a lot would become clear and much nonsense avoided. If Terence will forgive me: *Primatus sum; primati nil a me alienum puto.*

R. F.

Acknowledgments

This research started in 1960, and over the years many individuals and institutions have helped. I am bound to leave out some and I apologize for the omissions; none are intentional. The work was originally supported by the University of Exeter, and I would like to thank Professor G. D. Mitchell for his encouragement and Professor D. O'Connor for introducing me to Gaelic. Support was continued by the Anthropological and Geographical Research Division of the London School of Economics, where Professors Sir Raymond Firth and D. G. Macrae were always helpful.

In Ireland I received the usual warm and generous help and hospitality from many people and institutions. In Dublin from Trinity College, University College, the Institute for Advanced Study, the Folklore Commission, the Department of the Gaeltacht, the Land Commission, the Central Statistics Office, the Ordnance Survey, the National Library, the Commissioners of Irish Lights, and the Royal Irish Academy. In particular, I should like to thank Mr. P. Duffin and the staff of the Valuation Office. It will be obvious in the course of the book how much I owe to their help and enthusiasm.

In Donegal I was helped by the staffs of the Colaiste Uladh, and of the County Library and Land Registry at Lifford. On Tory itself I had more help than I can mention. The then curates, Father Michael Sweeney and Father Eoghan O Colm, and the Franciscan relief priest, Father David, were most kind. The nurse and her husband and the lighthousemen were always hospitable. As to the islanders, I would have list them all to be fair, and some who were most helpful would be embarrassed to be named in print. It is no secret that I stayed each time with Hugh and Mary Doohan, to whom I owe an overwhelming debt of gratitude. For the others, the book itself must be my thanks.

Some individuals were so especially involved that I must single them out: Séan O h-Eochaidh, the Folklore Collector for Donegal in Gortahork; Derek Hill of Churchill – artist extraordinary of Tory Island; Edward R. O'Connor, the Economic Officer at the American Embassy;

Professor E. Estyn Evans and Dr. K. Connell of Queens University, Belfast; Dr. D. McCourt of Magee University College, Derry. Many others could be mentioned, but one has to stop somewhere or acknowledgments turn into autobiography.

Had I not dedicated the book to the people of Tory, I would have offered it to my friend Séamus O Raghallaigh of Dunfanaghy. Séamus combines so many qualities in one person it is hard not to sound too eulogistic: scholar, grammarian, humanist, administrator, statistician, man of action. As a Field Officer for the Department of the Gaeltacht he has been as responsible as anyone for fostering economic development in the Donegal Irish-speaking areas, but his official duties have never swamped his active mind and his delight in searching out new ways of knowing and researching. I remember taking long drives with him to the Crolly Doll factory, which had the only calculator in the area large enough for him to pursue his research on county incomes and central-place theory. His lively, questioning mind was a constant tonic to me on my return from the isolation of Tory, and a constant stimulus to new questions of my own. The practical help he gave me is beyond calculation, and to this must be added the kindness of his wife and family. Without his enthusiasm, consideration, and example I doubt I would have seen it through. What is more, to me he represented the ideal of the Gaelic Irishman. He kept a Gaelic home, but without bigotry or unreasonableness, realizing that even Gaelic speakers live in a predominantly English-speaking environment. If there can be such a thing as a secondary dedication to a book, then I gratefully offer it to Séamus – not only for what he did, but for what he is.

In preparing the manuscript for publication, I am indebted to Deborah Graham for research assistance (through the Rutgers University Research Council), and to Linda Marchant and Jay Callen. Susan Fox (no relative) worked above and beyond the call of duty on the diagrams and maps, and my youngest daughter, Anne, brought all an eleven-year-old's perception and determination to help with the birth and death records. Professors Conrad Arensberg and Paula Rubel of Columbia University read the manuscript with painstaking care and I have gratefully incorporated many of their helpful suggestions. Karyl Roosevelt struggled brilliantly with the production of a difficult typescript.

Without the help of the president (the late Mason W. Gross), the chairman, the executive director, the board of trustees, and the staff of the Harry Frank Guggenheim Foundation, it would never have happened at all. To them my heartfelt thanks.

All the maps that follow concerning the land of Tory and its disposition and inheritance are based on the records of the Valuation Office, Dublin, by the kind permission of the Government of the Republic of Ireland.

Finally, I would like to thank Professor Jack Goody, Walter Lippincott, and the staff of The Cambridge University Press, who with patience and good humor saw a complicated task to its conclusion.

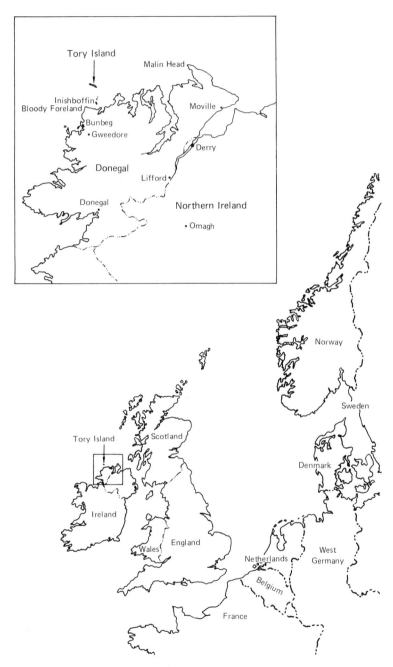

Map 1. Tory Island in relation to northwestern Europe

1

Prologue: myths and masters

Cá bhfuil an sneachta abhí chomh geal anuraidh?

At that soft, crepuscular edge of half-remembered time, where legend had not hardened into history and men and gods had easy intercourse, there, on the edge of the known world, at the northwestern corner of the island of the goddess Eriu, beyond which stretched only endless ocean, was another island; a tiny island not three miles long, surrounded by sullen, sometimes angry seas; an island hovering in elusive mists and filigree-fine rain that clouded it like steam from the cauldron of life itself.

The druids and the bards had called it Tor Inis: "the Island of the Tower"; but its people called it Torach: "the Towery Place" – Oileán Thoraí, "the Island of the Tors." And so it was: an island fortress; a Machu Picchu of the northern world; an island *de piedras escalares,* "stepped in stone"; a tower of crenellated rock nine sea miles from Cnoc Fola – the Hill of Blood. But that was not what the bards meant, being tedious and grave about these matters as bards and scholars will be. To them it was just an island; its castellated stance a fortuity of nature that, although it might awe the little dark people in sod cabins, did nothing to strike wonder into minds crammed with royal genealogy and the patronyms of kings. It was "the Island of the Tower" for them, not "the Towery Island," for it nursed the tower of a king; and some, with that pedantry that stems from a repressed love of wordplay, had held that its name was Tor Rí – "the Tower of the King."

The little people in the huts were as mad with words as their bardic superiors, and more so than their boastful and illiterate kings who lived in terror of the wordy bardic curse. The little people were the tillers of the coastal strip in the land of Conal – Tír Chonaill it was to distinguish it from neighboring Tyrone (Tír Eoghain, the Land of Owen). These people, who were there before the Gaels but who had long since absorbed Gaeldom (retaining only their un-Gaelic names to this day) knew that Torach was but a fancy back-formation from their own name –

The Eldest Duggan

Oileán Thoraí: "the Island of the Pirates" (brigands, robbers, thieves, outlaws). That tóraí – "thief," sounded almost like the genitive singular of torach – "towery," was not lost on them, even though they, unlike the bards, knew nothing of genitives, singular or commonplace. And so it was. For what had ever come to them from the Towery Island but murder, theft, and rapine?

The bards could, if they wished, exalt these brigands into kings, but the peasantry knew better. A tory was tory, a thief a thief, whether he wore a circlet of red gold or a winged helmet – or even plucked a twelve-string harp; for the bards were a caste apart and not above exploitation when it suited them. Bards, kings, Norsemen, pirates – all the same. "Aithníonn ciaróg, ciaróg eile," said the quiet people in the huts: One beetle knows another beetle.

When the mists had cleared and history emerged from the chrysalis of myth, their descendants would cry it out once more at those, who, pleading right of birth and conquest – *noblesse sans obligation* – would plunder them again, even if, in this late age, they called their loot by the quasilegal euphemism "rent." A tory was a tory. And what to them if Whigs should hurl it as an insult at the King's Friends, and that today it should be a name proudly borne by those who know nothing of its origins? Whigs, tories, labels, insults, words.

But plunderers there always were, and the winged helmets were the worst, perhaps. Were these Nordic robbers drawn to the island by strategy or philology, one wonders? For again, it has been said that they gave the island its name after their own god of thunder, Thor. Thor Ey, they called it: "the Island of Thor" (who, despite the "h," was "Tor"). These were people of the sword, not of the word, but they were superstitious. If into the old Celtic name they could read an omen as delightful as the name of one of their own gods, then why not take advantage?

But it was not Thor's island. The winged helmets left, but the tower and the dim memories of the "king" remained. What king? Tory is one of the earliest places mentioned by the bards. It was the home of the Fomors, the "Africans," the enemies of the Irish sons of Nemedius. And one king was Conán, and his tower Tor Chonáin – "the Tower of Conán." For does not Eochodius (thus to the Latins – Eochaidh to the Gaels, and Jock to us) tell, in his poem, of "Torinis, inis an tuir, cathair Chonáin"?

> Torinis, island of the tower,
> The fortress of Conán, son of Faobhar;
> By Fergus himself, who fought the strangers,
> Conán, son of Faobhar, was killed.

Finally, Morc the son of Dela, in the year of the world 3066, defeated the Fomors, and Tor Inis was free. But not for long. Another set of tales – the Battle of Muigh–Thuireadh ("Moira") tells us that Balor, in the year of the world 2764, killed Nuadha airgiod-lámh ("the silver handed") in that battle. Balor was also a Fomorian, of incredibly ancient descent, being the old Celtic god of death, Bel (he of the baleful stare), in another guise; even related, they say, to the Ba'al of the Semites, rival of Yahwe. Balor and the Fomorians were giants – at least to the little people; for is not the so-called Giants' Causeway in fact Clochan na bhFomórach – "the Causeway of the Fomorians"?

The legends of Balor are many and are talked of to this day by the people of the island. They point out Dún Balor, Balor's Hill Fort, and are not impressed when told it is an Iron Age remain. Who knows who might have used it *after* Balor? And the great cleft in the rocks at the eastern end of the island is still Balor's Prison, where he kept his daughter Ethnea, for fear of the prophecy: that her child would be the slayer of the Fomorian king. But of how Cian of the Tuatha Dé Danánn, lords of the mainland, came to her by magic; how they had a child who was to be the Celtic Apollo – Lugh lámh-fhada – Lugh the long handed, the fair haired, the gold savior of his race who has planted his name from Lyon to Luton; who was thrown into the sea by Balor, but saved by Manannán, the sea god to whom the Isle of Man is sacred, and reared by Gabhan the smith, the Vulcan of the Celts; and who indeed did slay his Cyclopean grandfather by hurling into his evil eye a sling ball made of the brains of enemies mixed with lime.

Many and contradictory are the tales of Balor, and a book could be made of them alone. Enough for us that he is remembered by the people of the island as if he lived there yesterday. And the people's memories are more homely. For was he not, although certainly a giant with an evil eye that had to be covered with plates of steel, also a sad old patriarch whose daughter got herself "into trouble" and produced an ungrateful grandson with murderous designs? It is all very familiar. And what, in the people's version, was Balor's crime? One might guess: Like Meadhbh of Connaught in the Táin Bó Cuailgne, he was, essentially, a cattle thief. In this case it was not a bull, although of course it was white: The great white milch cow Glas Gaibhnann, which he stole from the smith Gabhan, rested on Inis Bó Finne ("the Island of the Fair Cow" – the Inishboffin of today), and landed on Tory at Poirtín Ghlais. Now, in this tale, it is the brother of the smith, one Kineely, who, in revenge, impregnates Balor's daughter, with all the known consequences. (Except that there were triplets: Two were drowned; the third, Lugh, was saved because he fell from the sheet in which they had rolled the children when a thorn-pin came loose and dropped into the sea. The islanders today point to Port an Deilg – "the Harbor of the Pin.")

But what of Kineely? Balor wounded him on Cnoc Fola – bloody headland – and finally beheaded him on a stone that still stands, covered with the red veins, outside the town of Falcarragh in Cloghaneely – or in Gaelic Cloch Cheann-Fhaolaidh. This can be just "the Stone of Kineely" or "the Stone of the Head (ceann) of Faolach" (in the genitive, always used for surnames, Faolach is Faolaidh: "Feeley"). Now, with that love of wordplay we have encountered already, cannot the people again have juggled the "head" (ceann) of some unfortunate Feeley, and the name of the old God Cian? So a local chief, be he Feeley, or Kineely, or McKneely, or whatever, gets written into the record of the rise of the Celtic Sun God and his defeat of old grandfather death – he of the life-destroying eye. Even today in Donegal, the evil eye is Súil Bhaloir – "Balor's Eye."

Those who wish can consult the "high" versions of the tale, for the manuscripts abound in these. Here, Lugh was the great hero-warrior of the gods, who engineered their victory over the Fomorians. His father's liaison with Balor's daughter was strictly legal and the result of an alliance between the Celtic gods and their primeval enemies in which brides were exchanged. Bress of the Fomorians took to wife Brighid (a name later canonized as Saint Brigid), while Cian married Ethniú (Ethnea), the daughter of Balor. The alliance broke down through treachery, and, in the ensuing battle, Lugh killed his grandfather.

But the doings of the high gods have to be rendered on a human scale, one the people can grasp: rendered in terms not of cosmic principles and powers, but of "us" and "them." If this seems odd, then take a version I was told: that Balor hid his gold on Tor Mór. A lady read this secret in a book and came to dig for Balor's gold (which he robbed from boats going to America). She dug a while until the government heard and stopped her, because, of course, it wanted the gold itself. That the lady was a respectable archaeologist and that her account of the Iron Age fort on Tory Island appeared in a respectable journal does not impress the islanders. A clever front. But Balor kept his secret and his gold. They say, if you listen by the "prison," and the wind is right, you can hear him laughing. He is there still.

And so is Colmcille – Columba, the Dove of the Church, the descendant of Niall of the Nine Hostages who founded the Irish dynasty. Here we pass almost imperceptibly from the chrysalis of myth into the fluttering, painted glory of history and the written word. Columba has his dates, records, even manuscripts. Born of noble family at Gartan in Donegal in 521, drawn to the church, he founded over 300 monasteries, meddled in politics, and was banished to Scotland where, on Iona, he founded a famous and still-flourishing community. But en route, as a result of a mystical vision, he made the unlikely choice of Tory for "an extensive monastic settlement," as the books have it. "Usque Columbinam insulam quae Thorach dicitur." On the way to Tory he disputed with rival saints, and his position as saint of saints in Ireland was established when God opened the waters of Tory Sound for him and he walked across to the island. This conflicts with the Tory version that he landed in a curragh after being three times (of course) repulsed by the Danes. Either way, or neither, to Tory he came.

His tower, his church, his altars and relics are still there, as are the stone on which he rested his head with the impress still of his hands, and the stone that bears the imprint of a paw from the dog the islanders set upon him; the rock on which he landed helped by a man called Dubhgán (Duggan) and from which he expelled the Danes, turning *them* into rocks; the chapel where he buried seven shipwrecked nuns, the clay of whose grave he endowed with magical properties and put under the power of the Duggans who exercise it still: the power to cure, to still rough waters, to kill rats, and to prevent potato blight. The latter is surely a remarkable case of saintly foresight, but the blight indeed never came to the island in the forties and fifties of last century, and the potatoes were saved from destruction and the island from famine. The islanders carry the clay – which can be "lifted" only by the eldest Duggan – in their waistcoat pockets, and in little bags under the prows of their boats. When they enter foreign harbors, the rats flee.

Colmcille is still there, with Balor and the other ghosts. But despite the painted words, history tells us little of them. We know for certain that in 1595, in the aftermath of the Armada, George Bingham, governor of Sligo and president of Connaught, "devastated" the island that had harbored the Spaniards. The islanders boast of their mixed Spanish and Scandinavian blood – so some survived. The *Annals of the Four Masters* tells us;

> A.D. 1517 – Donagh, the son of Torlagh O'Boyle, the best gentleman of his means, who made the most warfare and performed the most intrepid exploits of any of his own tribe, went with the crew of a boat to Toraigh, and a wind having driven him westward to sea, no tidings of them were ever heard.

The O'Boyles ruled much of South Donegal and were enemies of the O'Roarties (Uí Robhartaigh), who were "herenachs" (churchwardens) of

Tory and built, records say, a tower there – inevitably. Even so, the lands of The McSweeny, who ruled in Donegal north of the island, were said to include Tuatha Toraí, or the district of Tory Island. O'Roarty, so the islanders say, tore down Balor's (or Conán's, or whoever's) castle to build his own. Neither remains. But the O'Roarties, the "descendants of Robert," left their name at least on the mainland opposite: Machaire Uí Robhartaigh (Magheraroarty) – "The Plain of the O'Roarties."

After Colmcille came Saint Hernan, or Ernan, or Ereneus, or Hernanus, or Erianus, or as many aliases as a modern crook. And the Annals have regular lists of "devastations" from 612 to 1041, when the unlikely Soenghasus *praelector et praepositus* of Torry," died. Before him was Maolcolainn O'Branain, Arneach of Torry, who died in 1002; while in 733 Dougall the Second, King of Scotland, thought fit to mount an expedition against this stronghold in the sea. In 732 he had done the same, and "violated Torrach," as the manuscript quaintly puts it. And on and on. The Island of the Tower, the Towery Island, sitting menacingly off the shore, was too tempting a refuge for every rebel, too juicy a plum for any tyrant, to be left in peace.

Why? Because for one thing it was the perfect stronghold, surrounded by difficult seas and with a natural defensive fort on its eastern extremity, where even the sod wall still extant would have been enough to hold back an army, never mind the numerous "towers" and "castles" that were reputedly built there. Also, whoever ruled Tory ruled the coast of Donegal – as it had become: "the Hill Fort of the Strangers," Dún na nGall. The coast could be ravaged or protected with relative impunity by daring seamen based on the island. So every king and petty rebel, every would-be chief, every trivial pirate and rival prince, tried his hand at holding Tory.

Meanwhile, the little people – the Duggans, the MacRuaris, the Doohans, and the Divers, kept their peace, hid in the caves during the devastations, and let their masters fight it out. They clung to Balor and to Colmcille, and hung on to life itself – or what their masters left them of it. They absorbed both blood and wisdom, but they kept their secrets: They survived.

The Ulster Inquisitions of County Donegal reveal new masters at work. On September 12, 1609, before various Chichesters, Ridgeways, Winches, Davies, and Parsons all assembled, evidence was offered on the island of "Torro." O'Rohertye was both "Herenagh and Corbe," they were told, "but being dead another of his sept should be elected to pay the tax of seven shillings to the Bishop of Raphoe on the two quarters of

Termone land and every balliboe inhabited." Yes – they were there with a vengeance, book and pen and measuring rod in hand, to tax and exploit again in the name of a different king. And again the people held their peace and survived.

In 1653, we hear from Sir William Petty in his great *Civil Survey of Ireland* that Tory had a garrison and was under the ownership of the coheirs of one Captain John Stanford, "English Protestant, Deceased." New masters, new names, new credos – old experiences (see notes).

The island disappears from history for long periods. Life must have continued much as always for the few hundred inhabitants – but only the killings and the rents seemed worth recording to the masters and the scribes.

From the early nineteenth century records increase; again records of the gains others hoped to make from the little island: tithes, taxes, rates, and rent. A lighthouse (1832) and a Lloyd's signal station pulled it onto the edge of the burgeoning industrial age. The Ordnance Survey surveyed it – producing those beautifully engraved maps of 1832, and the indefatigable O'Donovan tried to render the Gaelic place-names into something other than anglicized gobbledygook. A "reforming landlord," John O. Woodhouse, Esq., in his zeal reapportioned their lands and removed 100 islanders – for their own good, of course. In 1845, Mr. E. Getty visited them with the botanist Mr. Hyndman, and Mr. Grattan of Belfast. As a result, the "History and Antiquities" of the island launched the first volume of the *Ulster Journal of Archaeology* in 1853 (see notes).

Most significantly, in 1861 the island was purchased, together with bits of the mainland, for £6,500 by Benjamin St. John Baptist Joule – a Manchester businessman, known even now on the island as "the Jew man." Poor Joule. He collected scarcely any rents. Times were changing, and the idea of resistance – never far from the Tory mind – was fanned by "Fenian designs." After 1872 or so, Joule got not a penny. In 1883 he published a remarkable pamphlet to defend himself against accusations of cruelty and indifference to his starving tenants (see notes). The pamphlet consisted of reprints of letters to the press by the Rev. James J. O'Donnell, resident priest of Tory; Joule himself; and one letter ostensibly from the islanders (signed "The Torroneans") but probably, as Joule scornfully suggests, written by the priest. O'Donnell had appealed for funds to save the islanders from starvation, and Joule answered that this was a typical Hibernian swindle. The islanders were well off from the sales of lobsters and crabs; they were able to pay rent but refused to do so (they were £2,000 in arrears); they were stripping the sods from pasture to provide fuel for illicit whiskey distilling; they were putting stones in kelp to increase its weight and selling it at inflated prices. The islanders replied that they received little for the crabs and lobsters. Joule's estimate had been £600 for 1882: They would only admit to £35 12s per house. They maintained that they had offered a rent settlement that had been refused: They offered Joule £100 per annum instead of the £196 he was asking. They had, they said, ceased distilling illicit whiskey – a rejoinder that caused Joule much amusement. The price of kelp had dropped in their version and in 1882, they said, they received only 18s 4d for it: Joule had estimated £700 for 1881. On the whole, Joule gets the better of the argument – if they could indeed afford £100 a year for rent they were scarcely starving, he pointed out – but he never got the better of the islanders.

It is clear that they refused to pay rates as well as rent. The "collector of county cess" was driven off the island in 1871, and at Lifford Assizes it was decided that armed force should be used to collect the arrears (£263 15s 8d). This was easier to order than to carry out, and it was not until 1884 (the year after the pamphlet), and probably at Joule's urgings, that the expedition was mounted. A gunboat, the *Wasp,* was dispatched from Westport in County Mayo on September 22 of that year. According to admiralty records, the *Wasp* was wrecked in Tory Sound because of a "navigational error," but the islanders know better. They know that Heggarty the King called them to the cliff where the cursing stone is buried, put them in a circle round the stone, and chanted the spell for its turning – a spell contained in its runic writings; and that the stone turned, the cliff shook, the seas rose, and the miserable little gunboat was smashed on the rocks: those very rocks that were the unconverted Danes long since petrified by Colmcille.

The idea of "cursing stones" is not unique to Tory. Sir Samuel Ferguson records in a poem that, when the Druids were angry with King Cormac,

> They loosed their curse against the King,
>   They cursed him in his flesh and bones,
> And daily in their mystic ring
>   They turned the maledictive stones.

So the islanders were in a good tradition.

Be that as it may, more than fifty sailors lost their lives, Joule made no more attempts to collect his rents, and the county, from that day forward, abandoned the idea of collecting rates. When the Congested Districts Board for Ireland bought Tory from Joule in 1903, its inspectors noted that the islanders were "in occupation without paying rent from about 1878." Curiously, it is from this date also that the island seems to have had a permanent priest. A schoolmaster had been intermittently there since midcentury. But these outsiders sat lightly on Tory.

Even the Congested Districts Board – that exemplary body founded on funds from the disestablished Irish church by Balfour in his attempts to "kill Home Rule with kindness" – made not much deep impression. It built houses, slipways, a pier; made loans to fishermen; started a herring-curing station, and taught women commercial knitting. Tory even prospered by its own standards. But that brings us to the First World War; in 1917 a British garrison fired on a boatload of Dubliners who flew the tricolor and sang the "Soldiers' Song." And that is more than history (although it is the stuff of legend): It is us, and our time and a point of immediate contact with the descendants of pre-Christian kings who knew above all one thing – how to survive.

What follows is a relatively sober anthropological account of the social structure of Tory. But I mean it to be more than just that: I mean it to be, in some small way, a memorial to this unique and remarkable people who may not be able to survive the worst devastation of all: progress. Soon, for their own good of course, they may be removed forever. That is why I have dedicated the book "do Mhuintir an Oileáin": to the people of the island; and why I have given as a dedicatory quotation to this chapter the saying recorded by Robin Flower on the now deserted Blasket Islands, with its astonishing overtones of the most famous line of Villon: Ca bhfuil an sneachta abhí chomh geal anuraidh? "Where is the snow that was so bright last year?"

2

The island and the people

Is grá geal mo chroí thu a Thoraigh a stór,
'Do luí mar bheadh seoid ghlas 'san fharraige mhór.

The song quoted above – adapted from a song about Tír Chonaill proper – says: "You are the bright love of my heart, Tory, my darling; lying like a green jewel in the great ocean." From the mainland, Tory looks more grey and brown than green, dominated as it is by the towering cliffs at the East End, particularly Tor Mór, which gives it its name (at least in one version). But as one approaches, the green patches, which turn out on closer inspection to be cultivated fields, begin to shine in whatever hesitant sun there is; and Tory does indeed seem like a green turquoise set in dull silver: the epitome of some Navajo jeweler's art.

One travels, by open boat, more or less due north to the island from the little pier of Mín Larach at the foot of the hills of Machaire Uí Robhartaigh (Magheraroarty) on Cnoc Fola (Bloody Foreland). One passes three islands, close to shore: Inis Bó Finne (Inishboffin), of the Balor legend, which is inhabited; Inis dTuaidh (Inishdooey), which is a cemetery; and Inis Beag (Inishbeg), a refuge for birds. From the Tory viewpoint, Inishboffin – their closest neighbour – is always "the island." The Tory islanders speak of "going over to Ireland" when visiting the mainland, and one wag has commented that Tory belongs not to the Republic of Ireland, but to the Atlantic Ocean. The truth of this can be seen even on the calmest of days: An island totally in the grip of heavy, rolling seas, and guarded by swift crosscurrents in Tory Sound, it recalls uncannily Weber's lines from *Oberon* about "ocean, thou mighty monster, coiling like a green serpent. . . ."

As the little boat rides the waves, one begins to pick out the houses, first at the harbor where the boat is aiming – An Camus Mór (Camusmore Bay). One sees the fabulous tower of Colmcille's monastery, standing out above the cluster of roofs. Then, to the east, a few scattered houses can be glimpsed against the backdrop of the towers of rock. One sees that the island, two-and-a-half miles long running west to east, in

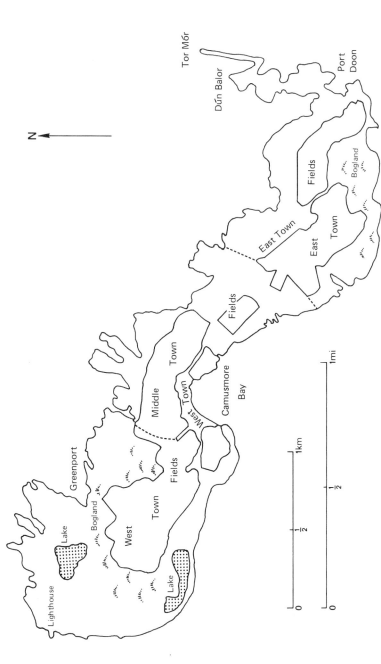

Map 2. Tory Island

fact slopes backward toward the great sea like a wedge of cheese. And this is its secret. Had it been flat, it would not have been, in its totally exposed position, habitable. Because of its shape, the northern "wall" protects it from the sea; soil gathers on the slopes – south-facing for the sun; precipitation is lower than on the mainland, where the clouds empty once they hit the Donegal mountains; and a little agriculture is possible.

Perhaps at most, 250 of the island's 785 acres can be used for crops and cattle, although sheep graze on the hillsides. There are no trees, although legend has it that there once were, and the bogs attest to that. The rest is bog itself (now virtually exhausted through overexploitation as fuel), scrub, rock, and water. That this land could have, at one time, supported nearly 600 people is amazing, and only made plausible by the harvest of the sea, Tory's great strength. The seas are literally "mackerel crowded": Stretch a hand into the water and touch one, or a glasan, or a herring.

The cliffs in the east are higher than those in the west. Tor Mór itself – the narrow spit of rock thrusting almost obscenely out to sea alongside the sloping ramp of Dún Balor – reaches 400 feet. Its steep sides are crowded with cormorants and puffins. The western end of the island, where the lighthouse stands, is broader and flatter, but protected even so by formidable cliffs, each with its own name – Mór ard, "The Great Height"; Miodh-aird, "The Middle Height." Just to the east of the light-house is the northern harbor Portín Ghlais (Greenport), unusable in winter. The whole Atlantic seawall of the wedge has been nibbled at as if by giant ocean rats of some Fomorian epic. Fjords, caverns, grottoes, inlets, and weird rock formations, including Tor an Bhoid – "Penis Tower," and Leac na Leannán – "Lovers' Stone," all witness the creatively destructive power of the sea. This is underlined by the many names of rocks that derive from wrecks: Feadán an *Wasp* (about which we know already); Boilg an *Fair Home;* Uaimh an *Chotton;* Poll an *Rutton*; Slodán *Echo* – and so on through the dismal catalogue. The islanders deny that they were wreckers; but they feel that there is nothing wrong in profiting from such disasters – it's all a matter of salvage after all, and what harm if they are first in the race?

Nowhere is the island more than three-quarters of a mile wide: In one place, at the foot of Dún Balor, it is only a few yards across. When the seas are really high – and winds of hurricane force and gale forces nine to twelve are common – the great cliffs are not enough; the whole island is drenched with salt spray; the piers are awash; the houses are threatened. But even on the worst of days the island is, from any angle

The Tory Islanders

and aspect, incredibly beautiful: Reflecting the pale sunlight or defying the waves, it stands a monument to nature's impeccable aesthetic sense and man's astonishing endurance.

As one approaches closer, the houses become more distinct. The main cluster is around the natural harbor into which the boat is maneuvering. This, the boatmen say, is West Town (Baile Thiar). There are really two towns (bailte), this one, and East Town (Baile Thoir) – the cluster on the ridge that we have seen. But, say others, there is also Middle Town (Baile Láir) – a town in its own right with its own fields. Physically, it is an extension of West Town, a ribbon development along the rough road to the east. Others again distinguish New Town (Baile Ur), but most count this as part of Middle Town, even if it is thought of as a new suburb of the metropolis. East Town is roughly three-quarters of a mile from West, and each "town," it turns out, was in fact, in the old days, a "clachán" – a group of houses whose owners held the land around them in common. This was the "rundale" system, once common in Ireland, to which we must return. But meanwhile, what of the towns?

West Town (including Middle and New) is indeed the metropolis. It has forty-two inhabited houses as opposed to East Town's twenty-four. It has the pier and the slipways built by the Congested Districts Board (CDB) in 1903–12, and since extended by the Irish government's Board of Works, the Department of the Gaeltacht, and the like. It has the antiquities so ably described by Mr. Getty (see notes, Chapter 1), dominated by the tower, and the "tau cross" set in a mill wheel over the slipway slightly above a torpedo washed ashore in the First World War. It has the church (Saint Colmcille's), the parochial house – painted a garish green; the school (Saint Colmcille's), with its beautiful copper roof; the church hall, which was once the church before the new one was built, and served for a while as a cooperative store; the three small shops; the nurse's surgery, which was once a herring-curing station; the life-saving station; and the graveyard.

East Town has none of these. But its inhabitants praise its rural charm, although they complain of having to go over to the West for everything. Some West Enders (as they call themselves) have never gone to the East and never want to. East Town has its own small harbor, Port an Dúin (Port Doon), where there is a tiny slipway and boats are simply turned over and beached – as was the case in Camusmore before the pier and slipway came. Landing in those days was very difficult, and still is in heavy swells and storms, despite the new facilities.

Before the CDB (or "the Board" as it is still affectionately known) began its good works, West Town was a cluster of houses – small thatched cabins – round the base of the tower. Some of these still exist, but are mostly used as byres and storerooms. The Board built one- and two-story houses, mostly along the road – the same in East Town. These new houses had sash windows, wooden floors, and slate roofs, and revolutionized the appearance of the towns. They stood out boldly from the land and did not hug it – even seem to grow out of it – as the old cabins had. No longer are the cattle kept inside in the winter for warmth, and by and large the chickens are kept out too. No doubt these stern houses are healthier, but there is still, among the old people, a nostalgia for the cabins, with their warmth and intimacy. The storytellers and genealogists – the seanchaithe – used to lie on the stone or earth floors with rocks under their heads for pillows as they relaxed and recited the long, rhythmical tales, accompanied by the lowing of the cows, the clucking of the odd hen, and the hum of a spinning wheel in the corner. No. It's not the same.

Around each of the towns are the arable fields, the grazing land, the bogs and lochs: Loch O Thuaidh (North), Loch O Dheas (South), Loch Thoir (East). The fields of East Town radiate out from it like the spokes of a wheel; those of West Town are arranged in north–south strips of suspicious regularity. There are few walls, except at the extreme boundaries; the strips themselves are usually separated by nothing more than a little ditch or a line of turf. The walls are to keep out wandering animals, and old and broken walls appear beyond the present ones – even up onto the cliffs – showing where older generations had pushed onto marginal land in their search for food.

The curious regularity of the "strips," we learn, is not how it always was. Under the old rundale system, the land was divided higgledy-piggledy into small lots, and everyone had bits and pieces here and there. In any case, it was periodically redistributed to ensure a fair allotment of the better land among the households. Clusters of households – containing persons related by blood – owned various portions of the fields around each town, and held them in common. But relationships and holdings got confused over the generations, and then an appeal would be made to the "king" (An Rí) to sort them out.

The king of Tory (Rí Thoraí) was probably a true descendant of the old Brehons – the lawgivers: those who knew the customary laws and usages particularly with reference to inheritance. Whether or not his position was hereditary or elective, no one remembers. In the old days, they say, he would have been "appointed" when necessary, but he would have had to have been of a "royal" (Brehon) family, and been literate. The last king of Tory was Paddy Heggarty, a dwarf. Heggarty is not one of the old Tory names like, for example, Duggan. But perhaps the requirement that the king be literate meant that an outsider – one who had married in – had to be appointed. The "Eldest Duggan" was already the ritual leader of the island. He was in charge of the sacred clay from the Church of the Seven, and the pilgrimage sites. He recited the prayers on Sunday mornings in front of Saint John's Altar, when there was no priest on the island. The king – as on other islands – was primarily an arbiter of land and shore disputes; the shore being as meticulously divided as the land itself, and like the land periodically redistributed: Common opinion has it that this was annual. It was understood that, for example, deposits of valuable driftwood landed at random as did other bits of wreckage – all usable. (The only iron on the island came from wreckage and was used for making plough blades.) The king therefore divided up the shore in secret and then assigned an object – a rag, a bone, etc. – to each portion. To the assembled islanders he called out "who's for the rag; who's for the bone?" and the first to respond received the object, the portion of shore that went with it, and his chances with the flotsam and jetsam.

The succession is now in dispute. There is one pretender whose claim is his exceptional literacy in both languages. He does write many letters for the islanders, but because he has abused his literacy by using his pen for illegal purposes and has done a spell in prison, his claim is suspect. The services of a king in any case are not so much needed now, for no one bothers with the shore and the land is falling into disuse. But that is to leap ahead of our story.

In the chapter on land we shall further explore its fortunes. Here only a picture is given. And the picture is of half-used strips of arable land enclosed at their extremities, growing oats, potatoes, and barley; outside these are the scrubby hillsides and the bogs. The bogs, which once held excellent turf for fuel, were as meticulously divided as the fields. But they are practically exhausted now. Here and there can be seen little stacks of drying turf, while everywhere are the piles of stones that, in more plentiful times, were the foundations of the stacks.

The turf, they say, was exhausted in the normal course of events because these were shallow peat bogs. But illwishers like the miserable Joule thought, and think, otherwise: It was the distillation of poitín (poteen) – illegal whiskey – from the overabundant barley, grown in preference to other more obvious crops, that caused the failure of the bogs; the pot stills needed powerful fires to keep them bubbling. More likely, it was the burning of kelp to produce crude iodine that did it. Kelp was one of the few cash crops on the Donegal coast, and it was turned into a flourishing industry between 1845 – when a Mr. Ward established a chemical works at Ramelton on Lough Swilly to process the iodine – and the turn of the century. The few horses now on the island, kept more or less as pets, are the descendants of those used to pull the large sleds on which the kelp was brought from the shore for burning. Nowadays only a little sea-rod is gathered by the children and sold to nylon manufacturers: The kelp trade has long since died.

But the effects of this, and of overgrazing by sheep in the nineteenth century (up to 200 on the hillsides), have rendered much land unusable; the hillsides are mostly barren scrub. With the failure of the turf and the complete lack of wood on the island, the islanders were reduced to soaking dry sods in paraffin and burning those. Even now, when the government has provided bogs for the islanders on the mainland, many still prefer the Tory turf, as it is affectionately known: Which does nothing for the preservation of grazing land. But to many of them, their days are sufficiently numbered not to care too much for such things. "When we are gone," one said, "there'll still be enough for the rabbits and the birds."

The idea that they might be evacuated is ever present to them. They take it in different ways: mostly stoically. They know that they survive largely on subsidies, and they know that migration and the loss of the young present them with very different problems from the problems of sheer survival that their ancestors faced. The problem now is not how to live with the sea and each other and not starve: The problem is how to keep the children on the island. Before we consider this, let us look at how the island population has fared over time.

For the period before 1841, we only have the island tradition that there were "six hundred and more souls." Woodhouse, we know, removed a hundred of them, and the 1841 and 1851 censuses show about 400, with a gradual decline after that. Details of these censuses, other than the gross figures, are not available, because the records were destroyed in the civil war (1922). There is some difficulty in establishing the "real" population of Tory because it is subject to fluctuations resulting from the absence of migrant workers for long periods. There tends to be a wave of young people returning home in the summer, and another slight increase at about the time of the Scottish New Year celebrations, when the boys from Glasgow and other Scottish towns return (weather permitting, of course). The official census figures for 1961 give 146 males and 118 females: a total of 264. The census was taken in the autumn and so probably represents a fair average: It would have been higher in the summer and lower in the winter.

The gradual decline of the Tory population is shown in Table 1. The island has declined to roughly two-thirds of its 1841 population. This

Table 1. *Tory Island population (census returns, 1841–1961)*

	Male	Female	Total
1841	191	208	399
1851	207	195	402
1861	201	185	386
1871	151	192	343
1881	140	192	332
1891	160	188	348
1901	149	186	335
1911	162	145	307
1926	134	116	250
1936	147	144	291
1946	141	124	265
1951	143	114	257
1956	148	125	273
1961	146	118	264

Note: Figures include a few nonpermanent residents such as the priest and lighthousemen.
Source: Central Statistics Office, Dublin.

compares with the drop of Ireland as a whole from 6,548,000 to 2,818,000 in 1961: a loss of more than half. The loss of females is most spectacular, their number having been practically halved. The drop of 50 males between 1861 and 1871 was probably the result of both emigration and a measles epidemic. The total drop between 1911 and 1926 (57) is said to have been the result of panic emigration at the beginning of the First World War, when it was feared that ablebodied men might be conscripted. Some of these returned later. Since then, the population has remained fairly stable.

Figure 1 shows the population pyramids for the island for 1901 (the first available breakdown by age and sex), and 1961. The change in age–sex structure is apparent and shows the classical development of a declining population from a pointed "pyramid" to a "rectangle." An increase in the number of old people is matched by a severe drop in the numbers of the working population, particularly young women. Indeed, in 1961, for the 20–24 age group there were *no* women; a situation masked by the grouping of the figures. This reflects the growing tendency for women to emigrate, sometimes for good (especially on marriage). Young girl migrants usually take jobs that require them to be away for most of the year, and hence will not figure in the census returns even if they do come back for Christmas.

This illustrates again the difficulty of arriving at an estimate of the effective population that besets anyone dealing with a migrant labor situation. But the decline is in many senses a real one and is reflected by the figures for marriages on and off the island. As a general rule, those islanders who marry away from the island never return to it as permanent residents. This is particularly true of women. Table 2 shows the number of marriages of people born on the island that were solemnized on or off the island. Glasgow, Edinburgh, and Omagh (Northern Ire-

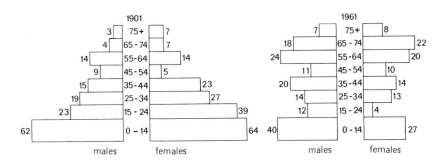

Figure 1. Population of Tory Island by age and sex. *Source:* Central Statistics Office, Dublin.

Table 2. *Marriages of persons born on Tory (by decades)*

	Solemnized		
	On Tory	Elsewhere	Total
1918–27	16	0	16
1928–37	15	1	16
1938–47	19	3	22
1948–57	14	17	31
1958–64	4	7	11
Total	68	28	96

Note: The record of marriages off the island is compiled from notes added to entries in the baptismal register. These give the date, parish, and names of the parties concerned in a marriage of a Tory parishioner that is solemnized elsewhere. There may be some omissions, but the overall trend is obvious.
Source: Marriage and Baptismal records, Saint Colmcille's Church, Tory Island.

land), were the most popular places for marriages off the island. Nineteen of the twenty-eight marriages were of women to nonisland men. Thus there has been a progressive loss of marriageable women, which set in during the war and accelerated after it.

This decline in the relative numbers of women is made worse by a natural imbalance that occurred in the 1947–56 decade. Table 3 shows the number of births (male and female) by decades from 1897. The ratio of males to females that had been fairly steady until 1947 suddenly swung in the male favor and produced more than two males for each female. This makes it unlikely that the men born in this period will marry on the island when they reach marriageable age. If one adds to this natural imbalance the fact that most of the marriageable girls now leave for most of the year, thus increasing their chances of finding husbands off the island, then the prospects for future marriages are bleak.

As regards net reproduction, the island more than holds its own. Between 1951 and 1961, for example, the ratio of births to deaths was 1.6. But emigration, mainly of young women, steadily erodes the island population and undermines its chances for survival. Tory is in fact Ireland in microcosm: high fertility (made higher over the past fifty years by a rapid drop from an infant mortality of 80 percent to less than 10), combined with a high rate of emigration.

Who then are the people represented by these dry statistics? They are Gaelic-speaking Roman Catholics, fishermen and crofters, living by the

Table 3. *Tory Island births (by decades)*

	Male	Female	Total	Male:Female
1897–1906	44	33	77	1:0.75
1907–16	18	25	43	1:1.3
1917–26	31	28	59	1:0.9
1927–36	19	25	44	1:1.3
1937–46	15	16	31	1:1.06
1947–56	32	14	46	1:0.4
1957–64	22	22	44	1:1

Source: Baptismal records, Saint Colmcille's Church, Tory Island.

sea and the land and by subsidies from the government at home and a little from relatives abroad. Their ancestry – or the ancestry of the more ancient lineages – is lost in the proverbial mists of prehistory and myth. But if the legends of Colmicille are to be even half-believed (and he *did* have a monastery on the island), then the Duggans at least have been there since the fifth or sixth century A.D. Even the Duggans will sometimes admit that the MacRuaris (Mac Ruadhraigh) are the oldest "family." They use various anglicizations to approximate the Gaelic name – as do all the families – and it comes out sometimes as McRory, but most often just as Rogers or Rodgers. In any case, they are the "red" people (rua = red) as opposed to the "black" ones, the Duggans, the Uí Dhubhgáin (dubh = black). One other accepted ancient name, that of Doohan, is thought by the folk-etymologists (the "sloinnteoir" is literally the "surname person") to be derived from O Dubhgáin by a process of "softening" the "g" to produce "gh" and the modern Irish O Dubhgháin. Lastly, of the venerated names, there is Diver – O Duibhir – pronounced with a short "i" to rhyme with river. These four surnames account for nearly 80 percent of the islanders. Other names have come in, as they say, at various times, and it is agreed and attestable from records that the next most ancient names date from the latter half of the eighteenth century: McClafferty (Mac Fhlaithbheartaigh), Meenan (Míonáin), Whorriskey (O Fuaruisce) and Herraghty or Heggarty. Later in the nineteenth century came Mooney, O'Donnell, Doherty, Carrol, Dixon, and Ward; and in this century McGinty, Boyle, Burke, and Hendron. Several came and disappeared (Carrol, O'Brien, Gallagher), and others are now extinct – like Heggarty, Ward, and Mooney – that were prominent until recently. Burke and Hendron are adopted boys and Boyle and McGinty married in (although according to the records there had been McGintys on Tory before).

What this shows is a hard core of ancient names that persist, a few eighteenth- and nineteenth-century stocks that have grown, and a few men who married in, or settled, and whose names do not survive. On the whole, there has been relatively little immigration to Tory from the mainland, and in few cases has this been of women marrying Tory men: It is usually the other way around. Most marriages in fact are endogamous to the island, and in this, as in most things, the island is pretty self-contained. The number of dispensations granted by the church over the last forty years (for which figures are available) shows that 12 percent of marriages were within the prohibited degrees.

The islanders speak, as a first and everyday language, the northern dialect of Irish Gaelic – very close in some ways to Scots Gaelic, which, indeed, derives from it. It retains, for example, the negative particles "char" and "cha" as opposed to Irish "níor" and "ní." Tory Gaelic also has many archaic usages all its own that delight scholars. Most noticeable is the use of the words for "man" and "woman" ("fear" and "bean") to refer to masculine and feminine nouns respectively when saying the equivalent of "one of those (masculine or feminine)." Once, the islanders took a play about the island they had prepared themselves to a festival in Gweedore. They had used best "book Gaelic" in the dialogue, but one of them forgot himself and lapsed into dialect when talking of a cow – "bo," feminine noun. "Tá bean ag an tSagart i dToraigh," he said. To him this was "The priest has one (of those) on Tory"; to the audience it was "The priest has a woman on Tory." The resultant uproar can be imagined.

English is spoken to some degree by all except the very old (particularly the ladies) and the preschool children. But fluency varies greatly. Because, despite schooling in Gaelic, many people never have occasion to read or write it, the standard of literacy in the language is low, and any additional vocabulary after school is likely to be in English. The language, then, although very much alive and vigorous, is riddled with English loanwords, all suitably Gaelicized. In many cases, the islanders are unaware that Gaelic words exist for many items in common use, and even when they are, they prefer the English word that is familiar through use. This can be seen by purists as a "decline" of Gaelic, but perhaps this is the wrong view. Gaelic is still the first language of the people, but it is locked into English now in a dynamic way – which is a natural process common to many languages.

This is all speeded up by the use of English by the lighthousemen, officials, visitors; by the English of the radio (the Gaelic of Radio Eireann is not well received, being in "foreign" dialects); by the reading of English-language newspapers, reports, etc; and above all by the use of

English by returning migrants, who use it extensively in England and Scotland – even if they continue to speak Gaelic among themselves. Significantly, those who write home always write in English, even if, once home, they speak nothing but Gaelic.

The language situation is a reflection of the social condition of the island as a result of migration. This affects all aspects of island life. But it has not always been so, and the economy has not, until fairly recently, been so dominated by migration and subsidies. For most of Tory's history, the problem of sheer physical survival must have been uppermost. A population of over 400 crowded onto this shelf of rock, supporting itself at subsistence level from sea, shore, and farmland. The sea was limitless and there was room for all to fish, but the two-man curragh, which was the standard vessel, was unsuitable for deep-sea fishing and dangerous in bad weather. The cost in human life was high and the returns negligible. The fish, however, did enable the islanders to survive when many on the mainland starved. As Joule's pamphlet shows, there was some trade in lobsters and crabs, which were sold to coastal steamers and taken to Liverpool. Whether this trade ever realized the relatively large profits – over any long period – that Joule mentions is doubtful. No large-scale fishing industry could be developed on the basis of small two-man canoes, and the building of larger boats required capital the fishermen did not have.

A few yawls were built from imported timber at the end of the nineteenth century, but it was not until the Congested Districts Board instituted loans for fishermen that fishing really got under way. About the turn of the century, large sail- and oar-powered herring-fishing boats began to be built, and fishing for profit began. These boats required large crews and kept most of the able-bodied men, and even older boys, employed. A group of men would form a syndicate to run a boat on a profit-sharing basis with one man as manager. About eight or ten boats were in use at any one time with an average crew of nine or ten men. According to the 1901 census, this would have stretched the manpower resources to the full, there being certainly not more than sixty to eighty men of working age available. Many things made the marketing of fresh fish difficult, and it was again only after the establishment of a herring-curing station by the Board that fishing became a boom industry (by island standards, that is). Women found employment for the first time in gutting and salting herring, shops made their appearance, and for a time Tory prospered.

However, the herring were uncertain and the First World War intervened. As early as 1917 a motor-powered boat had been built with capi-

Young people, mostly young women, leaving the island to seek work.
The Franciscan relief priest accompanies them.

tal accumulated from fishing. After the war, motors became more common, and in the 1930s the Sea Fisheries Board provided two "Bollanders" under island management. The motors made large crews of oarsmen redundant, and drove men to migrate. Also, after a brief season of success with matjes herring in the early thirties, the elusive fish made one of their knight's moves to another and warmer part of the great sea, and were not seen again in commercial quantities. In Chapter 6, more will be said about fishing, its history and its problems; for now I can only note its decline and the changing pattern of what remains.

People had always emigrated from Tory. There is not a household that does not have relatives in America, Canada, Australia, or Britain. In fact, the island was something of an entrepôt in the emigration trade. Mící Mac Gabhan, in his incomparable autobiography *Rotha Mór an tSaoil* ("The Great Wheel of Life"), describes how the emigrant ships used to anchor off Tory. The departing peasants were rowed out to them, weeping; and Tory was often the last glimpse of Ireland they ever had. What Tory had never been involved in was the annual summer migrations to Scotland and England for harvesting, which characterized the rest of Donegal. But, during the First World War, men took to going off for fairly long periods to gather capital for boats and equipment. They were mostly employed on public works in Scotland. Gradually, truly *migrant* laboring became the pattern, the periods away becoming progressively shorter. At one time men would stay away working for anything up to ten or fifteen years, finally returning to marry and settle down at about age thirty. The average period of exile gradually shortened to two or three years, with brothers and cousins taking turns being away.

The exploitation of the lobster market altered this pattern still further. After the Second World War, lobsters began to dominate the economy. The lobster season is convenient in that it coincides with the summer homecomings of the men, and is relatively short (June–September). The return is high relative to the effort and investment, compared with other forms of fishing. All the fishing is inshore, and the lobsters can be stored in floating boxes (with their claws disabled to prevent fighting) and so preserved fresh for market in a way impossible with fish. The demand is so high that boats will come around to pick up the catches and merchants, in return for a monopoly of the catch, will even supply pots. Other forms of fishing have not completely stopped. Several nonmigrant men run one quite successful herring- and salmon-fishing boat. Market fluctuations and salmon gluts in recent years have, however, rendered this less profitable than lobstering.

The economy of lobster fishing, although attractive, is precarious. It requires a high capital investment and the risk of total loss over a season is discouraging. A gale can take away all or most of the pots, hold up fishing, and ruin a season's work. Some of the men must then go off to work in Scotland for the winter to provide new equipment. The actual cost of petrol, oilskins, rope, etc., is often barely covered by earnings. One suspects that the attraction of the lobster/laboring complex is not its economic, but its social advantages: It provides a self-sustaining cycle of migration that suits the taste of the young men.

Table 4 shows the involvement of households in migrant labor and in fishing and/or ferrying. Because all shopowners have boats, the figures for boatmen include shopowners. Thus at least a third of the households have active or intermittent migrant laborers, and a third also have interests in shops and/or fishing. There is a good deal of overlap between these two groups, and between them they account for about half the households. The rest – largely consisting of older people or chronic nonmigrants – live on subsidies in the form of pensions, unemployment benefits, remittances from relatives, and hidden subsidies of various kinds. A surprisingly large number of the islanders are officially blind. Because there is a pension for this disability, one can only conjecture about the official standard of blindness and the islanders' ability to meet it so successfully. One wit has suggested that the eye-testing charts being in English, the islanders can't read them anyway.

As well as the sea and the earnings from migrant laboring, they have always had their land. But this has provided subsistence and little more.

Table 4. *Households having at least one migrant, boatman, or shopkeeper*

	Total households	Households with migrants		Households with boatmen/shopowners	
		Active	Intermittent	Active	Intermittent
East Town	24	5	2	6	2
West Town	42	16	3	14	4
Total	66	21	5	20	6

Note: "Boatmen" is used rather than simply "fishermen," as some men employed on boats are employed for ferrying, collecting mail, etc. The 1961 Census lists seventy-eight adult males as "fishermen," which works out as exactly three per household involved.
Source: Author's fieldnotes.

In the chapter on land, we shall look more closely not only at its use but at its ownership and its meaning for the people. For the moment, it is enough to note its declining use and the growing dependence on the shops. The shops extend credit, and so the islanders become locked into a typical peasant debtor–creditor relationship with the shopkeepers. The shops used to accept fish as payment – this being salted, packed, and sold. But falling prices have ended this practice – a great blow to many people who otherwise had an extra string to their meager economic bow. At one time, on a fine Friday evening, the bay would have been full of curraghs and rowboats out catching glasan to be traded at the shops for weekend supplies.

But despite the evidences of "decline," the Tory people remain cheerful and stoical. One of them put it to me, "We've had a good run from Balor to the Board and after; and we'll be running awhile yet, you'll see!" There is almost a careless sense of a gambler's defiance of the odds in their attitude, which is, contrary to mainland notions, far from magical and superstitious. They are a pious people, but pragmatic. Priests sit lightly upon them. They did without for centuries and are not much awed by formal religion. They feel proprietary about "their" priest, and take good care of him, but they know he will not last. Should he go against "the custom of the island," he can expect quiet noncooperation and even open defiance.

One priest, from Malin, tried to stop them having dances that went on all night: starting at midnight usually, after the evening's visiting was over, and going on until dawn. But he was told that the church hall was built by Tory men not Malin men, and the Tory men would make their own rules about it. It was not "béas an oileáin" – the custom of the island – to dance early, and that was that. The priest backed down. But the people are considerate. They humor the priest and will ask his advice in quarrels and like matters, listening gravely to his words and usually very politely disagreeing. Also, they do not like to hurt his feelings too much. Rather than upset him with a "bad" confession, some of the worst sinners refrain from confessing at all until the relief priest – usually a Franciscan father – comes over in the summer, when they pour out such misdeeds as they have stored up all year.

There are no other real "statuses" on Tory. Good dancers and singers are much admired and there are firm ideas about good and bad character in both persons and families. But to think oneself better than others is considered both stupid and wrong. Outsiders have some status – the nurse for example; and the Ward family, when it was there, which kept a hotel and entertained Sir Roger Casement. The nurse, perhaps the postmistress (an outsider who married an islander), and the lighthouse-men are respected for their official salaries; but they are not real islanders. Otherwise, Tory goes its own way and pays little heed to the outside world's notions of class and authority.

There is, of course, faction, dissension, and dispute. But over time these things even out. However disunited they may be over an issue that concerns their internal relations, they unite to a man when threatened by the outside. When the pretender to the Tory throne was sought by the police, however much they might have disapproved of him not one of the islanders would take the price offered to ferry over the Gardaí. In the end, the Irish navy had to send one of its two corvettes – in the night.

This sense of island identity is very strong and noticed by outsiders; there is a terrible sensitivity that it is almost impossible not to offend in the defensiveness that the people feel about themselves and their much misunderstood "customs." But there is a pride also in being a "Tory man" that will be asserted, with fists if necessary, against all comers.

From being an island pretty much turned in upon itself, Tory has gradually come to be more and more involved in the affairs of the world. It could not now survive, with its aging population, if there were not government subsidies and migrant earnings, and both these things push Tory into a relationship with the bureaucratic outside world. From a system of intense face-to-face relationships in which problems had to be solved in customary terms with the help of kin, Tory has moved into a system of involvement in a wider and more impersonal network. Dependence has shifted from the kinship group to various agencies, and outside forces of law and authority can be invoked in disputes. For example, a legal will can be drawn up in favor of one child despite customs of equal inheritance. But the very impersonality of the outside makes home all that more attractive, and most young people, at least at the beginning of their migratory career, come back as often as possible. Here at least they have the comfort of knowing that their talents as singers and step-dancers will be appreciated.

The lobster/laboring complex works well enough for the men, but female migration is beginning to threaten island survival. It has been common since the First World War for girls to work away, often for years at a time, and many settled down and married outside. However, enough girls stayed home to provide wives for the men who, after their intensive period of migrating, wanted to settle down and marry. Of late, however, the majority of young girls have been following the migratory pattern also. In 1962, all the marriageable girls left for winter jobs. Girls' migrations are usually of longer duration than those of the men, which involve only casual work. The young men still average three to four months on the island each year; the girls three to four weeks. The chances of the girls ever marrying on the island then are slim. For them, Tory is no longer a firm base for expeditions to the outside world, but a childhood home to return to at the holidays.

For the present generation of schoolchildren, the future pattern of life is established. With very few exceptions they will go away to work. This is a conscious ambition for most of them. Only the inadequate will stay. "Working away" has become a part of the life cycle, a *rite de passage* as firmly established as baptism and confirmation. It is the initiation into adulthood.

All this erodes the traditionally strong authority of the old. The young are now the breadwinners. They know that they will leave sooner or later and so the sanctions of the old have less force. Loyalty to parents is fierce and contribution to their upkeep large, but obedience to their stricter tenets, for example over marriage choice, is not so automatic as it might have been. Indeed, the old rarely try to exert authority any more; they have become dependent, and the young are the adaptive and successful.

The old people are ambivalent about migration. They feel that the young should migrate to earn money, but at the same time they want to keep them at home. If anything, fathers are keenest for their sons to migrate, and mothers most anxious to retain them. No one wants the girls to go, but they are resigned to the exodus. The feeling is that "there is nothing for them here." But here, as in so many things, we face a paradox: A son who does not stay at home is disloyal, but one who does not go away to work is lazy.

There could be opportunity for some enterprise in the sphere of boat building in which both fathers and sons might join. The Tory men are skilled boat builders and the boats they build for themselves are much admired around the coast. However, most of the likely candidates are relatively permanent islanders who receive the "dole" (unemployment compensation), and this has come to be regarded as a regular subsidy. Any kind of profitable self-employment would mean the end of the subsidy, and this is greatly feared. Wives put great pressure on their husbands not to "lose the dole." They prefer this very small but reliable income to the uncertain prospects of high profits from industry. In a sense, the certainty of unemployment benefits inhibits risk taking, and so perpetuates unemployment; a problem not unique to Tory.

Despite all this there is still the gambler's gaiety. During the long and often harsh winters, it was common to eat the older cattle. But rather than do this prudently, the men would gather in the houses and amid great excitement gamble for the beef, a cow at a time. Man cannot, as we know, live by beef alone. There has to be some kind of spirit, even if only the uncertainty and thrill of a gamble, or there is no human life at all. Perhaps in the rather dry pages that follow some of the spirit of Tory will emerge as well as the facts, figures, and countless names. If the reader is patient with the details, he or she will be rewarded by an insight into the remarkable adaptability and ingenuity of what I call, for want of more precision, the "society" or "social structure" of Tory Island. And if it turns out to be the last of the Tory epics, it will certainly not be the least.

3
Genealogy: principles and practice

Le h-anmanna na seacht sinsear d'fhág tú!

The Reverend Patrick Dineen, in his monumental dictionary *Foclóir Gaedhilge agus Béarla,* quotes the above saying – "for the souls of the seven generations before you," and comments: ". . . seven generations, about 210 years, is in the popular idea a measurable ancestral period." The saying is well known and often used on Tory as a blessing, and in this chapter we shall see how true his comment is, and look at the way the islanders map out their genealogical relationships.

We must start here if we are to understand the islanders' social world, because this is where they start themselves. How do they decide who is related to whom on an island where everyone is related to everyone else? Well, there is relatedness and relatedness, as we shall see. This problem is not peculiar to Tory, but pervades any small community that chooses to base some of its most important social transactions on the fact of relatedness or kinship. "We are all related," they say, laughing. At the same time, they say such things as, "When a man dies, his land goes to his relatives." "Does that not mean it goes to everyone, then?" asks the naive observer. "Oh surely not," comes the reply, "only to his own people." So there are relatives and relatives, own and other, close and "far out." Some of these categories will be discussed in the next chapter; here I shall be content to show simply how the islanders *see* their universe of relatives by observing how they actually trace relationships when indulging in this as a formal activity – seanchaíocht.

When taking genealogies from the islanders, I found they were very ill at ease with the standard genealogical method; that is, starting with the informant and working out to his closest kin, then to his more remote, and so on. They would try this, but would soon become confused, and there would be much discussion and debate about exact links and forgotten persons. At length, after we had become thoroughly bogged down, one of them suggested to me that I should put down the genealogies in the manner in which the islanders recited them; that is, I should take an

Boys gathered round an ancient altar and remains of a "tau" cross, after Sunday Mass. Bloody Foreland is in the distance.

"old one" (seanduine), or "ancestor" (sinsear) and trace out all his descendants (clann). Methods of doing this varied, but two of the most common were as follows.

An ultimate ancestor would be picked, because no one knew of a yet more remote one for the particular group of living descendants that had been fixed on. Then the names of his children would be given – or at least the names of those who themselves had descendants. Sometimes the names of childless persons would be given with the comment "gan clann" – without offspring. Then, one of the children would be chosen and his children named, and so on until all the present descendants were reached, or at least until that line became exhausted. The narrator would then go back to one of the other children of the original ancestor and repeat the process.

Less common, and usually used only for groups of shallow generational depth, was the method of taking all the children of the ancestor, then all their children, all their children's children, and so on. If the group was small and had relatively little segmentation, this method was favored. It treated the whole group, in effect, in the same way as a "segment" of a much larger group would be treated.

If, on the other hand, the group was extremely large, with a founding ancestor many generations back, then it was often necessary to treat the various segments, each of which would be exhausted before going on to the next. This is very important because it illustrates the islanders' own conception of the nature of genealogy and the structure of these groups. For the moment, I will concentrate on the structure, and discuss any possible functions later.

To make this graphic and to aid discussion, I offer Figure 2. Let us concentrate on the ancestor (or ancestress) A^1. He has children, 1, 2 and 3, who in turn have issue. The genealogy would start with him, and his three children would be named. (The squares indicate either individuals, or groups of individuals, of either sex or both sexes.) Then, the descendants of 1 would be named until exhausted; then those of 2; then those of 3, in the order suggested by the numbers. The recital would go as follows:

> Ancestor, 1, 2, 3
> (1), 4, 5
> (2), 6, 7, 8
> (3), 9, 10
> (9), 11, 12
> (10), 13, 14

The alternative method would go:

> Ancestor, 1, 2, 3
> 9, 10, 6, 7, 4
> 11, 12, 13, 14, 8, 5

If this group were merely a segment of a larger group, then the recitation would have started, for example, with ancestor A^2, continued with his children – A^1 and A^3, after which the procedure just outlined would have been followed for A^1 until this genealogy had been exhausted; then the narrator would have turned to A^3.

The order in which the various segments would be taken was more or less agreed on by the various narrators, who, incidentally, were all older men who styled themselves quite consciously "sloinnteoirí" – genealogists. There was some sense that the order had implications of seniority, although no one was clear about the criteria. Sometimes it was said that one segment was "bigger," although often this was not the case as far as sheer numbers were concerned; sometimes that the senior segment was descended from the oldest son of the ancestor. This was

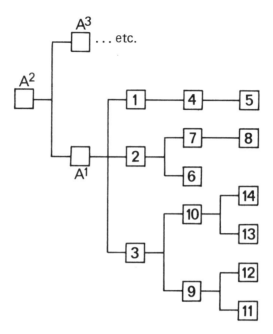

Figure 2. Ideal scheme for reciting genealogies

often impossible to verify, but where it was possible, the statement was not always true – the senior segment was sometimes descended from a woman. Again, it was said that it might be first because it was "more important" – and this seemed to mean that it owned more land. Because men were more likely than women to own land – or at least to be credited with ownership, as we shall see – then land now owned by several descendants of an ultimate ancestor would probably have been more likely to come through his male heirs, and this might help establish seniority of lines. The idea of seniority, however, was not very strong, and nothing much seemed to follow from it except that the senior line might get recited first in the genealogy.

On request, spouses were included, and often they helped to remind a narrator of an exact relationship, particularly because so many names are the same. The narrator would also check by means of the naming system described below. But he usually preferred to give the consanguines first and then add the affines later; otherwise it was too confusing. One of the problems with taking the genealogies was the speed at which the names were given; a narrator in full flow not wishing to be interrupted lest he lose the thread. I managed to get some of them to slow down enough to take the names hurriedly, and even to persuade some to write down their own versions that we would then discuss. But the recitation of genealogy was not something intended for writing down and the convenience of an anthropologist, hence there were always many omissions in the written versions.

It was unpredictable whether the spouses of older members of genealogies would be remembered. Often there was hesitation and dispute about a spouse's name – but never if she or he came from an important group. Lastly, it should be noted that genealogical knowledge was the preserve of a few old men, and other people reckoned not to know much about the "old ones" and the niceties of relationship. Although they may not have known all the details of the connections, however, they certainly knew to whom they were related and with what degree of closeness.

Let us now go back to the beginning and ask who these "ultimate" ancestors were and why they are chosen as the starting point of genealogies. The islanders themselves have no real answer to this question. In some cases, they can point easily to a founding ancestor because he was an immigrant who arrived at a known time and all his descendants are known. But in other cases, where the ancient names of the island are concerned, it is simply asserted that X is the oldest known of the MacRuadhraigh family, or whatever, and that no one knows who came before him. Again, this is not always the case; sometimes the father and even grandfather of an ultimate ancestor might be named, but only the descendants of the ancestor in question would be remembered. If, for example, his father had other sons, their offspring would not be recorded. With a number of ancestors of the same surname, the genealogists will assert that they were related "far back," but that the links are lost. So, for whatever reason – and that will have to wait on our discussion of land – some ancestor is fixed upon as the starting point of the genealogy. He usually must have lived at about the turn of the eighteenth century – certainly between 1780 and 1830 – to judge by the generational depth and documentary evidence (for example, the death records and the Tithe Applotment Rolls of 1830).

All the genealogists were agreed that there were four key genealogies to which most of the others, if not all, could be related: The Clann Eoin, the Clann Neilí, the Clann Fheilimí and the Clann Shéamuis Mhic-Fhlaithbheartaigh. (The names following "clann" ("descendants") will always be in the genitive in Gaelic. Sometimes this is the same as the nominative, as with Eoin, sometimes it requires only a modification of the initial consonant, as with Feilimí (producing a "silent" F), and sometimes it affects both initial *and* final consonants, as with Séamus. In this latter case, the whole name would sound something like "Clan hamish viclaverty.") The first genealogy represents the descendants of one Iain, or John Duggan; the second of Ellen or Nelly Doohan; the third of Phelim or Phillip Rogers; and last of James or Shamus McClafferty – to give them their English and Anglicized equivalents. The Duggans, Doohans, and Rogerses are of course ancient names, and although the McClaffertys are considered relative newcomers, they were certainly on the island in the 1780s and were established as landholders of substance in the 1830s. But that is recent by Tory standards. They definitely "came in" at some point, probably in the eighteenth century.

I will take them in this order because this is the order in which they were regularly given. Subsequent genealogies were then referred to them. Thus, for example, a genealogy would be started with a man who had a son and a daughter, but the son married a member of Clann Eoin. The marriage would be mentioned and I would be told "Tá sin agat faoi chlann Eoin" (you have that under Clann Eoin). Obviously, these genealogies endlessly overlap, and the method of taking the four most prominent and referring the others to these achieves a great economy of memory and time. All in all, some twenty-three ultimate ancestors were referred to and if all the offspring of all of them had been given, it would have involved endless repetition of the same facts. I present the genealogies therefore exactly as they were presented to me, and without intruding any analysis of my own to achieve this economical mode of presentation: It is an exact replica of the islanders' mode of conception of their own genealogical system. (I will occasionally refer to people by their first name and the name of a parent, thus Caitlín–Eoin, "Caitlín daughter of Eoin." The significance of this will appear in the section on naming.)

Readers should note that in the genealogies, land maps, boat crews, etc., that follow, the same person may appear with a slightly different version of his first name. This might be a little confusing, but as the chapter on names explains, in the local naming system there is no cause for confusion; this results from the attempts to adapt to the Anglo-Gaelic bilingual world that the islanders have to live in for a lot of the time. Some of the following more common variations should be noted.

Gaelic	English
Pádraig, Paidí	Patrick, Paddy, Pat, Patsy
Aodh, Hiúdaí	Hugh, Hughie, Hughdie
Bríd, Brídín	Bridget, Biddy, Bridey
Gráinne	Grannia, Grace, Gracie
Caitlín, Cáit	Cathleen, Kate, Katie, Kitty

Eibhlín, Neilí	Ellen, Nell, Nellie, Nelly, Eileen
Nábla	Isabella, Isobel, Belle, Bella
Eamonn	Edmund, Eddie, Ned, Ed
Róise	Rose, Rosie
Donnchadh	Dennis, Denis, Dan, Danny
Brian	Brian, Barney, Briney, Bernard, Bryan
Uilliam, Liam	William, Willie, Billy
Seán, Seánín	John, Johnny
Eoghan	Owen, Eugene, Gene
Feilim, Feilimí	Phelim, Phillip
Séamus	James, Jimmy, Jim, Shamus
Anton	Anthony
Micheál, Micí	Michael, Mike, Mickey, Mick
Eilís	Elizabeth, Betty, Betsy
Máire	Mary, Moira
Máiri	Marie
Tomás	Thomas, Tom, Tommy
Anna	Anne, Annie, Ann
Máiréad, Máirgid	Margaret, Maggie, Madge
Ruarí	Rory, Roger
Cormac	Cormick, Cormic
Domhnall	Donal, Daniel, Dan

Clann Eoin is given as Genealogies 1a and 1b (it is too large to give as one). Its recitation would start with Eoin himself, then, in order, his children, Anton, Hiúdaí, and Caitlín (Anthony, Hughdie, and Cathleen). Then the children of Anton would be named – Anton, Niall, and Paidí. Then the children of Anton Jr. would be taken *per stirpes* until his offspring were exhausted. The narration would then pass to Niall and his descendants, then to Paidí (Paddy). After this segment (craobh – branch) was finished, Hiúdaí would be briefly dealt with because he had but one childless child, and the narration would pass to Caitlín, and her children Gráinne (Gránnia or Grace), Bríd (Bridget), James, and John. Sometimes Hiúdaí would be last, but this was not considered important; effectively there were only the two branches – those of Anton (1a) and Caitlín (1b). When we come to discuss naming, we shall see how Caitlín's children were considered as much Clann Shéamuis–Nance, after their father Séamus (Doohan) Nancy, as they were Clann Chaitlín–Eoin, after their mother. But when the genealogies were given, the complete Clann Eoin were given first, then Séamus Doohan, son of Nancy, was referred to this genealogy.

It will be obvious at a glance that the spouses of members of Clann Eoin enable many other genealogies to be referred to this one. Thus,

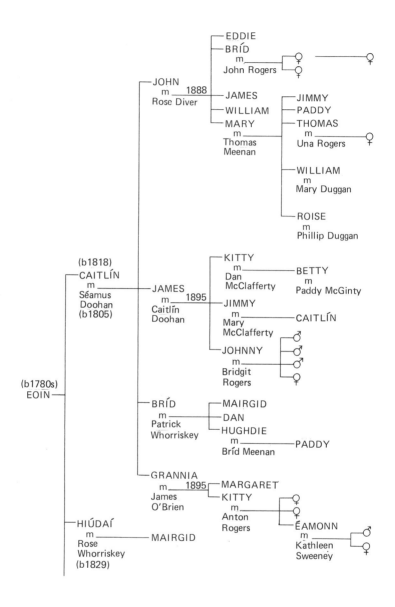

Genealogy 1a. The Clann Eoin

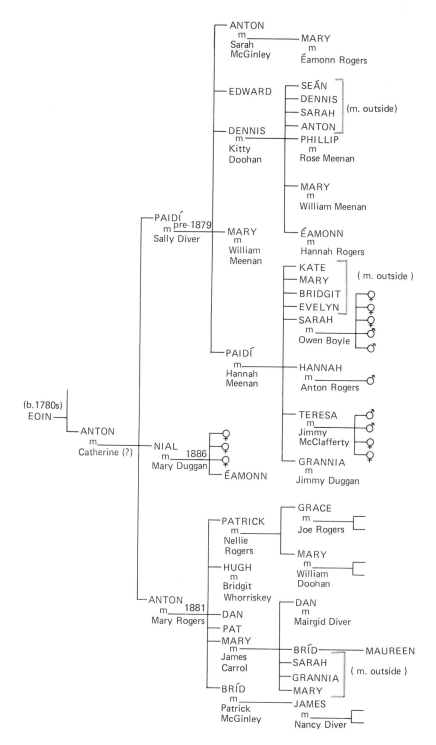

Genealogy 1b. The Clann Eoin *(cont.)*

Paidí, son of Anton, married Sally Diver, and their offspring over three generations constitute a major part of a Diver genealogy. The same is true of the offspring and descendants of Rose Diver, who married John, son of Caitlín and Séamus–Nance. In the generation below this, Thomas Meenan married John's son Mary, and Thomas's cousin, Hannah Meenan, married Paidí, son of Paidí–Antoin. In the generation below this, the children of Thomas and Mary – William and Róise – married the grandchildren of Paidí and Sally – Mary and Phillip. The Divers continued their connection with the marriages of Nancy and Mairgid to James and Dan of the branch of Anton. This constant interweaving, this marriage of a pair of siblings to a pair of cousins, etc., locks certain genealogies together, and the one is constantly referred to the other in recitation. Thus here, substantial portions of the McGinley clann can be accounted for through the marriages of Sara and Patrick McGinley, brother and sister, to the Duggan cousins Anton and Bríd. Note also Mary and Dan McClafferty, brother and sister, married to Jimmy and Kitty Doohan, the children of James, son of Caitlín. (The use of surnames here is merely for convenience of reference. All the descendants of Eoin are not Duggans, of course, and should perhaps be referred to as something like "the Iains" to be correct. Note also that I have given the names as they were given to me, without regard for "correctness" in spelling. There is thus a mixture of unreformed Gaelic, modern versions, "gaelicized" English, various English renderings, and some that hover between all three categories.)

Other things should be noted, such as the number of unmarried people; the number recorded as "married outside"; the number simply recorded as "away" or specified as in the United States, etc.; the number of "forgotten" names – usually of people who died young; and the free mixture of Gaelic and English versions of the names. The forgotten names include, for example, the wife of Anton–Eoin. This is seemingly odd, because the wife of the relatively unimportant Hiúdaí is remembered as is also, of course, the husband of Caitlín. The clue here is the inheritance of the land. When we come to discuss this we shall see how crucial was Hiúdaí's wife and why, therefore, she is remembered. Some people thought they remembered the name of Anton's wife, but it was disputed. Some thought she was from outside, some that she came from a branch of a family that died out. All were agreed that she had no land and that none "came down" from her. It is for this reason – the inheritance of land – that the children of Séamus–Nance and Caitlín have the virtual "dual nationality" that has been mentioned.

The next genealogy – the most extensive – is that of Clann Neilí. It is given as Genealogies 2a, b, and c. Nelly Doohan was an old widow with three children (who are remembered) – Eoin, the eldest (2a), Liam (2b), and Máiri (2c). They would be given in that order, and recited in much the same way as the Eoins. Máiri married Paddy Heggarty, and her branch almost exhausts the Heggarty genealogy. Caitlín, the daughter of Liam, married James Doohan, who was the son of Séamus Doohan Nancy and Caitlín, and has already appeared in Genealogy 1. When the Neilí genealogy was being narrated, however, even if it followed directly on the Eoin, these descendants were given in full. The system of referring one genealogy back to another was reserved for the lesser clann. Even so, it would be pointed out that this branch had already appeared. Liam's other daughter, Neilí, married Séamus Meenan, usually known as Séamus Bán ("Fair James"), who occupies in this genealogy much the same place that Séamus–Nance did in the last. His children were associated strongly with his name, as well as with their mother's. But they were indubitably Clann Neilí when the genealogy was being given, and the Meenan genealogy of their father would be "referred" again to this one. The children of Neilí and Séamus, Hannah and William, who married the Duggan cousins, Patrick and Mary, have appeared already on the Eoin genealogy. Of the descendants of Eoin – the "senior branch" – Nábla married Barney McClafferty, thus providing a link-up with that genealogy – one of the big four.

The next important genealogy is that of Clann Fheilimí MhicRuadhraigh, or more simply, Clann Fheilimí: Genealogies 3a, b and c. The four children of the ultimate ancestor – Phelim or Phillip – are two brothers and two sisters, Paidí and Liam (3a), Bella (Belle, Isobel, or Nábla) (3b) and, possibly, Mary (3c). The doubt about the latter is interesting. She is remembered as definitely being a "sister of Belle," but there was argument about her name. She definitely married Eoghan Doohan, and his connections are known – we will return to them later. But the genealogists preferred to move quickly on to the more certain ground of her daughter, Ann, who married Ned Diver. And this is interesting. The Divers (O Duibhír) are, of course, an ancient name on the island, but they seem to have difficulty in providing a "key" genealogy. They are constantly referred to others. The descendants of Ann, here, are definitely also known Clann Eamuinn after their father, and are therefore "Divers"; but the genealogists at least do not forget that ultimately they are, through two female links, members of the Clann Fheilimí. The matter is complicated, for of Ann's three children, only Eddie carried on the name of Diver; Isabella married a Whorriskey and thus there is a great overlap with that clann, and Rose, as we have

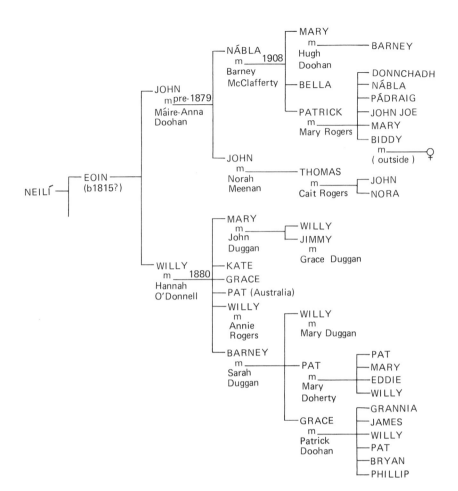

Genealogy 2a. The Clann Neilí

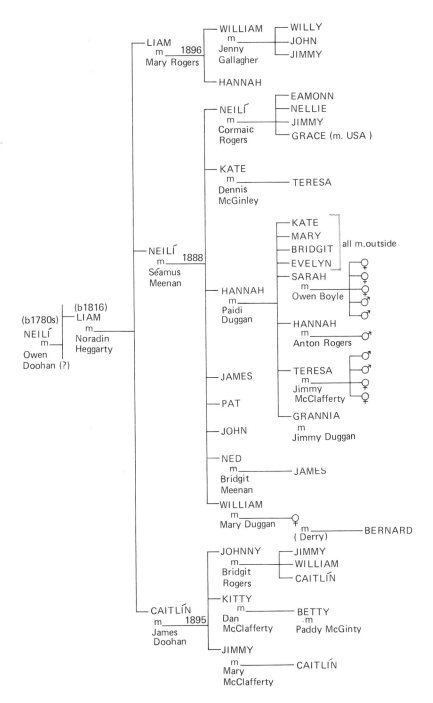

Genealogy 2b. The Clann Neilí *(cont.)*

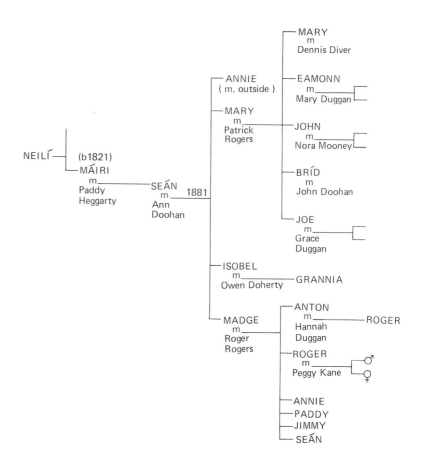

Genealogy 2c. The Clann Neilí *(cont.)*

already seen in Genealogy 1, married John Doohan, son of Séamus–Nance and Caitlín, and thus is also linked strongly with the Eoins. Thus, this particular branch of the Clann Fheilimí is more invaded, as it were, by other genealogies than are its sibling branches.

The less rigorous of the genealogists would sometimes give the descendants of Ann and Ned as a separate genealogy and then explain its links to the Feilimí genealogy. But the more strict did not regard this as correct. "Separateness" in social terms (and again here it may well turn out that "Mary" had no land and this weakened the link) has nothing to do with the correctness of genealogy. If one starts with Feilimí, then one must recite all his descendants, even if this does do violence to notions of Diver separateness.

There is also a problem here of generation turnover. Mary was, it seems, a very much older sister to the other children of Feilimí, and her daughter Ann was effectively of their generation rather than the next. I have compensated for this graphically, so that the balance of the genealogy represents the effective alignment of generations. Thus we can fix Ann's birthdate from the death records (supplied by the Central Statistics Office, Dublin Castle) as 1836. By extrapolation, Mary was probably born about 1812. She is remembered as much older than the other children of Feilimí, and it is possible that there were intervening siblings who died. From the marriage records, we know that Ann's daughter Rose was born in 1864 (although the death records would make it 1862). Eddie dates from 1856 and, if he is Ann's eldest, which is assumed, then she married at twenty like her mother, who must have married at roughly that age. There is then a tradition of very young – by Irish standards – marriages here, but that does not explain the seeming oddity of both Isabella, and Eddie's wife Máiréad Rogers, who, if the death records are to be believed, were born in 1861 and 1862 respectively, and yet who were married before 1879. Even if they were married in 1878, that makes them seventeen and sixteen respectively – very young by island standards. This is not impossible, however, for women often did marry young in those days, especially if they were expecting a child as evidently was often the case. Of course, the death records could be in error, and we have examples of this, but it is this series of very young marriages that explains the extra generation in this branch, in any case.

The rest of the genealogy is not problematical. The reader by now will be able to pick out some familiar name and see where it connects into the other two. I will only point out the marriage of Bella's granddaughter, Kitty, to Dennis Duggan, which we have already come across in Genealogy 1.

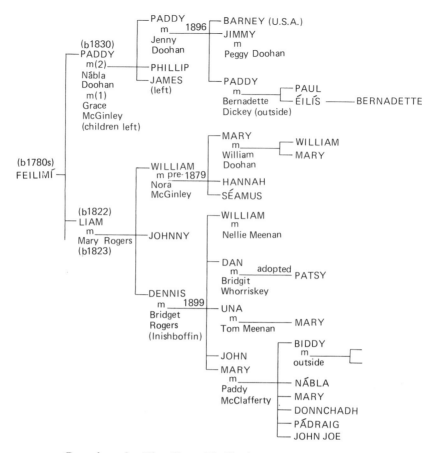

Genealogy 3a. The Clann Fheilimí

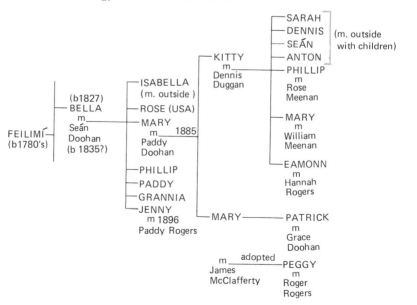

Genealogy 3b. The Clann Fheilimí *(cont.)*

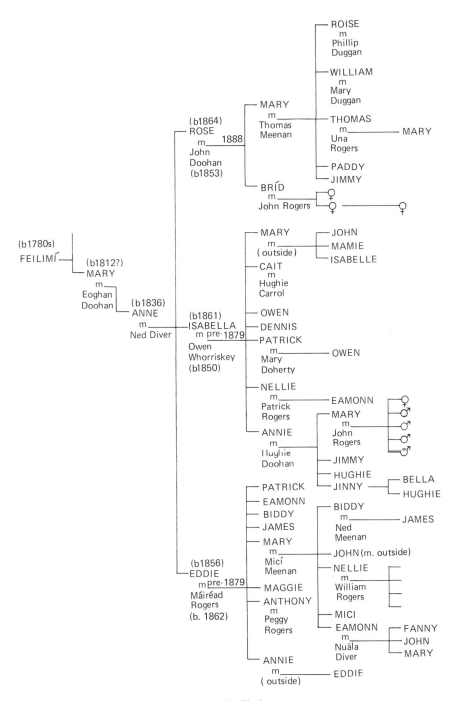

Genealogy 3c. The Clann Fheilimí *(cont.)*

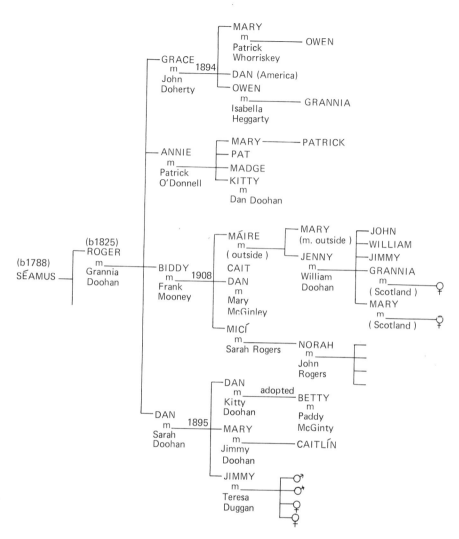

Genealogy 4a. The Clann Shéamuis

The last of the big four is the Clann Shéamuis MhicFhlaithbheartaigh, or Clann Shéamuis, shown in Genealogies 4a and b. Séamus (Shamus or James) had two sons, Roger (4a) and John (4b). John married twice and the son of his first marriage, Barney (Brian), married Nábla Doohan of the Ncilís and has figured in that genealogy. The marriage of Dan and Mary McClafferty, to Kitty and Jimmy Doohan, has already featured in both the Eoin and the Neilí genealogies. The Mooneys and Doherties are absorbed in this one by the marriages of Grace and Biddy, daughters of Roger.

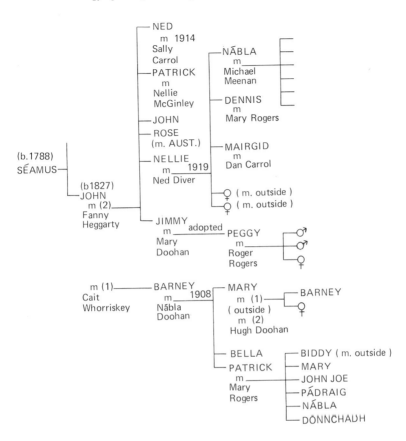

Genealogy 4b. The Clann Shéamuis *(cont.)*

To give an idea of the location of these genealogies in time, I have added the dates of certain marriages in the second generation down from the founders. Marriage records for the island start in 1879, and births in 1882. (These records were made available to me by the curate of Tory, Father Sweeney, and were cross-checked with those provided by the Central Statistics Office.) Where any of the marriages of this generation are not recorded, it is simply assumed that the marriage was pre-1879. This is confirmed by birth records showing children of these couples in the 1880s.

If we start with Genealogy 1, we can read off the dates of the relevant marriages: Anton to Mary Rogers, 1881; Niall to Mary Duggan, 1886; Paidí to Sally Diver, pre-1879; Gránnia to James O'Brien, in 1895; James to Caitlín Doohan, 1895; John to Rose Diver, 1888. In 2: Seán to Ann Doohan, 1881; Caitlín to James Doohan, 1895; Neilí to Séamus Meenan,

1885; Liam to Mary Rogers, 1896; Willy to Hannah O'Donnell, 1880; John to Máire-Anna Doohan, pre-1879. In 3, Eddie Diver and Máiréad Rogers, pre-1879; Isabella to Owen Whorriskey, pre-1879; Rose to John Doohan, 1888; Mary to Paddy Doohan, 1885; Dennis to Bridget Rogers, 1899; William to Nora McGinley, pre-1879; Paddy to Jenny Doohan, 1896. In 4, Barney to Nábla Doohan, 1908; Nellie to Ned Diver, 1919; Ned to Sally Carrol, 1914; Dan to Sara Doohan, 1895; Biddy to Frank Mooney, 1881; Grace to John Doherty, 1894.

The bulk of the marriages took place, then, between 1875 and 1900. Of the earliest recorded marriages, the priest took the care to note the age of the partners; for forty people so recorded, the average age was twenty-nine. This was for marriages up to 1896, and so roughly takes us back to the 1850s as the era in which the oldest of this generation were born. (The late dates of the marriages of Nellie and Ned McClafferty result from a late second marriage by their father, which puts them behind the rest of their generation.)

For the generation previous to this, some absolute dates can be obtained from the death records that also start in 1879. Some of the ages at death that give an idea of the time depths involved are of people not recorded in these four genealogies. For example, Mary Whorriskey died in 1880 at an age of "about 104." The cause of death is boldly given as "old age." This takes us back to 1776. An Owen Doohan, who may have been the husband of Neilí, died in 1879 of the same cause, aged 94, taking us to 1785. Denis McGinley died in 1883 aged 105, thus having been born in 1778 – and so on.

If we take our genealogies in turn again, in Genealogy 1 we have firm dates for Séamus Doohan and Caitlín: 1805 and 1818, respectively. Rose Whorriskey dates from 1829. Where the deaths are not recorded, it must be assumed that they occurred before 1879, and therefore that most of our first generation of ancestors were born around the turn of the century, or at least in its early years. In 2, Máiri dates from 1821, Liam from 1816, and Eoin from 1815. In 3, Paddy is perhaps 1830, Liam 1822, Mary Rogers whom he married 1823, Mary 1812 (uncertain), whereas Bella died in 1929 at the age of 102, thus dating from 1827. Her husband was perhaps born in 1835. In 4, the death of Séamus McClafferty is one of the first recorded – in 1879 aged 91, thus placing his birth in 1788. Of his sons, John was born in 1827 and Roger in 1825. This generation, then, occupies the first half of the nineteenth century, and that of its children the second half. Relatively late marriage leads to a relatively slow turnover of generations. The generation of the founding ancestors, in its turn, occupied the latter half of the eighteenth century.

Séamus McClafferty was known to have been one of the younger of these, so they must have been born before 1788. If the average age of marriage is about thirty, and Eoin–Neilí, for example, was born in 1815, then it is likely that his mother was married in the previous year and hence born around 1784–5. This is assuming that Eoin was her firstborn, which he may not have been, but it is a reasonable guess because the Owen who was her husband (probably) was born in 1785.

Most of the "founders," as we shall see, appear on the land records from 1830 onward, and the whole discussion of land inheritance will refer constantly to these genealogies, as will the discussion of kinship and naming to follow. For the moment, let me discuss some of the genealogies that are important but not of the big four and see how they are referred. In this way, we shall cover most of the living islanders.

(The general reader, who by now has the general picture, might wish only to look at one or two of these to see how the "referral" system works, and then go on to the conclusions at the end of this chapter. Both general reader and specialist will have need to refer back themselves to the genealogies that follow when we come to discuss land, which is why – along with making for completeness of the record – they are given.)

Let us take some of the 'immigrant' genealogies – those of the McGinleys, Dohertys, O'Donnells, etc., and see how they are quickly exhausted by cross-referencing. Patrick McGinley (Genealogy 5) was born in either 1843 or 1845, and is taken as the starting point. He is not the earliest McGinley on record. Sarah was born in 1814; Dennis and Cathleen appear on the applotment rolls in 1830. Dennis was born in 1778 and in 1857 he is still the holder of the McGinley land, Patrick taking over sometime shortly after. It is agreed that Dennis was Patrick's grandfather, probably the brother of Sarah and Cathleen, but that there were no other children who survived and had children; so the genealogy starts with Patrick in 1843–5. He married a Diver, variously Mary or Norah, born in 1858 of a branch of Divers that died out, although there may be survivors in America. I have given the two genealogies together as Genealogy 5, for the Divers here illustrate how a branch can just disappear through death and emigration.

We can pick up from this the Dohertys, because Patrick's daughter Bríd married Ed Doherty. But of the other children of Patrick who themselves had children, all are referred to two of the big four. Pat and Sarah married Duggans and are referred to Genealogy 1; Mary and Dennis can be found in Genealogy 4.

The Dohertys start with Paddy in 1825, and no earlier Dohertys can

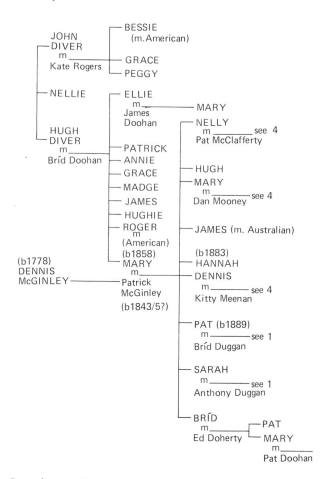

Genealogy 5. Patrick McGinley and a branch of Divers

be found. Genealogy 6 shows how easily this line is absorbed, with the marriage of John (1864) to Grace McClafferty being referred to 4 and that of Edward and Bríd McGinley to 5.

Another immigrant group with a known starting point is the O'Donnells (Genealogy 7). Patrick was born in 1830 and moved to the island on marrying Bríd Duggan, born in 1836. Of his children, some left for America, and of those who married, Patrick is accounted for by the McClaffertys, Genealogy 4, and Hannah by the Neilís of Genealogy 2.

The Carrols came to the island in the shape of Owen, who was not there in 1830, but who appears on the landlord's list in 1845 as a tenant. He bought land, which passed to his sons James and John, born in 1837 and 1845, respectively. Their offspring are shown in Genealogy 8, and are quickly accounted for by the marriage of James (born 1874) to Mary

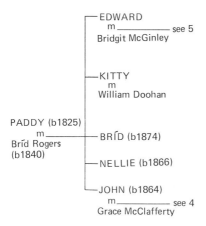

Genealogy 6. Paddy Doherty

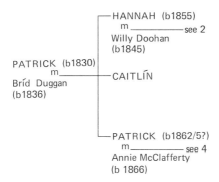

Genealogy 7. Patrick O'Donnell

Duggan, which appears in Genealogy 1. Sally married Ned McClafferty, but they have no children. This does, however, link up with 4. John's line died out, but Hughdie (born 1869) married into the Whorriskeys, whom we will consider next.

The Whorriskeys, as we have seen, are long established, having the earliest documented birth, that of Mary in 1776. But she was probably the wife of one of the two original Whorriskeys, brothers or cousins, who came to the island in a smack late in the eighteenth century, married, and stayed. They were Tomás Dubh and Domhnall–Shiubhanna (Dark Thomas, and Donal, son of Susan). Their clann is given as Genealogy 9. There is some uncertainty about the spouses of the sons of Tomás, but a number of Whorriskeys appear in the death records, and these, it is agreed, might have been the spouses in question. These have been tentatively added. If John, the eldest son of Tomás, was indeed born as early

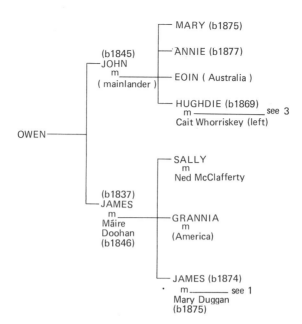

Genealogy 8. Owen Carrol

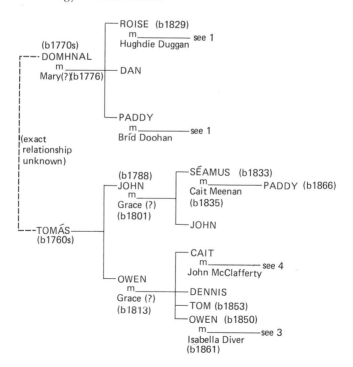

Genealogy 9. Whorriskey

as 1788 – and this seems well attested, that puts Tomás's birth back at least in the 1760s. Domhnall, his younger brother, was probably then born in the 1770s. There is an Owen recorded who should have been born in 1832, but he would not quite fit the Owen on our chart. Many Whorriskeys (Mary 1857, Susan 1847, Susan 1824) are either women who died without marrying, or spouses of otherwise unrecorded male Whorriskeys who left no issue (Patrick 1848, John 1860, Anton 1835, etc.) The line has a record of young deaths, and as we saw above, there is a tendency to leave out of account members of genealogies who leave no issue. This is less true of the big four than of the more peripheral genealogies.

However, with the Whorriskeys, the line of Domhnall is continued through the marriage of Paddy to Bríd Doohan, which refers to Genealogy 1, but of this line only Paddy remains, and he is unmarried. Róise's marriage to Hughdie Duggan has been noted in 1. The line of Tomás continues, but is totally referred to the McClaffertys in Genealogy 4 and the Diver branch of the Feilimís in Genealogy 3.

Of the other immigrants, we have seen how the O'Briens are largely accounted for in Genealogy 1, although there are older O'Briens than James (born 1863) recorded: two Kates born in 1829, Grace (probably James's sister) born in 1859, as well as George, born in 1845 (elder brother). The Mooneys are entirely referable to the McClafferty genealogy, 4, Frank being the original immigrant. The Heggertys or Heraghtys – who once supplied the "kings" of Tory – were in evidence as considerable landowners in 1830 (Sarah, Edward, James, and Niall). Margaret, sister of our ultimate ancestor Paddy, was born in 1839. But no descendants except those of Paddy are recorded and they are all referred to the Neilís – Genealogy 2. Another name frequent in the records is Curran or Curren. There were several at the beginning of the nineteenth century (Patrick 1800, Ellen 1801, Bridget 1805, Bryan 1815). But the name peters out, the members of the line have been absorbed, and there are no distinct genealogies.

Of the more recently established names one should note Ward and Dixon, which appear largely as affines to the main genealogies, and, having no prospects of further offspring, are not thought to merit genealogies at all.

What remain are the fragmentary genealogies of the well-established names – Rogers, Duggan, Doohan, and Meenan. The last is interesting because it represents an important and long-standing island group, but again has failed to generate a key genealogy, much like the Divers. One

Meenan genealogy starts with Tom, of uncertain dates but appearing on the records for 1845 and 1857. A Sara Meenan (widow) appears on the 1830 records. A Kate Meenan was born in 1807, which establishes the antiquity of the Meenan line. Genealogy 10 effectively starts with Tom, and his three sons John (1855), Tom (1848), and James (1861). The last is the Séamus Bán who appears in Genealogy 2, and whose descendants comprise such an important branch of the Neilís. John, it seems, had no offspring – or at least none to survive, but is remembered in land transactions. Tom married Peggy Duggan (1852) and of his children, the one with offspring was Tomás, who married Mary Doohan and who thus is referred to both 1 and 3. James and Nellie had Hannah, who married Patrick Duggan; thus this branch is referable to both Genealogies 1 and 2. William Meenan in turn married Mary Duggan, thus further entwining this branch with the Eoins.

The other line of the Meenan family – known to be related to the one just discussed – is commonly referred to as the "Micís" because the eldest son has always been Mickey. There were Mickeys before the one recorded in Genealogy 3 (who married Mary Diver – daughter of Ann, daughter of Mary, daughter of Feilimí), but again they left no other offspring and the Micí Meenans are referred in their entirety to the Feilimí–Diver genealogy.

The other established names present many fragmentary genealogies. The genealogists are agreed that ultimately they would link up, but the links are mostly forgotten. It is vaguely remembered that the "West End Rogers" are more related to each other than to the "East End Rogers" and so on – but the exact links are forgotten or, as the islanders would say, "fuar," "cold." Thus, the younger McClaffertys have no real idea that the East Enders and West Enders are linked through Séamus. He is known only to the old genealogists, which is not surprising for someone born in 1788. Ultimately he will be forgotten, and the various McClafferty lines or branches will know only that they are "related" but not how.

Let us take the "fragmentary" Doohans. One genealogy that is quickly disposed of is that of John Doohan (Genealogy 11), known as Seán–Bhrianaigh – John, son of Brian (or Barney) born in 1802, probably. Although the "Seán–Bhrianaighs," or indeed properly the "Brianaighs" or "Brineys," are recognized as a group, and "William Doughan, Bryan's son" is recorded on the rolls of 1830, the whole group is quickly referred to the two genealogies of Feilimí – through the marriage of Seán Doohan to the famous and long-lived Bella Rogers (Genealogy 3), and that of the Carrols through the marriage of his sister Máire to James Carrol –

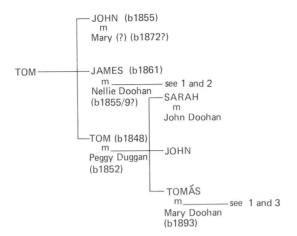

Genealogy 10. Tom Meenan

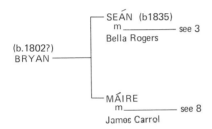

Genealogy 11. Bhrianaigh (Bryan Doohan)

Genealogy 8. Alternatively, the "Carrol" line here would be recited as part of the Seán–Bhrianaighs and then this branch of the Carrols referred when they were recited. It did not seem to matter which, and depended on which genealogy was recited first. But the Seán–Bhrianaighs were always referred to the Feilimís.

Again, the descendants of "Eamonn Rua" (Clann Eamuinn) are similarly the offspring of two siblings, Eamonn himself and his brother Eoghan. These are given as Genealogy 12. Eoghan's line is immediately referred to the Feilimís through his marriage to Mary, daughter of Feilimí and sister of Belle. Eamonn's wife is unknown (perhaps an outsider), but her daughter Máire-Anna (Mary-Ann – unique name) married John Doohan, son of Eoin–Neilí, and that line similarly is absorbed in the Neilis (Genealogy 2). Eamonn's son Hughdie married a Sally Doohan and continued the line that still exists in the person of the unmarried Nábla but is continued through the Whorriskeys by the marriage of Hughdie's son Hugh to Annie Whorriskey (see Genealogy 3),

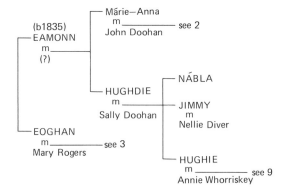

Genealogy 12. Eammon Rua (Edmund Doohan)

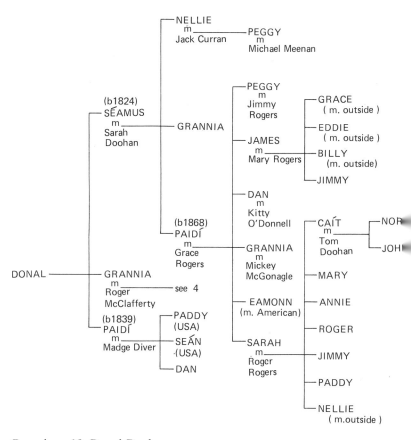

Genealogy 13. Donal Doohan

because Annie is the daughter of Isabella Diver. Note also the complication that Hugh Doohan, here, and Isabella are second cousins, both descended from the pair of siblings Eamonn Rua and Eoghan Doohan. Isabella's mother, Anne, was the daughter of Eoghan.

Another set of Doohans are the Clann Dhomhnaill, the descendants of Donal Doohan. Because one branch, that of Paidi–Dhomhnaill, is extinct, they are usually known as Clann Shéamuis–Dhomhnaill after Donal's other son James – as shown in Genealogy 13. The "referral" here is a major one: that of Donal's daughter Grannia and her marriage to Roger McClafferty, which takes in the whole of that McClafferty branch. The line through Séamus, however, is not referable, and the Séamus–Dhomhnaills have a distinct existence, taking in some Currans on the way.

A strange branch of Doohans are the Pircíns ("Pirkeen") – given in Genealogy 14. For a long time, the name did not make sense to me, even though the descendants of Domhnall–Phircín ("Donal–feerkeen"), etc., were often referred to. It was eventually explained that this was the Gaelic rendering of "Perkins." How Mr. Perkins gets into the picture I am not sure – perhaps he was with the lighthouse – but as a result of his liaison with an unknown Doohan, the line of the Pircíns was started. It is quickly absorbed in two branches by the marriages of Sara to Dan McClafferty (4) and Ann to Séan Heggarty (2). The third branch, that of Dennis – Domhnall–Phircín, continues – just.

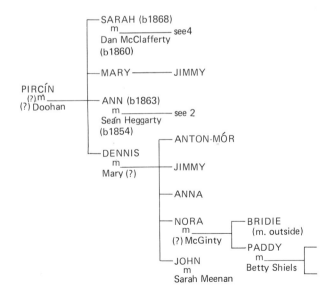

Genealogy 14. Pircín (Doohan)

We have already seen how Divers are absorbed in both Eoins and Feilimís. We must briefly examine the line of Divers that includes the Sally who married Paidí Duggan and created so many Eoins. She was from the line of Donnchadh–Shallaigh (Dennis, son of Sally), given in Genealogy 15. Sally's son, Dennis Diver (born 1833), married twice. From his first marriage, he produced Ned, who married Nellie McClafferty and is referred to Genealogy 4. The other line, through John, is petering out. Through his second marriage he produced a line through Bríd that is also declining, and one through the already well-known Sally, whose marriage with Paidí Duggan we have discussed, thus referring this line to Genealogy 1.

All that remain are the remnants of the Rogers group. Genealogy 16 shows the descendants of Anton, who fall into two groups: the descendants of Edward (1849) and of Patrick (1846). The former are largely accounted for by reference to Genealogy 2, whereas the latter overlap

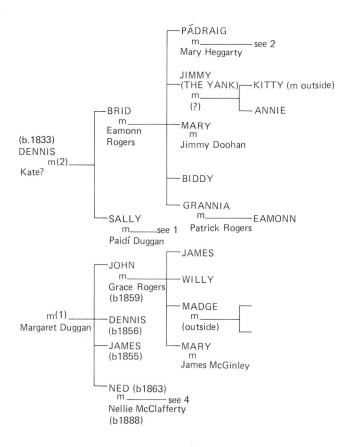

Genealogy 15. Donnchadh–Shallaigh (Diver)

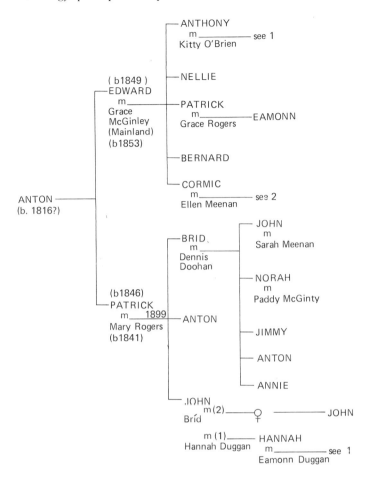

Genealogy 16. Anton Rogers

briefly with Genealogy 1. It is noticeable, as in this case, that when the overlap is several generations deep and involves a large number, the reference is felt to be obligatory.

Genealogy 17 shows the descendants of Paddy Rogers (approximately 1832), known usually as Paddy–Dooley–Thoraí (Paddy son of Dooley of Tory) to distinguish him from Patrick Doherty, who is Paddy–Dooley–Mhallainne [Paddy, son of Dooley of Malin (Inishowen)]. Who the two Dooleys were is a mystery, but they probably get into the picture in the same way as the equally mysterious Mr. Perkins. No one was inclined to elaborate. Paddy's son Ruarí (Roger) continued the line with two marriages, linking with 13. His other son Eamonn (1856) married Bríd Diver and is usually referred to Genealogy 15, which itself links up with Genealogy 2.

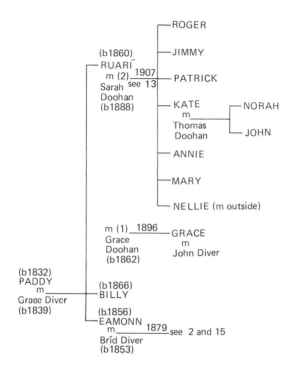

Genealogy 17. Dooley–Thoraí (Paddy Rogers)

Finally, Genealogy 18 dates from another Paddy Rogers (approximately 1821). His line through his son Anthony (1854) is ultimately referred to Genealogy 2, and that through his daughter Kathleen (1851) also to Genealogy 2 and Genealogies 16 and 1.

With these genealogies we almost exhaust all the living islanders, except for some odd names such as McGonagle, Gallagher, etc., which have been discussed above. This in itself is the aim of the prouder genealogists: All the living islanders must be linked ultimately to an ancestor – one of the twenty-three I mentioned above. I list below these apical or ultimate ancestors who are agreed upon.

1. Eoin (John Duggan)
2. Neilí (Nellie Doohan)
3. Feilimí (Phillip Rogers)
4. Séamus (James McClafferty)
5. Patrick McGinley
6. Paddy Doherty (Dooley–Mhallainne)
7. Patrick O'Donnell
8. Owen Carrol

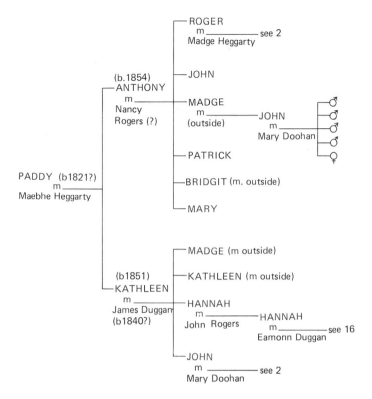

Genealogy 18. Paddy Rogers

9.   Whorriskeys (Tomás Dubh and Domhnall–Shiubhainne)
10. Tom Meenan
11. Bryan Doohan (Brianaigh)
12. Eamonn Doohan (Eamonn Rua)
13. Donal Doohan (Domhnall)
14. Pircín (Doohan)
15. Dennis Diver (Donchadh–Shallaigh)
16. Anton Rogers
17. Paddy Rogers (Dooley–Thoraighe)
18. Paddy Rogers
19. James Doohan (Séamus–Nance)
20. James Meenan (Séamus Bán)
21. Paddy Heggarty (An Rí)
22. Ned Diver
23. Frank Mooney

Ancestors 1 to 18 are those in the genealogies of the same numbers. The remaining five are ancestors contained within the big four who are regarded by the genealogists as worthy of independent recital. This applies particularly to Ned Diver, as we have seen, but quite strongly to the two Séamuses, 19 and 20. Perhaps because the Heggartys are the "royal" line, they too are considered an entity. The Mooneys are too long established to be ignored or simply subsumed under the McClaffertys. The ultimate ancestor of the Whorriskeys is not known, but they are treated as one genealogy with the ancestor "assumed."

That only one ancestor is a woman is an artifact of the current situation. If, for example, Nancy the mother of Séamus had had two sons, then there may have been two lines converging on her and known collectively as Clann Nance – as was the case with Neilí. It is significant that no one remembers much about Neilí. She is simply a name. Her two sons and her daughter are remembered, and hence she is enshrined as an ancestress. Ultimately, some of the ancestresses of present lines will become independent as older links are forgotten, and there will be more female ultimate ancestresses. If we go one generation down from the founders, to the founders of the effective branches, we find that of forty two, eleven are women.

The "seven generations – 210 years" of Dineen's proverb are realized in some genealogies but not all. Generations turn over at different rates, and when they turn over quickly, as with the Mary–Fheilimí branch or with the descendants of Biddy McClafferty, we do get a compass of seven generations. When they turn slowly, we manage five. But the span of roughly 200 years is there, because the effective ancestors were born in the 1780s. The genealogists will happily discuss older connections, but confess these to be speculative. They are concerned with relationships of greater depth than those shown here, but not as part of the structure of genealogy itself; they discuss them as an extra item. One reason, as we shall see, is pragmatic: Connections beyond those shown here are irrelevant for making claims on land.

But it is not only pragmatic concerns that move the "seanchaithe" to weave their verbal webs, spinning out the names like intricate connected threads. There is sheer devotion to the details themselves, and to the perfection of their articulation. A "seanchas" is not only a "story," but also a "tradition," a "genealogy," a "law," an "act of tracing pedigrees," a "telling of tales," and just plain "gossiping"! Father Dineen may not have exhausted the meanings, but they tell their own story as they stand. When a "storyteller" launches into his tale, it is law, tradition, pedigrees, and gossip that are always involved. Even the highest of the high tales sound at times like gossip about the doings of the gods and heroes – including the interminable discussions of their ancestries. There is no such thing as *idle* gossip; it always works overtime. For it is but one name for that endless fascination with each other, with relationship one to another, and with the traditions and laws that govern this, that consume all little communities. And consume the keepers of knowledge in little communities like Tory more than the rest; for knowledge-for-its-own-sake – the highest expression of man's humanity – is often most treasured in the lowliest of settings. It is, along with song and dance, often the only manifestation of the human spirit that the masters cannot suppress – although even here they try, by banning the language and the songs. Aodhagán O Rathaille, teaching Latin, Greek, and the Gaelic epics in the hedges to the sons of starving peasants, was one of this lineage; the old men of Tory, lying on their backs on the dirt floor with stones under their heads for pillows, gossiping about heroes and pedigrees until the dawn, were of it also.

I put this in the past tense because they are almost all dead, the Old Ones with the knowledge and the ferocity of fascination in imparting it. The young men (those around sixty or so), and the boys (anyone under forty), have only fragmentary information and no such fascinations. We, the scholars of another tradition, have caught the last spark of the old fire, but can only blow on it with dry and analytical breath; unlike the Old Ones we do not have the breath of life – of the lifeblood of the people who inhabit these elaborate nominal schemes, these conceptual scaffoldings. But inadequate as it is, it is the best we have, and I must do them what honor I can as I conduct my own form of seanchas in the ensuing pages. For what we have here is untold riches for the anthropologist and historian. We have a living example of well-articulated "cognatic" or "bilateral" descent groups; but not those belonging to a remote tribe; these belong to a people rich in history, to part of our own history. What is more, we can plug them *into* history via the existing records, sparse as these are, and see how they are the framework for the articulation of land ownership and inheritance. And from this we can read them back into more remote history, for Tory is, in a sense, a living fossil of ancient land-tenure and inheritance practices that have never been fully understood.

I must commence this seanchas, however, by first looking, in the next chapter, at Tory categories of kinship, and then at how the genealogical scheme fits with both the reckoning of kinship and, more remarkably, with the system of personal names.

4
Kinship and naming

Fir is mna óga, is seandaoine is páistí;
Muintir mo mhuintire, 'gus cairde mo chléibhe.

This song celebrates the "sean reilig bheannaithe," the "blessed old graveyard," where sleep "men and young women, old people and children; people of my people and friends of my bosom." But in trying to translate we are in trouble immediately with the Gaelic categories. Take the word "muintir," for example. I have had to translate it twice as "people," and in its widest sense it does mean the same as the English, as when one is talking of "the People of Ireland" or something such (see the dedication of this book). It cannot stand alone, but must have a qualifying word or words. Thus it can perhaps be translated accurately, although not elegantly, as "people of a social category." Thus, when a Gaelic speaker refers to "mo mhuintir," it is in the sense that English speakers used often to refer to "my people," meaning "my close relatives." Bertrand Russell, in his autobiography, does it all the time; now it is not used so frequently. Thus the singer is playing on the word; buried there are "people" who are "my people," that is, my close relatives.

There is, however, another word (not in the song) that refers specifically to relatives: "gaolta" (singular gaol), those of my blood. In the singular it refers specifically to kinship: "Tá gaol eatartha," "they are kin." But its adjectival form, gaolmhar, although meaning "related," also means "kindness" and "friendship." This is similar again to English, where "kind" derives from "kin" – indeed they are the same word. But it comes first as a surprise, then a delight, to the English speaker to find that when an Irish countryman refers to his "friends," in fact he means his relatives. In Gaelic, he could distinguish, because he has the alternative words "gaolta" and "muintir," and the other word used in the song, "cairde" (singular cara), "friends"; that is, those who are *not* related. (Its Latin affinities are obvious and it might be a loanword.) One islander put it to me, "Is iad mo mhuintir mo chairde is mo ghaolta": "My 'people' are my 'friends' and my relatives" – or something such; and he was strug-

The dying art of spinning.

gling. So again, the singer is playing with the words – as they love to do – because he is not only contrasting the two meanings of muintir with each other, but both with cairde – nonrelated "friends."

He does not stop there, because the other contrast is between muintir, again, and "daoine" (singular duine), as in the word "seandaoine," "old people" or "old ones." Daoine can stand alone, unlike muintir, and means people in the more general sense of "human individuals": "Bhí daoine go leor ann," "There were a lot of people there." To make matters clearer (or more confused), when referring to his close relatives, a speaker will often call them "daoine muintire," which drives us to writing "people people" and has really no translation except something cumbersome like "people of my particular social group" – usually kinship group (although this could more exactly be "daoine gaolmhara" – "related people" – and so on through the combinations).

There are yet other ways of referring to the bulk of one's relatives, or one's close kin. Usually someone will say "mo lucht gaolta." "Lucht," like muintir, is used with another word, and also means "people" or even "persons" in the barbarous contemporary usage. Thus "lucht oibre" could be literally translated as "work-persons," for example, because it does not specify sex; thus we can avoid "workmen." But it is always a company, or party – an organized group of persons. Perhaps then "mo lucht gaolta" could be best translated by the anthropological jargon as "my kinship network," or by the plainer and older English, "my kindred": all the people on both sides related to me personally.

"Lucht" contrasts sharply with "clann," which we have come across already in the previous chapter. But before tackling that crucial distinction, we must look at two other words. "Dream," a "tribe" (much less often "fine," same meaning), is used to refer to a surname group, and often translated as "crowd" – "the Rogers crowd," "dream Mhic Ruadhraigh." This is sometimes divided up by towns or "ends" – the West End Rogers, the East Town McClaffertys, etc. Nothing much follows from this except that certain qualities are supposed to go with certain names, and there is some dispute about which is the oldest "crowd" on the island. But a surname group is not really a social group, and nothing is assumed except a common relationship "i bhfad amach," "far out," by virtue of the common name, even if such a link cannot be traced. The other word in common use is "teaghlach," "family" or "household." Gaelic does not easily separate out these two, because it is assumed they would be the same. The more bookish term "líon tí" means the "number" or "full complement" of the house. In the chapter on marriage and household, we shall see what difficulties there are in applying this on Tory where "family" – in the sense of the nuclear family – and household do not always coincide. In the Tory scheme of things, there is really only "household" and beyond that the other categories of kin such as muintir. The nuclear family of parents and dependent children does not merit a separate concept. The term "bunadh" is also often used and can be roughly rendered as "folk," something like muintir. Thus "an bunadh óg" – the young folk; "bunadh an tí" – the folk of the household; "bunadh Uí Dhónnaill" – O'Donnell's folk, etc.

Again, when referring to relatives, a Tory islander will often speak of "clann agus ua", "children and grandchildren," literally; but both words have the meaning of "offspring" or "progeny." Clann, although meaning "children," means it always in this sense of "offspring" or "descendants," as opposed to the word for children generally that again we have seen in the song: "páistí" (singular páiste – child). There is no singular of clann, although there is a plural, "clanna." This cannot be "offsprings," of course, and is perhaps best rendered "progenies"; the plural would therefore mean "several clann": groups of people related by common descent. We have come across these in the previous chapter and seen how they are conceptualized by the Tory genealogists. Thus the Clann Neilí, and the Clann Fheilimí, were the descendants of their respective ancestress and ancestor. Although the word can be used in a literal way to describe the descendants of anyone – "tá clann go leor aige," "he has many offspring," when used as in the last chapter it refers specifically to this kind of social group: a body of people related by common descent from a known ancestor.

It *can* be translated as "clan" or "sept," but is rarely used in Gaelic this way. If a person refers to "mo chlann," he means his own offspring; if one asks him of whom he himself is a descendant, he will reply that he is "clainne Fheilimí," or something such: "of the offspring of Phillip (Phelim)." The way of referrring directly to a sept or clan is to call it "clann mhacna": "Mo chlann mhacna" would then be "my clan" in the English sense. But on Tory this is rarely said except by the more literate. For a start, everyone has more than one clann affiliation, so "my clan" would be relatively meaningless. Nor would they say "mo chlanna" – "my various progenies," which would make no sense except in some bizarre polygamous circumstances. On the other hand, it would make good sense to talk, for example, of na clanna Fheilimí: "the progenies of Phelim." These would be the various branches of Phelim's clann. If a man lived to be very old, he might conceivably speak thus of branches of his own offspring; but usually it is used in this way only to refer to branches stemming from an ancestor. I am treating this at some tedious length, because it is necessary to avoid thinking of the Gaelic category clann as the same as English "a clan." The difference can be put graphically by pointing out that one cannot ask someone "what is your clann?"; one has to say, "of whom are you clann?" Thus, when asked to describe her muintir to me, one islander answered crisply that she was "clainne Eoin, Neilí, agus Shéamuis Bháin": "of the offspring of Eoin, Neilí, and Séamus Bán." She could have put it: "na clanna Eoin," etc., "of the progenies of Eoin, etc," using the plural. A useful English equivalent for the word used in this sense might be "stock," but again this has passed from regular English usage.

The English word "clan," however, is borrowed directly from the Gaelic, and usually associated with the Scottish clan system. But the Scottish clan was more of a fine or tribe; only the central line of chiefs would have been in fact clann, or direct descendants of the epomynous ancestor: The Clann Dhomhnaill, for example, "the MacDonalds," would be, strictly speaking, the descendants of Donald. But the whole clan would consist also of accretions through marriage and fealty of people of other surnames. Even so, the word causes us some embarrassment, because it has been adopted into anthropological usage to mean a group claiming descent from a common ancestor *in one line only,* the male or the female. There is no such implication in the Irish word. The descent is through both males and females equally. It is *all* the offspring of the ultimate ancestor, or of anyone for that matter. I must continue to use it that way, then, and will continue to spell it the Gaelic way with two "n's" to keep the distinction clear. I suppose I can claim to be the only anthropologist who is using the word correctly, to describe the one form of descent group that anthropologists would *not* call a clan: a cognatic or bilateral descent group that traces links to the ancestor through either sex indifferently. It differs from muintir or gaolta in that the point of reference is the ancestor, not the individual. We must go on now to look at the use of the concept "Ua," noting that what I share with people who are "clan agus ua" is that traceable relationship to a common ancestor.

The idea of relationship to an ancestor dominates the system of genealogical reckoning, as we saw in the last chapter. Here we must go on to see how it dominates the system of kinship reckoning, and even of personal naming as well. Arensberg and Kimball, in their beautiful ethnographic description of County Clare, note how kinship there was reckoned, as in most of Gaelic Ireland, by degrees – "col" – from the individual. This is of course the commonest form of reckoning for all Indo-European peoples, and was adopted by the church for fixing prohibited degrees ("col" in fact means "prohibition"). The authors refer also to another form of reckoning, that in terms of relatedness to a common ancestor, but say they found it "only in dictionaries" and not in Clare itself. The dictionary in question could only be that of Dineen (Professor Arensberg confirms this) and the entry under "O" or "Ua," "grandchild" or "descendant," describes this way of reckoning kinship, with examples taken from the novel *Caisleán Óir* (The Castle of Gold) – a Donegal story by Séamus O Grianna. It is doubtful if this method survives outside Donegal.

It might be termed the method of reckoning "grandchildship." The word "O" – and for all its brevity it is a word – is of course the well-known Irish surname prefix, as in O'Reiley or O'Neill. In Gaelic it is separate from the name itself, and takes the genitive case after it ("descendants *of* so-and-so"), thus giving rise to the Irish names with which we are familiar. (The Scots favored almost exclusively the surname with Mac, "son," whereas the Irish were divided.) When written as a word in its own right, the form "Ua" (plural and genitive Uí) is used. (When pronounced alone it sounds roughly like "awe," the plural like "we".) Thus, on Tory, two first cousins, that is, descendants of a common grandparent, would say of each other, "támuid i n-ua amháin," "we are grandchildren," or "we are in our first grandchildship." More specifically, they might add that they were, for example, "clann dearthair agus deirfiúir," "offspring of brother and sister," or perhaps "offspring of two brothers," and so on. Second cousins would say they were "an dá ua," "second grandchildren," and would likewise state the exact relationship by saying somethng like "my mother and her father were the offspring of two brothers," etc. ("Bráthair" in Gaelic can mean "kinsman," but more usually means a friar or monk; a "brother" in the ecclesiastical sense. When referring to a sibling one has to specify a "true" (dearbh) brother; similarly with sister. Thus "dearthair" is short for "dearbh-bhráthair.")

Now here we come to a peculiar usage. In most gaeltachta, they would go on to say that third cousins were "third grandchildren," and so on. On Tory, however, third cousins were "fionn ua," "fair grandchildren," and fourth cousins "dubh ua," "dark grandchildren." No one could explain this to me, and one can only refer it to that Irish love of this particular contrast between dark and light, black and white, as in Fionn Gall, "Fair Stranger" (Fingall), and Dubh Ghall "Dark Stranger" (Dougall), epithets applied to various foreign races. Thus the former were the Norweigians, and the latter the Danes. These were also Finngheinte and Duibhgheinte, the fair tribes and the dark tribes, and, for that matter, Fionnlochlannach and Dubhlochlannach, "Fair Norseman" and "Dark

Norseman." We shall come across this dualism again. But after this, the count would resume, with fifth cousins as "fifth grandchildren," and so on. Figure 3 shows how this would work with reference to the original grandparent or ancestor (sinsear). The squares refer to individuals of either sex. The original descendants would be the original clann of the ancestor. There is no way of saying "siblings" in Irish any more than there is in English now that that useful Anglo-Saxon word has dropped out of common usage and into the jargon of psychology. Siblings would say of each other, "támuid i n-ár gclann. . . ." of whoever: "we are in our (immediate) offspringship of . . ." This diagram can easily be related to Figure 2 in Chapter 3, and we can see how the genealogist can quickly tick off the degrees of cousinship between people on the genealogies in terms of their distance, in generations, from the ultimate ancestor. Thus a particular generation of one "craobhóg," or "little branch" of a clann, was often said to be, for example, Fionn Ua to the same generation of another branch. It is easy to imagine the hapless anthropologist's confusion at such an explanation, until such time as the whole system of reckoning was explained.

I said above that in giving genealogies, the old men not only used this

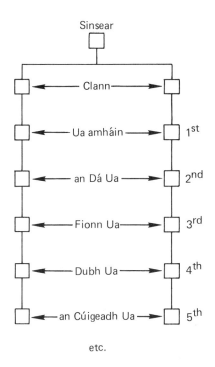

Figure 3. Method of describing degrees of cousinship

system of mnemonics, but also recited personal names to remind themselves of connections. Before we delve into this, let us remind ourselves of the categories so far. We have seen, in effect, a series of rough oppositions that can be set out as follows, with the singular of the noun given where it exists:

—	muintir	:	daoine	(duine)
(gaol)	gaolta	:	cairde	(cara)
—	clann	:	páistí	(paiste)

Those on the left usually refer to kin; those on the right need not. Those on the left always denote a social group or category; those on the right do not. Yet in terms of translation and "meaning" in that sense, the words on each line can "mean" the same thing. The conceptual distinction, however, is clear enough.

We must now pass on to the naming system, which on Tory acts much as the system of kinship terms does in the societies more familiar to anthropologists. Kinship terms are little used on Tory, except for the immediate family, and it would not be worth our while to spell these out because they operate in the same way as their English counterparts. Even the terms for "uncle" and "aunt" have been borrowed, although some older speakers remember that the mother's brother should be "amhnair" (a word appropriated for "uncle" by ardent Gaelophones who do not understand the Omaha type of system for classifying kin from which Indo-European systems all derive). Personal names, as used on Tory, in themselves help to fix a person's kinship status, and although the system in essence is known elsewhere in Ireland, it seems to be more elaborated on Tory than anywhere else; and in a way consonant with the concept of genealogy and the reckoning of kin.

J. M. Synge, in that perfect little account of another island outpost of Gaeldom, the Aran Islands, made these observations on the system of personal names in use when he was there (1898–1902):

> When a child begins to wander about on the island, the neighbours speak of it by its Christian name, followed by the Christian name of its father. If this is not enough to identify it, the father's epithet – whether it is a nickname or the name of his own father – is added. Sometimes when the father's name does not lend itself, the mother's Christian name is adopted as epithet for the children . . .
> Occasionally the surname is employed in its Irish form, but I have not heard them using the "Mac" prefix when speaking Irish among themselves; perhaps the idea of a surname which it gives is too modern for them, perhaps they do use it at times that I have not noticed.

Sometimes a man is named from the colour of his hair. There is thus a Seaghan Ruadh (Red John), and his children are "Mourteen Seaghan Ruadh" etc. . . .

The school master tells me that when he reads out the roll in the morning the children repeat the local name all together in a whisper after each official name and then the child answers. If he calls, for instance, "Patrick O'Flaharty" the children murmur, "Patch Seaghan Dearg" or some such name, and the boy answers.

If an islander's name alone is enough to distinguish him it is used by itself, and I know one man who is spoken of as Eamonn. There may be other Edmunds on the island, but if so they have probably good nicknames or epithets of their own.

Synge, marvelous ethnographer that he was, had caught the spirit of the system beautifully; his description would do well enough as a first approximation to the Tory situation if one did not delve deeper. I am not sure whether on the Aran Islands delving deeper would help at all, for it is not clear that the Aran kinship system is like that on Tory; it is probably nearer that of County Clare proper, of which it is a close neighbor. But what Synge describes would do as a summary, for Tory, of everyday usage. There would be this exception: The islanders know about, and use, the formal surname system with "Mac" and "O," but only on very formal occasions: calling someone's name in church; writing on documents when using Gaelic; requesting someone to sing or dance in the hall; carving on a tombstone. The full formal name would be of the kind we have seen already, such as Pádraig Mac Ruadhraigh, etc. A woman keeps her own name on marriage and adds the descriptive phrase "wife of so-and-so." Thus Mary Doohan, who married Paddy Rogers, would be Máire Ní Dhubhgháin bean Phádraig Mhic Ruadhraigh, in full formal dress. For short, she might retain her own maiden name (Mary, daughter of Doohan), or be known as Máire bean Mhic Ruadhraigh (Mary, McRory's wife) depending on the degree of attachment she was seen as having to either her natal or her husband's family.

As we have already seen, some kind of English equivalent is picked for the Gaelic name; sometimes this sticks almost like a nickname, and someone will be known as "Mary" or "Paddy" or "Johnny" even when speaking Gaelic. Men going to England or Scotland like to pick English-sounding versions of their surnames that the foreman will recognize. Thus the Mac Ruadhraigh people usually opt for "Rogers" and the Whorriskeys (O Fuaruisce) settle for "Waters" – the name means "Cold-water." Mostly, however, as with O Duibhir and "Diver," the English is a rough phonetic rendering. With Christian names the problem is easier for there are, with some exceptions, obvious English equivalents.

We should pause very briefly to look at the choosing of the Christian name. The tradition, which Séamus O Raghallaigh tells me is strictly adhered to throughout the Donegal Gaeltacht, is that the father names the firstborn after his father or mother and the mother the secondborn after hers. They alternate until the parental names are used up. Then they use the names of brothers and sisters, then uncles and aunts – but always alternating. Thus any child's first name immediately links him with another generation of his kin, and names have to be taken from the "pool" of names available in the kindred. The eldest children in particular are firmly linked to the grandparental generation, and thus an "alternating generation" cycle of Christian names is set up.

The kind of personal name that we are interested in, however, is basically like that described by Synge, in which two or more names, either Gaelic or English or both, are strung together. The simplest way is the one he describes: The name of the father or the mother is added to the child's name. Most children do take the father's name, but a significant minority take the mother's – 30 percent of males, and 16 percent of females. Sometimes, again, the father's nickname will be added, or the child given a nickname of its own and then the father's name added, and so on. This produces simple names like the ones quoted by Synge, or like some of these Tory names:

John–Tom	John, son of Tom
Seámus–Uilliaim	James, son of William
Peigi–Thomáis	Peggy, daughter of Thomas
Anton–Eamuinn Rua	Anthony, son of Red Edmund
Máire–Shéamuis Bháin	Mary, daughter of Fair James

The second, and any subsequent, names and adjectives will be in the genitive case if the name is Gaelic, and will often be "genitivized" if the name is English. The genitive of Séamus, "James," when appearing in compounds like these, is – Shéamuis – the source of the Scottish name "Hamish" (deriving from the vocative, which is the same as the genitive). The genitive of Seán ("John") is in compounds likewise – Sheáin (giving rise in its vocative form to the name "Shane"). Thus, the meaning of any two or more names is, literally, "X of Y of Z . . .

I am talking now, as was Synge, essentially of the daily names by which islanders are referred to: the ones used in ordinary conversation to locate an individual. Compounds of three names are not uncommon:

Jimmy–Mháiri–Bhilli	Jimmy (of) Marie (of) Billy	("Jimmyvurryvilly")
Johnny–Dhonnchadha–Eoin	Johnny, Dennis, Iain	("Johnnyonahooian")
Anton–Phaidí–Antoin	Anthony, Paddy, Anthony	("Antonfwadjiantin")

Four names are known:

Peigi–Phaidí–Shéamuis– Dhomhnaill   Peggy, Paddy, James, Donal
("Peggyfwadijihamishownil")

"Epithets" of various kinds get thrown in. Thus the clann of Dooley–Mhalainne are known by his name and epithet:

Eoghan–John–Dooley–Mhalainne   Owen, son of John, son of Dooley
                                       of Malin
Mary–John–Dooley–Mhalainne   Owen's sister
Cait–Dooley–Mhalainne   His paternal aunt – Kate

Another variant we might note in passing is to tack the Christian name of a parent onto the English version of the name. Thus two paternal cousins might be respectively known, after their mothers, as Jimmy Diver Nancy and Jimmy Diver Mhadge. But this is simple compared with the mouthfuls that one often gets from the genealogists that cause laughter even to the owners of the monstrosity, but which they recognize as their "complete" name. Take an example from the Neilís. In the branch of Eoin–Neilí, there is a woman, easily located on the genealogy, I always knew, as did everyone, just as Nora–Thomáis (roughly "Norahomish") – Nora, daughter of Tomás. When her status in the genealogy was being discussed, however, one sloinntear clinched the matter by reciting her full genealogical name: Nora–Thomáis–John–John–Eoin–Neilí ("Norahomishjohnjohnianelly"). Said in one breath at speed this is impressive, but unintelligible until explained. Her father had always been known to me as Tomás–John, but again he was here referred to as Tomás–John–John–Eoin; the Neilí was not always included, but it might be. Needless to say, his father, no longer alive, was referred to as John–John–Eoin, or John–John–Eoin–Neilí. The first had been his "everyday" name.

To follow this up, I worked systematically through the names of all the Neilís, and subsequently all the other genealogies, until I had the names of all the members of all the clanna. I give those of some of the Neilís in Figure 4 (it would be both difficult and redundant to give them all). We can illustrate the principles involved from this genealogy. As we saw in the previous chapter, there are three branches of the Clann Neilí, those of Máiri–Neilí, Liam–Neilí, and Eoin–Neilí. Eoin–Neilí is immortalized in a place name – Boilg Eoin–Neilí, "Eoin-Neilí's Leap." His descendants' names refer back to him in the manner described. One of his sons was called by the English "John" – of which Eoin is one version of course, the other being Seán (Shawn). Most of his descendants, then, traced their "everyday" names back to him, although in many cases the "Neilí"

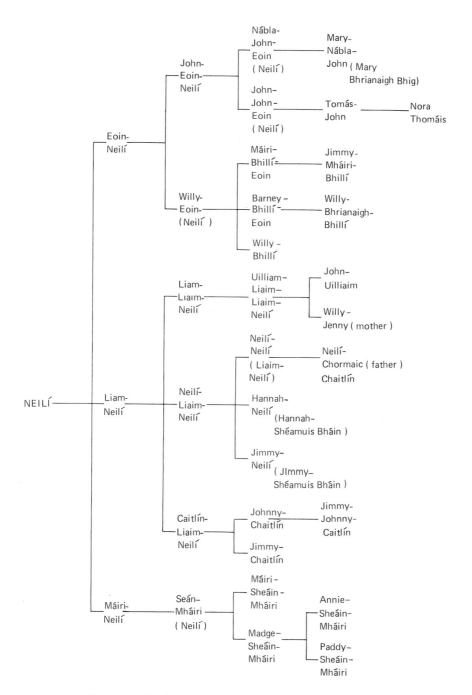

Figure 4. Naming system of the Clann Neilí

was not added, except as we have seen, by the genealogists who are particular about these things.

With the immediate children of Liam–Neilí, things are also quite straightforward. Their names all go back to Neilí through him. This suggests strongly that he was known as Liam–Neilí only, although this need not be the case. He may have had Neilí's father's or mother's name as well, of course; it is not necessary for a child to take the complete "string" of parental names, and as Synge says, they tend to take as many as will distinguish them from all others; for everyday use, that is. We do not know what Neilí herself was called; whatever it was it has not survived. The older genealogists said firmly she was a Rogers, related to the Clann Fheilimí, and that she married Owen Doohan; but her personal name was not known. The names, in any case, as they say, have to stop somewhere.

With the children of Neilí–Liaim–Neilí, the plot thickens. She married James Meenan, known as Séamus Bán, and as names of first choice – that is, the everyday names we have been talking about – their children were known more readily after their father: Jimmy–Shéamuis Bháin, for example, rather than Jimmy–Neilí. I have heard them spontaneously referred to by both sets of names, but usually only by the Neilí set when the context specifically demanded it. When, for example, there were discussions going on that concerned the relations of this branch to other branches of Neilís, then the discussants would readily talk in terms of Jimmy–Neilí–Liaim–Neilí, rather than Jimmy–Shéamuis Bháin.

In the youngest generation of the branch of Liam–Neilí, I have illustrated how two children have departed from the scheme, again in terms of everyday names. Willy–Jenny took his mother's name and Neilí–Chormaic her father's, when logic demanded the other way round. This is because in these cases the principle that each islander should have a distinct name quarreled with the principle that names should converge on the clan founder. But, for reckoning purposes, Willy–Jenny was uncompromisingly Willy–Uilliaim–Liaim–Liaim–Neilí. (Because Liam is an abbreviation of Uilliam, and "Willy" an English alternative, we have four Williams in a row here).

If we go back to the branch of Eoin–Neilí, we find that Mary, daughter of Nábla, who is a McClafferty, is just as readily known as Mary–Bhrianaigh Bhig, after her father "Wee" Brian (Barney) McClafferty, as she is Mary–Nábla–John(–Eoin). In some cases, then, people have two readily available sets of names, from mother's and father's sides. In others, they have one set they use, and another that can be used for reference if other connections need to be made. In yet other cases, they seem to be firmly known by one set and to have no others. The children of Sean Heggarty, son of Máiri–Neilí and Paddy Heggarty, were all firmly known after Máiri–Neilí herself, to the extent that her great grandchildren skipped their parents' generation and were known as Seán–Sheáin–Mháiri and the like. This skipping of a generation happened sometimes in other cases, and was usually done when the grandparents had reared children in loco parentis, but not always.

In the genealogists' conception of the ideal universe of names, all names of a clann would ultimately converge on the ultimate ancestor. In reciting their genealogies, this is how the names would always go. Thus, my clue to the attachment of the Divers to the Feilimí genealogy came when, in discussing the place of Eddie Diver, he was referred to as Eddie–Annie–Mháire–Fheilimí, thus filling in the missing links. In everyday usage, however, he was probably more often Eddie–Eddie, or Eddie–Annie. The people themselves have some notion of this ideal scheme, and would recognize that they ideally possessed sets of names that in practice they were never known by. In this charmingly Platonic scheme, the genealogists could use the "ideal" names for reckoning membership in descent groups. It was pointed out to me that the nearer the actual naming of members of clanna approached the ideal, the stronger was the group in question. A measure of its ability to draw members away from their other clann allegiances was the continuity in names it established from the ancestor downward. The Neilís, as we have seen, are quite strong in this respect, except for the intrusion of the equally strong clann of Séamus Bán. Other groups are weak and disparate in their name continuity, and the sloinntear would shake his head and say, "tá na h-ainmneacha caillte": "The names are lost."

If the ideal universe of the genealogists were realized, then everyone would have several sets of equally balanced names: two sets from the parents, four from the grandparents, eight from the greatgrandparents, and so on. This is nowhere the case in practice, and so the naming system faithfully reflects social reality: Of all the allegiances and their accompanying names that theoretically exist for an individual, he only in effect claims one or two; if he claims more, then this will not be reflected necessarily in his use of names or even in his knowledge of them. For this he must refer to the genealogists.

The principle that clanna – or in anthropological jargon "cognatic descent groups" – will endlessly overlap is elegantly expressed in the naming system. We have seen examples of this already, but let us look quickly at the Clann Eoin for confirmation. Figure 5 shows part of the complement of names for this clann. With the branch of Anton–Eoin, we

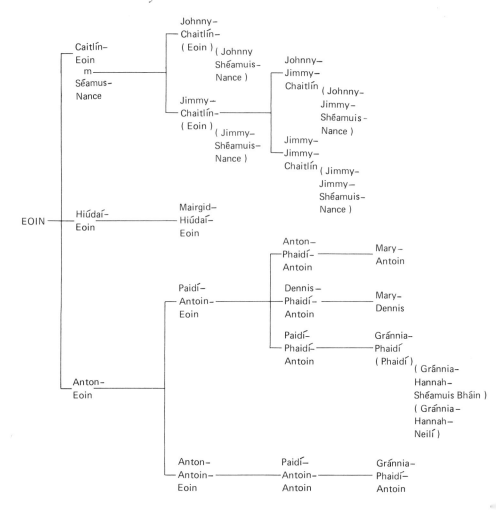

Figure 5. Naming system of the Clann Eoin

see a firm continuity with the incredible play on the names of Anton, Eoin, and Paidí. The continuity is only broken somewhat by the marriage of Paidí–Phaidí–Antoin to Hannah Meenan, who was Hannah–Shéamuis Bháin (see the Neilí names). Séamus Bán intrudes here too, and Hannah's children took his names as readily as their father's; they also were known by their mother's alternative name, Hannah–Neilí (–Liaim–Neilí). If we look at the branch of Caitlín–Eoin, we see the intrusion of Séamus–Nance, and hence the existence of two sets of names among the descendants. The Eoin names had some precedence, as far as the genealogists were concerned, but in practice the children were known by the names stemming from Séamus–Nance. They were very conscious, however, of their Eoin allegiance: "We are Caitlín-Eoin's," they would say.

One could go on citing more such examples, but only a few are needed to establish the point that the naming system is itself a form of genealogical reckoning in which everyone, ideally, has as many strings of names as he has clann allegiances. This ideal scheme is the one used for genealogical reckoning by the experts; it is manifested partially in the everyday use of the islanders. It reflects both the continuities and the discontinuities in the system of descent; and particularly it reflects the overlapping of clann groups. A quick reference back to the system of counting cousinship will show how perfectly the naming system also locks in with it. Ideally, again, if two people are "Ua" then they should, at some point, share a common name – as do all the Neilís, for example, if they extrapolate back far enough. The ideal, however, is usually only actualized by perfection-conscious genealogists.

We have seen how the rendering of genealogies coincides perfectly with the conceptualization of kinship, in both the reckoning of cousinship and the construction of personal names. This exquisite system of classification, based on the principle of common descent through both males and females from an ultimate ancestor, is not only material for "seanchaíocht" – "gossiping about pedigrees" – on the island, and a source of pleasure for any student of human cognition, but is used for settling stern questions of ownership and the like. So we must now turn to see how these ideal schemes work out literally "on the ground" – but also on the high seas. And we shall find that in the slow unfolding of history over many generations that is involved in land inheritance, the genealogies – the clann – are supremely important. When it comes to the matter of recruiting boat crews, however, the urgency and relatively short-term nature of the operation forces the islanders to turn to other principles. First, then, to the land.

5

The land: use, ownership, and inheritance

Féar leath-bó, asal, agus a chuid práití

The above can be translated as "Half a cow's grass, a donkey, and some potatoes." This represents the minimum a man needs to survive, according to this island proverb. Land is measured according to the amount needed to graze a cow: thus, "a cow's grass" – "féar bó" – is the basic measure; half of this, as in the proverb, is "féar leath-bó," whereas this bisected yet again is "a cow's foot" – "féar coise." Some informants think that the size differs between East Town and West, but most agree that the grass of two cows is about an acre, whereas a minimum holding for decent agriculture – as opposed to sheer survival – is the grass of three cows, about one and a half acres. This is called a "cut," and does indeed represent the minimum available size of holding.

In this chapter, we shall be concerned largely with the inheritance of land and its relation to genealogy. But before we get to that, we have to look at the land itself and the use the islanders make of it, as well as the sources of information we have about its inheritance and the history of its division.

Of the island's 785 acres, roughly 250 are cultivable. Map 3 shows the inner and outer field boundaries as they appeared between 1858 and 1910, and these have changed little to the present day. What has happened, from the evidence of the earliest Ordnance Survey maps onward, is a progressive decline in the amount of land ploughed. The surveys of the 1850s show 250 acres under cultivation and much marginal and hill land under the plough; in 1911 this was 233 acres, and in 1961, 160.

Along with this decline in use has gone a concomitant decline of holdings, so that now, with less land than ever cultivated, there are more owners with smaller holdings. The Tithe Applotment Rolls of the 1830s show fifty owners with some 400 acres on which tithes were levied. This is much more than the amount of cultivable land and must have included poor-quality grazing and bog land. A figure of perhaps 4 acres per owner would be more realistic. The rating valuations of the late

View of West Town from the harbor, showing the graveyard, round tower, and "tau" cross at left. The houses were mostly built by the "Board" between 1903 and 1912.

1850s show some sixty tenants sharing approximately 250 acres; an average of about 4 acres. The Congested Districts Board records of 1911 show sixty-nine tenants with 233 acres (excluding commonage); an average of about 3 acres. In 1911–12, to take advantage of the CDB housing schemes, twenty-six tenants registered their land with the Land Registry at Lifford, and again the average holding was 3 acres. The agricultural census for 1961, however, shows only 160 acres in holding and only 26 currently under cultivation, with some 34 acres as pasture. With around seventy tenants, the size of the holding, used or unused, is only a little over 2 acres. We will explore below exactly what this "tenantry" and "holding" mean. For the moment, it is enough to establish the overall decline in land use.

Land, in effect, has ceased to mean the difference between life and death for the islanders. They could exist without it if necessary. Wages, subsidies, pensions, shops, emigration, have all reduced dependence on

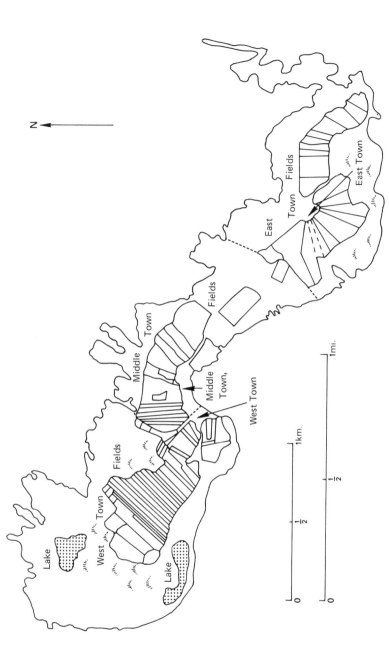

Map 3. Disposition of holdings of arable land, Tory Island, 1858.

the land, and less and less is ploughed every year. Even between Hunter's survey in 1959 and my own in 1965, much land had ceased to be used, and was turned over to the easier grazing of cows and sheep. This contrasts with the nineteenth-century situation – or even with the earlier part of this century – when every available scrap of land was used, even that not suitable for crops.

Yet, despite this decline, ownership of land is still a matter of importance for Tory people. To be without land is a disaster. Without at least a cow's grass, one has no stake in the island, no place in the social scheme of things which includes, as we shall see, membership in a group of landholding kin. Also, memories are deep of hunger and the failure of the herring. Land is still equated with security and is jealously regarded; its disposition often a matter of dispute and always of debate.

The naming of the land

The Tory people lavish names on the land. There is not a rock or a cleft or a hollow that goes unnamed. The same is true of the arable land, and without a knowledge of the names we cannot follow the intricate discussions of land use and ownership. I shall describe here the naming of the land as part of the ethnographic record, but also as another illustration of the conceptual schemes of the islanders.

Maps 4 and 5 show the divisions of the land with their names. The approximate meanings of the names are given in the captions. On the maps, these names have been superimposed on the 1865 field outlines, since informants claimed they fit better with the older boundaries. We shall see why this is so in the subsequent discussion.

The use of the land

In discussing land use, I lean on the work of Hunter who made, for his thesis in 1959, a complete survey of land use on Tory. I have adapted his maps of land use in East and West Town, and these appear as Maps 6 and 7.

Because the area of cultivable land is limited, crops that give a high yield are preferred, and as we shall see, only oats, barley, and potatoes are grown. Some vegetables, but not too many, are grown in gardens near the houses. A good deal of land over which dispute has raged concerning inheritance is either not used, or is rough grassland used for

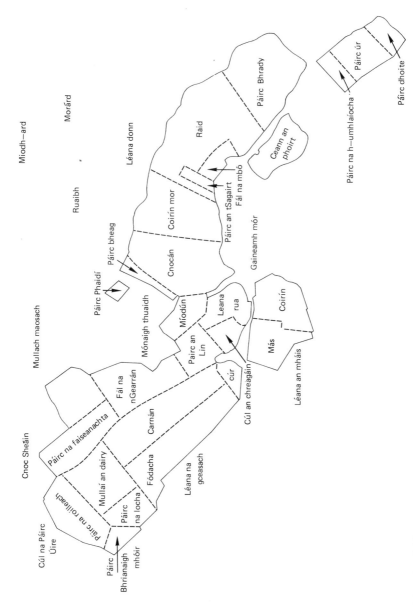

Map 4. Field names and meanings, West Town

Land outside the field boundaries

1.	Cnoc Sheáin	Sean's Hill
2.	Cul na páirc úire	The back of the new (verdant or exposed) field
3.	Léana na gceasach	Meadow in which there are stepping-stones over a boggy patch
4.	Léana an mháis	The small meadow at the foot of the long low hill
5.	Gaineamh mór	Big strand
6.	Mórard	Mór ard: big height
7.	Miodh-ard	Mean ard: medium height
8.	Léana donn	Brown boggy meadow
9.	Ruaibh	Spot where either rue or marshmallow grows
10.	Mullach maosach	Wet or soggy summit of the small hill
11.	Mónaigh thuaidh	Northern turf-bog

Fields inside the boundaries

12.	Páirc na roilleach	Field of the oyster catchers
13.	Páirc Bhrianaigh mhóir	Big Bryan's field
14.	Páirc na locha	Field of the lake
15.	Páirc na faiseanachta	Field where crops were damaged by grazing cattle
16.	Páirc bhuí	Yellow field
17.	Mullaí an Dairy	"Dairy" is a loanword – related somehow to the summits of little hills. "Hillocks of the Dairy"?
18.	Fál na nGearrán	"Hedge-field of the geldings." Fál is a hedge or wall
19.	Carnán	Cairn – heap of stones; possibly a boundary marker.
20.	Fódacha	Smooth grassy field
21.	Cúr	A point at which froth blows up (from the sea?)
22.	Cúl an chreagáin	The back of the rocky place
23.	Páirc an lín	Flax field
24.	Míodún	Meadow – ready for cutting
25.	Léana rua	Red meadow
26.	Más	Long low hill
27.	Coirín	Little crescent-shaped promontory
28.	Páirc Phaidí	Paddy's field
29.	Páirc Bheag	Little field
30.	Cnocán	Hillock
31.	Coirín mór	Big crescent-shaped promontory
32.	Ráid	Obscure. Could be a field of bog myrtles.
33.	Páirc an tSagairt	The Priest's field
34.	Fál na mbó	Hedge-field of the cows (see 18)
35.	Ceann an phoirt	Head of the harbor
36.	Páirc Bhrady	Brady's field. He was a bailiff in the nineteenth century.
37.	Páirc úr	New field
38.	Páirc dhoite	Burned field
39.	Páirc na h-umhlaíocha	Field of the genuflectors; one of the stations of the island turus or pilgrimage.

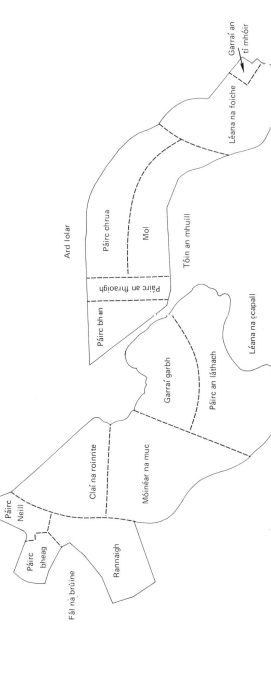

Map 5. Field names and meanings, East Town

Land outside the field boundaries

1. Ard Iolar   Height of the eagles
2. Fál na bruine   Ditch (hedge) of the fight or dispute
3. Léana na gcapall   Grazing land of the horses
4. Tóin an mhuil   The back of the hillock
5. Leachach   Flags of stone

Fields inside the boundaries

6. Páirc bheag   Little field
7. Páirc Neill   Nell's field
8. Cl

9. Móinéar na muc   Grazing field of the pigs
10. Garraí garbh   Rough garden
11. Páirc an láthach   The muddy field
12. Páirc bhán   White field
13. Páirc an fhraoigh   Heather field
14. Páirc chrua   Hard field (could in fact be Páirc rua, see West Town 25)
15. Mol   Hillock, mound
16. Léana na foiche   Field of the wasps (?)

Map 6. Land utilization, West Town

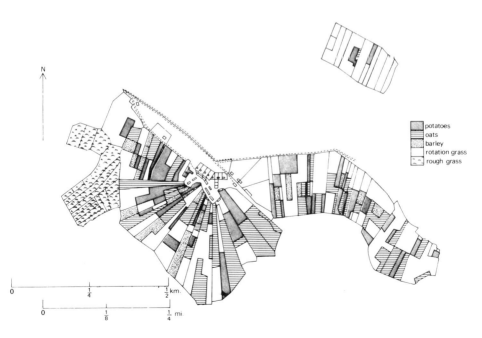

Map 7. Land utilization, East Town

occasional pasture. Oats are favored as a high-yield animal-food crop, and the potato type – Aran Banner – is again used for its high yield rather than its quality. Hunter notes that both crops give remarkably good yields, considering that the only rotation is from grain to potatoes, and the only manure is dried seaweed and a very little farm manure. Formerly, a good deal of rye was planted and used for thatching. Slate roofs have killed this crop, but barley, despite the unsuitable climate, is still very much in evidence. The islanders insist that it is fed to the chickens, but cynics suspect it is put to other and more interesting uses.

The land receives a top dressing of seaweed about the beginning of April, and is then ploughed. The lack of warmth may delay the planting of potatoes until the second week of April – two weeks later than the mainland. Saint Patrick's Day (March 17) is the beginning of farming operations, and Halloween the end; both marked, of course, by considerable festivity.

The islanders make their own ploughing instruments with driftwood and with iron from wrecks. Harrows and grubbers are skillfully manufactured from bolts. The donkey is preferred to the horse, being lighter and smaller and so better adapted to the narrow strips that have to be farmed. Crops are cut by sickle and scythe and threshed with a flail consisting of two sticks fastened together by a leather thong. The grain is separated and then cleaned in a circular riddle made from sheepskin with the wool removed by steeping it in a lime solution. The skin is stretched on a round frame, dried in the sun, and then punched full of holes by a red-hot wire.

Farming, then, is arduous, the land not good, the crops limited, and the methods of planting and harvesting, although ingenious, definitely primitive. Recently, a tractor has been introduced, but it comes too late to be of much use, and many people still prefer the donkey. A number of horses are still kept, although they are not used for anything. They are a hangover from the kelp-hauling days, and I suppose must be regarded as pets.

I will not discuss livestock much, for we are here concerned with the inheritance of arable land, and livestock are usually grazed on the common land. Sometimes, however, they are grazed on a fallow field, and often the right to graze a donkey or a cow is important in land disputes. Most households keep at least one donkey, and because two are needed for ploughing, a system of reciprocal lending operates. Otherwise, domestic livestock are kept in the yard near the house and fed on grain and scraps. Geese were abolished by the king many years ago because they raided the gardens and the grain; and pigs, it is reckoned, require too much feeding and so compete with humans. Many, but not all, households have a cow that is grazed on the common land or on pasturage in the infield. Some households derive a small income from the sale of milk and butter. Others give away to relatives what they do not use themselves.

The problem of rundale

Having looked briefly at the use of the land to see just what resources are involved in inheritance, it is to the latter we must now turn. The peculiar interest of landholding patterns on Tory for scholars of many disciplines lies in the persistence of the village or "clachán" arrangement, with its "open" fields and "common ownership." This has disappeared in the rest of Ireland, with a few exceptions, and been replaced by the "family farm." Nowhere has it persisted as on Tory. The question then is, how much of the older system of land tenure, the much-debated *rundale* system, persisted as well? This is difficult to estimate because we are not altogether sure just how rundale itself worked in the matter of inheritance. Getty says that land in 1845 was held on the "old rundale tenure, by virtue of which, each individual tenant has a proportion of every kind of land, and no one a permanent possession of a separate part." He adds in a footnote: "Since the above was written the proprietor has induced a considerable number of the inhabitants to leave the island, and abolished 'rundale' entirely, and the land is now divided into farms, as in other parts of the country." A somewhat exaggerated claim, it turns out.

Indeed, the earliest Ordnance Survey maps show little by way of internal field divisions. That of 1848 shows the beginning of consolidation in a few places, but the valuation maps of the early 1860s show that Mr. Woodhouse's energetic plans had come to full fruition, and the land had been elaborately rearranged into strips (or "stripes") on the same lines as that of the more notorious Lord George Hill in Gweedore (Refer back to Map 3) (see notes). The point of arranging it into strips was everywhere the same: The "strip" covered all qualities of land – poor at the top end, better at the bottom – and so ensured each owner a variety of land while keeping all his own in one piece. This at least was the theory, and Woodhouse forbade subdivision. But the Tory islanders never paid much heed to landlords, and as we shall see these rules were rapidly broken. The pattern of the strips was maintained, however.

Whatever had been the pattern of inheritance before the Woodhouse reforms, we can only be certain of actual devolutions after the advent of the rating valuation records in 1857. The Tithe Applotment Rolls give us a list of owners and acreages, but because there were no attached maps, we cannot follow any subsequent developments. The list of owners (see Appendix 1) is useful, however, in indicating who held land in the two clacháns, East Town and West Town. By 1857, it was found necessary to regard these as three, West, Middle, and East Towns, but this was largely for determining who had a share of commonage. For the islanders, Middle Town is simply the eastern extension of West Town. Mr. Woodhouse also supplied Getty with a list of owners' names that was published in his 1853 article. This list also is given in Appendix 2.

If a clachán, in D. McCourt's definition, is "a group of blood kin who own the land in common," then West and East Towns are not representative, because they contain several groups of different "blood kin." But the larger clacháns must always have been like this, and what I suspect is that each group held a certain area of the land and made its own internal arrangements about it. But a close look at these suggests that, for example, in West Town at least, the lands of the Eoins, the Ncilís, and the Feilimís were adjacent and internally subdivided; a pattern that Mr. Woodhouse modified, but did not destroy. Let us then proceed to the elucidation of this point.

The basic data

Our basic data are the maps and records of the Valuation Office, and the CDB. R. Griffith made the basic survey sometime before 1857, but he only listed the owners in each clachán *en bloc* and gave no details of the subdivisions (See Appendix 3). A subsequent survey a few years later (1865?) gave the field division in numbered detail. "Griffith's Valuation" is the "basic" valuation for rating purposes in Ireland, but because the islanders had no intention of paying rates, it was, literally, an academic exercise: It has been of use only to scholars. Indeed, so hopeless was the situation that year after year, according to the Valuation Office records, no attempts were made to revise the valuations. "Inclement weather" or something such was usually cited as the reason for the failure of the assessors to make the crossing, but one suspects that they simply abandoned the idea as useless. The change of landlord was noted in 1861, and occasionally the name of the priest was changed. But the next survey was that of the CDB when it purchased the island. The Valuation Office, in 1911, amended its records and maps and added the following note.

Tenants names and areas taken from C.D.B. maps and schedules and applotments made in office without inspection on the ground. The valuation and references of buildings copied from existing valuations and to be altered on appeal if necessary.

24/11/11 Ja. McGrath

So the assessors were saved another wet and pointless trip.

This revised valuation based on the CDB records is, then, our third set of data. The maps are excellent and detailed, but the notions of "ownership" entertained by bureaucrats, and those held by the islanders, differ somewhat, and make interpretation difficult sometimes. Also, there were in some cases quite considerable alterations in field boundaries between 1865 and 1911, and this makes it difficult again to look for continuities in ownership. Add to this the facts that plots were sold, used to pay debts, handed over to nonrelatives in return for services, swapped to achieve consolidation, and abandoned on emigration, and we have even more difficulty in tracing inheritances. However, there is enough continuity in enough instances for us to establish the pattern, and to this we must now proceed.

I will first lay out the basic data from the two sets of surveys in 1865 and 1911 (this latter was based on the Ordnance Survey map of 1910, which is of course our basic map of the island). The 1865 valuation is shown on Maps 8 and 9 for West and East Towns respectively, and Table 5 shows the list of owners. Maps 10 and 11 show the 1911 Valuation and Table 6 shows the owners. A third useful set of data is the "Final Schedule" of the CDB before it handed the island over to the Irish Land Commission after the achievement of Irish independence in 1922. This survey, made probably in 1922–3, consists of alterations and additions to the existing CDB Schedule. It uses the same map numbers as the 1911 map and therefore can easily be referred to that map. I give this list in Table 7. The fourth set of data are my own fieldnotes for 1961–5. These will emerge as we discuss the various cases of inheritance.

By cross-referencing the maps and lists with the genealogies we can learn a great deal. But unfortunately the confusion of names makes it impossible to be sure which "John Doohan" or "James Meenan" we are dealing with, and here I had to check and cross-check with informants. As a result, I know the history of each strip of land from 1857 onward. But diminishing returns would soon set in if I tried to give the total history of each piece, and in some cases it is wholly uninteresting. I shall, therefore, deal with those parcels of land that involve the four major

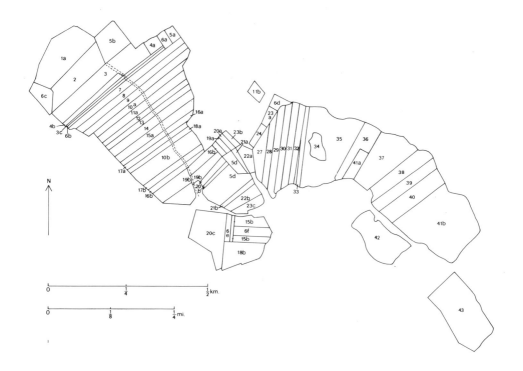

Map 8. West Town fields, 1865. *Note:* Land ownership by field number is shown in Table 5.

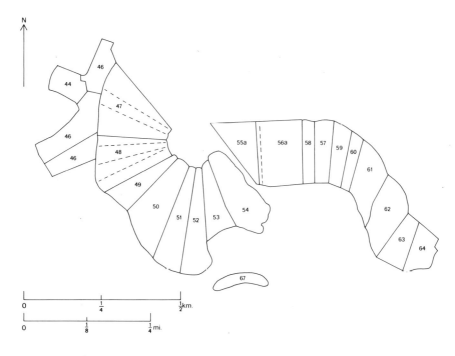

Map 9. East Town fields, 1865. *Note:* Land ownership by field number is shown in Table 5.

Table 5. *1865 valuation: list of owners*

West Town		Middle Town (cont.)	
1	Lighthouse	35	James Doohan (Shimagan)
1a	Catherine Dougan	36	Owen Whorriskey Snr.
2	Hugh Dougan	37	John Doohan (Nelly)
3	Daniel Rogers	38	Bryan Curran
4,a,b	Catherine Diver (Shane)	39	Catherine Diver (Shane)
5,a,b,c,d	Hugh Diver	40	Denis Diver (Gracey)
6,a,b,c,d,f	Bryan Dougan (More)	41,a,b	Benjamin St. J. B. Joule
7	Daniel Whorriskey	42,43,44	Patk. Doohan
8	Daniel Dougan		Roger McClafferty
9	John Doohan		James McClafferty
10,a,b	William Rogers	*East Town*	
11,a,b	Ed. Macken Rogers	46	Neal Heraghty
12	William Doohan (Red)	47	Patrick Rogers (Bailiff)
13	William Doohan (Nelly)		Grace Rogers
14	Owen Whorriskey		Pat Doherty
15,a,b	John Doohan (Bryan)		James Diver (Sally)
16,a,b,c	Patk. Rogers (Phillip)	48	Edward Dougan
17,a,b	Nancy Mooney (Mick)		Patk. Diver
18,a,b	Thomas Whorriskey		Ed. Doohan
	Grace Dougan (Bryan)	49	John Gallagher
19,a,b	James Doohan (Packet)	50	Owen Doohan (King)
20,a,b,c	Alex. Doohan		Mary Rogers (Widow)
	Edward Doohan (Red)	51	James Carrol
21,a,b	James Doohan (Nancy)	52	Ed. Diver
22,a,b	Roger Doohan (More)		James Diver (Neddy)
23,a,b,c	Widow Heraghty (Pat)	53	James Diver (Neddy)
24	James Doohan (Shimagan)	54	John Meenan
			James Doohan (Perkin)
Middle Town		55	Denis Diver (Sally)
27	Nancy Doohan (Roger		John Dougan
	Shane)	56	Denis Diver (Sally)
28	James Doohan (Nancy)	57	John Dougan
29	Roger Doohan (More)	58	Bryan Doohan (Hudy)
30	James Doohan (Danl.)	59	Patrick Diver
31	William Doohan (Red)	60,56,a	James Diver (Neddy)
32	Denis Maginley	61	James Diver (Hugh)
33	John Whorriskey	62	Patrick Dougan
34,a	James Doohan (Packet)	63	Thomas Diver
	(representatives of)	64	Patrick Curran

Note: The names are given exactly as recorded by the valuation officers.

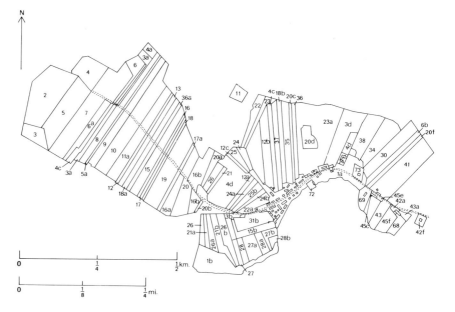

Map 10. West Town fields, 1911. *Note:* Land ownership by field number is shown in Table 6.

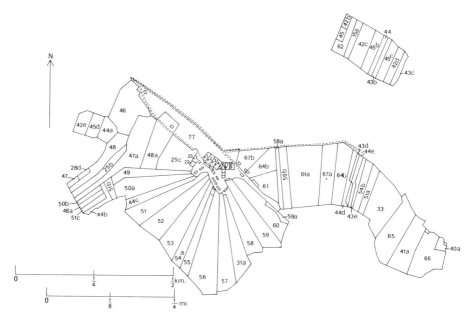

Map 11. East Town fields, 1911. *Note:* Land ownership by field number is shown in Table 6.

Table 6. *1911 Congested Districts Board list of owners*

1.	Land held in common	40,a	Owen Collum
2	Neil Duggan	41,a	Thomas Diver
3,a,b,c,d	Neil Ward		Denis Dixon
4,a,b,c,d,e	Hugh Diver	42,a,b,c,d,e,f	John McClafferty
5,a	Rose Whorriskey	43,a,b,c,d,e	John Doherty
6,a,b	George O'Brien	44,a,b,c,d,e	Roger McClafferty
7	Anthony Duggan	45,a,b,c,d,e,f,g	Daniel Doohan
8	Hugh Whorriskey	46	Ellen Heraghty (Reps.
9	Daniel Duggan		Margaret)
10	William Rogers	47,a	Patk. Rogers (Dooley)
11,a	Patrick Rogers (Mackin)	48,a	Patk. Doherty
12,a,b,c	James Doohan (Nancy)	49,a	Tom Meenan
13	Mary Doohan	50,a,b	James Meenan
14	John Doohan	51,a,b,c	Michael Meenan
15,a,b	Isabella Doohan	52	John Gallagher
16,a,b	Ptk. Rogers (Phillip)	53	John Meenan
17,a,b	Michael Mooney	54,a,b	Ed. Diver
18,a,b	William Doohan (Roe)	55	Dennis Doohan
19	John Rogers	56	James Carroll
20,a,b,c,d,e,f	James Doughan	57	Patk. Rogers (Anthony)
21,a,b	Daniel Doohan (Alec)	58,a	John Doohan
22,a	John Heraghty	59,a,b	Patk. Duggan
23,a	Ed. Rogers (Anthony)	60	Mary Doohan
24,a,b	Roger Rogers	61	Mrs. John Doohan
25,a,b,c,d	Ed. Rogers (Dooley)		Denis Diver (Sally)
26,a,b,c	Hugh Doohan (Roe)	61a	Mrs. John Doohan
27,a,b	William Doohan (Grace)	62	John Doherty
28,a,b,c,d	Denis Dixon (reps. Barney)		Roger McClafferty
30	James O'Brien	64,a,b	James Duggan
31,a,b	Owen Whorriskey (Beg)	65	Kate Rogers
	(Reps.)	66	Kate Curran
33	Denis Doohan	67,a,b	John Carroll
	Mary Doohan	68	John Doherty
34	Nabla McClafferty		Daniel Doohan
35	Patk. McGinley		Roger McClafferty
36,a	James Whorriskey	69	John McClafferty
37	Patk. Doohan (Shamus Donal)		Daniel Doohan
38,a	John Doohan (Nellie) (Reps.)		Roger McClafferty
39	Patk. Doohan (Shamus Donal)	70	Lighthouse

Table 7. *1922–3 Congested Districts Board "final schedule" of owners*

2,a	Neil Duggan	37,a,b	Patrick Doohan (Seamus
3,a,b,c,d,e	Ellen Ward		Donal)
4,a,b,c,d,e,f	Patrick Dever (Hugh)	38,a	John Doohan (Nellie)(Reps.)
5,a,b,c	James Doohan (Nancy)		(John Doohan)
6,a,b,c	Anthony Rogers (Ned)	39	Patrick Doohan (Seamus
7,a	Anthony Duggan		Donal)
8,a,b	Hugh Whorriskey (Patrick)	40	Priest
9,a	Daniel Duggan	40,a	Thomas Meenan (Mary)
10,a	James Rogers (William)	41,a	Denis Dixon
11,a,b	James Doohan (Paddy)	42,a,b,c,d,e,f	John McClafferty
12,a,b,c	James Doohan (Nancy)	43,a,b,c,d,e	John Doherty
13,a	Dennis Duggan (Paddy)	44,a,b,c	Roger McClafferty
14	John Doughan (Klondyke)	45,a,b,c,d,e,f,g	Daniel Doohan
	to Bridie Shields	46	James Meenan (James)
15,a,b,c	Isabella Doohan (Widow)	47,a,b	Patrick Rogers (Dooley)
16,a,b,c	Patrick Rogers	48,a,b,c	Patrick Doherty
17,a,b,c	Mrs. Sarah Mooney	49,a,b	Tom Meenan
18,a,b,c	William Doohan (Roe)	50,a,b	James Meenan
19,a,b,c,d	Daniel Rogers	51,a	Michael Meenan (Mick)
	Mrs. Bridget Rogers	51,b,c	Ed. Meenan (Mick)
20,a,b,c,d,e,f	Ellie Doohan	52,a	John Gallagher
21,a,b,c	James Rogers (Paddy)	53,a,b	John Meenan (James)
22,a,b,c	John Herraghty	54,a,b	Edward Dever
23,a,b	Patrick Rogers	55,a	James Doohan (Dennis)
	Anthony Rogers	56,a,b	James Carroll
	Cormic Rogers	57,a,b,c	Patrick Rogers (Anthony)
	Ptk. Euggan (son-in-law)	58,a	William Doohan (John)
24,a,b,c	Patk. Rogers (Roger)	59,a,b,c	Patrick Duggan
25,a,b,c	Patk. Rogers (Ned)	60,a	James Doohan (Mary)
26,a,b,c	James Doohan (Hugh)	61,a	James Diver
27,a,b,c,d	William Doohan (Grace)	62	John Doherty
28,a,b,c	Dennis Dixon	63	Patrick Rogers (Ned)
29	John Rogers (Nancy)	64,a,b	James Duggan
30,a,b	James O'Brien	65	Ptk. Rogers (Kate)
31,a,b	Owen Whorriskey (Beg)	66	Thomas Meenan (Mary)
	(des.)	67,a,b	John Carrol
	Isabella Whorriskey	68	John Doherty
32	Patrick O'Donnell		Daniel Doohan
33,a	James Doohan (Dennis)		John McClafferty
34	Ptk. McClafferty (Bryan)	69	John McClafferty
35,a,b	Patk. McGinley		Daniel Doohan
36,a,b	James Whorriskey		Roger McClafferty

Note: The appearance of many more lettered numbers on this list is due to the assessors assigning letters to house and garden land, to make a complete inventory.

genealogies, with side glances at other pieces that were fed into the mainstream represented by the genealogies. In the process, we shall discover just how the clann operates as a land-inheriting unit, and this in itself may give us clues to the nature of the functioning of the "blood group" under the old rundale system of which the Tory system today is a direct heir, despite the interference of Mr. Woodhouse and the CDB, and the decline of land use.

The inheritance of land

What then of inheritance? The islanders' own version is simple: Every child of a landholder has a right to a portion of his or her land, and no matter what happens to the land all the heirs retain a claim to it in the event of its falling vacant through intestacy or emigration. But that every heir has a right, and can make a claim, does not mean that every heir gets a portion. Some will, some will not. Some will press their claims and be denied, others simply will not press them at all. But, in the end, every household will end up with *some* land; the amount of land each household has is indeed roughly the same.

In its ideology, the system contrasts markedly with the rest of Ireland, where the inheritance of the farm by one son, the emigration of the rest, the dowry for the daughters, and the provision for the old people are the traditions classically described by Arensberg and Kimball. And the system also differs in practice. Although there are no dowries, males and females can inherit land equally, and do. This is not always reflected in the records. There, males account for between 80 and 90 percent of ownership. Thus the percentages of female owners would be as follows: 1830s, 13; 1850s, 10; 1860s, 15; 1900s, 16; 1920s, 11. However, in the 1960s my own records give 33 percent. This may of course represent a real change, but the islanders doubt it. I believe an estimate of between 20 and 30 percent for previous years would not be far wrong. As women are far more likely than men to relinquish claims, men must predominate. When one investigates some cases of land recorded as belonging to a man – for valuation purposes – it turns out to have "come to him" from his wife; but it has been treated as his by the evaluators. Even now, a piece of land may be spoken of as "belonging to" a man, but will on analysis turn out to belong to him and two sisters, for example. Even though a man may farm a plot and be known as its owner, it may turn out again that it "came down to" him and another brother and a sister, all of whom have a perfect right to a share if they want it. But because the men usually work and manage the land, they appear to monopolize its ownership. Evaluators cannot be expected to record all the "claims" to a piece of land, nor are they worried about where it "came from" and hence, where it will ultimately go. They are interested in recording an "owner" who will, it is hoped, pay the rates for the land, and this is usually the man who works and manages it as far as they are concerned. On the Tithe Applotment Rolls the same must have held. It was probably one prominent kinsman of a group of kin who was picked as the "owner" for tithing purposes, even though the islanders knew that many of his relatives were as much "owners" as himself; at least according to island conventions.

This is best brought out by the analysis of cases, as is the function of the clann – the cognatic descent group with which we are familiar from Chapter 3. This will require some patient sifting through the details, but it is essential, if we are to see just how the land is indeed inherited, and what ownership means. Once we have this information, we can think about rundale per se, because many of its characteristics, including its inheritance patterns, were adapted to the newly striped landscape. Let us take in turn the fate of the lands belonging to Séamus McClafferty, to the children of Feilimí Rogers and those of Eoin Duggan, and finally to the Neilís. I will use the numbering systems on the two sets of maps here presented, but will also provide a small map to illustrate each case for the sake of clarity. The actual devolution of the land will be shown, but constant reference back to the major genealogies will, I'm afraid, be necessary as well.

The land of the McClaffertys

We must begin in the period of Griffith's valuation, when the three plots of land marked 42 (Ceann an phoirt), 43 (Páirc úr), and 44 (Páirc bheag) were regarded as being the joint ownership of James McClafferty (Séamus), Roger McClafferty, and Patrick Doohan. It had, according to the islanders, previously belonged to Séamus, and to Patrick's father, Donal Doohan. This latter is the founding ancestor of the small clann of Domhnall, shown in Genealogy 13. How the two men came to be in joint possession is not known, but such a system for working fairly large acreages was not uncommon. "It must have come to them" was the island interpretation. It is likely that when Mr. Woodhouse came to rationalize the fragmented system, he found these two men with many plots adjacent to each other and simply assigned them as joint owners. Because the external boundaries of these pieces of land have not changed in the meantime, it is fairly easy to follow the subsequent events.

Even if Griffith did not show the subdivisions and simply held the three men jointly responsible for the rates none of them were going to pay, I suspect that subdivisions existed, for it was not long after the valuation, according to the genealogists' records at least, that the various lesser areas of the land were reassigned among other owners. However, we can only guess at how Séamus McClafferty and Donal Doohan divided the land if they did. Páirc úr was divided into Páirc úr proper and the two ends, which were Páirc na h-umhlaíocha and Páirc dhóite. Some people say that Donal had the center, and Séamus the two end pieces. But again, this may have been a rationalization of the naming.

Looking forward to Figure 6, we can see how the subsequent division of the land occurred. Donal died, passing some of his land to his son Patrick, who in turn died and passed his share to his son Dan. The other son, Séamus, got a small plot not involved in the joint ownership (number 30 on 1865, number 37 on the CDB.) This passed to his son Paddy, who married Gránnia Rogers. For the moment we must leave them, but they will pop up again when we discuss the land of the Feilimís.

All this was in the lifetime of Séamus McClafferty, and in 1865 the land is recorded as being divided between Séamus, his son Roger, and Patrick Doohan. Roger had married Patrick's sister Gránnia, and on his marriage Séamus, Dan, and Roger split the land three ways. The situation was then as in Figure 6. At this point Séamus, Dan, and Roger shared the holdings that had been divided up as shown on Map 12. (For convenience, I have used the numberings and divisions of the 1911 maps, but in 1870, for example, plots 62 and 15a were probably not divided, and plots 44 and 43b certainly were not.) This must have been in about 1870 (Séamus died in 1879). Our next set of records, the CDB Valuations of 1911, shows the land owned by John McClafferty, Daniel Doohan, and John Doherty. We must trace how this happened.

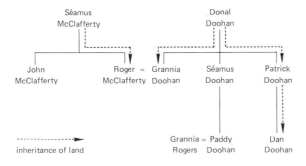

Figure 6. McClafferty–Doohan land, 1855–65

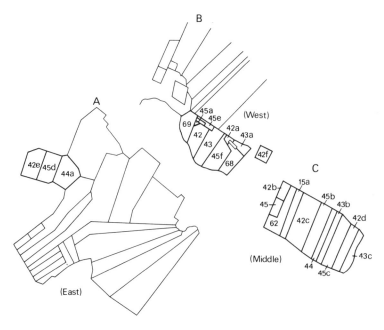

Map 12. McClafferty–Doohan land, ca. 1870–9

Key: A (This section was No. 44 in 1865):
      42e – Séamus McClafferty
      45d – Dan Doohan
      44a – Roger McClafferty
      B (This section was No. 42 in 1865):
      68 and 69 – all three owners jointly
      42, a, f – Séamus McClafferty
      43 – Roger McClafferty
      45f – Dan Doohan
      C (This section was No. 43 in 1865):
      42b, c, d – Séamus McClafferty
      62; 44; 43b, c – Roger McClafferty
      45, b, c – Dan Doohan

On Séamus's death, the remainder of his land went to his other son, John McClafferty. Thus the land was divided exactly as before but with John, Roger, and Dan Doohan as the owners. Figure 7 shows what happened subsequently. Dan had no children, but he took in a relative of his wife's, Jimmy ("the Yank") Rogers, to look after him in his old age, and the land went to Jimmy. Roger had two children, Grace (Gránnia) and Dan; when Grace married, it was to the younger son of an immigrant who had no land, because his brother had received what land their

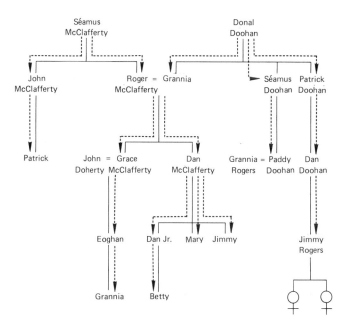

Figure 7. McClafferty–Doohan land, 1870–95

father had obtained. Roger therefore passed on some land to Grace for her use: "land of the marriage." This is always recorded as the land of her husband, John Doherty, jointly with her father, and so appears in the CDB records in 1911, but it was undoubtedly her land from her father. John Doherty later died and the land passed to his son Eoghan. On Roger McClafferty's death, his land went to Dan McClafferty, his son. John McClafferty had three sons but his land went to one of them, Patrick.

Sometime before 1895, Roger McClafferty had acquired three other plots in the East Town fields, probably by purchase (these are plots 44b, c, d, e and 43d, e, 1911 map). He divided one with his son-in-law, John Doherty, and passed on the other two to his son Dan. Dan had three children: Dan Jr., Mary, and Jimmy, and the land was passed largely to Dan and Mary (although recorded as Dan's) with a smaller share to Jimmy, because he had a wife with land. But he retained the right to graze a cow or a donkey on any of his father's land.

Map 13 shows the final disposition of the land in 1963. The numbers of the plots are those of the CDB valuation. (I have avoided mentioning plot 15a, which lacks an owner from this little group. It fell into the hands of the redoubtable Isabella Doohan of the Feilimís as a payment

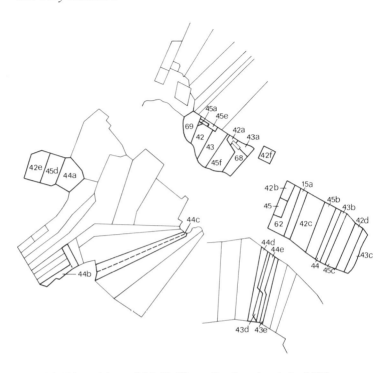

Map 13. Disposition of McClafferty–Doohan lands in 1963

Key: 42, a, b, c, d, e, f – Patrick McClafferty (from John McClafferty)

43, a, b, c, d, e, and 62 – Eoghan Doherty (from John Doherty and Grace McClafferty)

45, a, b, c, d, e – Jimmy Rogers (from Dan Doohan)

44, a, d, e – Dan McClafferty

44b, c – Dan and Jimmy McClafferty (from Dan McClafferty Sr.)

68 and 69 – Patrick McClafferty, Eoghan Doherty, and Jimmy Rogers

for a debt, and has come down to her heirs subsequently, as we shall see below.) Plots 69 and 68 remained in joint ownership, preserving the original pattern. Of the land of Roger, which was most subdivided, essentially the "44" plots went to Dan and his descendants, and the "43" plots to Gránnia and her child by John Doherty. Plots 44 and 43b, which had been one plot in 1879, for example, resulted from an exact bisection between the two heirs; and the curious alternating division of 44d, 43d, 44e, 43e is the result of similar minute partitioning in the next generation.

The fate of the land is problematical. Jimmy Rogers has two daughters and Eoghan Doherty one daughter. None of these is keen to stay on the island. Dan Jr. adopted a daughter who married an outsider who lives in Dan's house. This son-in-law now farms the land, and it is regarded as virtually his. Patrick McClafferty has no children, and it is generally agreed that his land will revert to the children of his brother Barney or his sister Nellie, should they want it. There is, however, reason to suppose that they will not, in which case it is agreed that it would then revert to the descendants of Roger McClafferty. There is much discussion and dispute about how exactly this would work out, but the order of precedence, as far as inheritance is concerned, is clear. Similarly, it is agreed that Jimmy the Yank's land should revert to the descendants of Roger McClafferty and Gránnia Doherty, should his daughters not want it.

If we look to the McClafferty genealogy (Genealogy 4) we will see that a number of offspring did not receive a share of the original land. Of the children of Roger, neither Biddy nor Annie received any. Each one married an immigrant, and each of these immigrants managed to acquire some land. Annie's husband was prominent in the fishing industry, whereas Biddy's was the enterprising entrepreneur who introduced motor-powered boats, so perhaps it was reckoned they had no need of the land. Of the children of John McClafferty, several died or emigrated or married into land themselves. Both Barney and Ned married women who shared in the inheritance of land with brothers. We will see how this worked in the case of Barney's wife when we discuss the land of the Neilís. There was a considerable dispute over her entitlement, but she was a strong-minded woman who pursued her claim to half her father's land in return for an agreement to succour a relative who might return from America. An "agreement" was drawn up and witnessed by the priest and several prominent islanders – the only time such a document has been used in the otherwise totally oral culture of land transactions on Tory. And there the matter rests. Both Barney and Ned have died; Ned was childless. Barney's daughter took his house, and his son took the land that had come through the marriage – a kind of compromise that is often reached. But this is to jump ahead. We should perhaps note for the record that Ned's land came to him as a result of his marriage to the Carrols. Of the sons of Owen Carrol, John held plots 67a and b (1911), and James Carrol held plot 56 (1911). When James's daughter Sally married Ned McClafferty, he divided 56 with him and with son James Jr. When Ned died, the land, being Carrol land and not McClafferty land, reverted to James's son Dan (see Genealogy 1). Dan McClafferty, having married Sarah Doohan of the Pircíns (Genealogy 14), established a claim for his descendants on their land. This was realized when the land was divided, with plot 55 (1911) going to Dennis alone, but plots 33 and 60 (1911) going to Dennis and his sister Mary jointly. The land of Dennis, 55, passed on his death to his sons Jimmy and Anton Mór (recorded as Jimmy's in 1923). But Mary hung on to her share and finally disposed of 33 to her sister Sarah's children, Dan Jr. and Jimmy McClafferty, and of 60 to her son Jimmy (see 1923 list).

Already, in the discussion of this case, we can see some principles forming concerning the choice of heirs from the many possible claimants. Chiefly, there is the consideration of "the land of the marriage." The amount of land is limited and each household needs much the same. If all claims were pressed, then ultimately there would be endless fragmentation, and some people would end up with a lot and some with little or none. But all claims are not pressed. It is seen that each "marriage" requires land and this is provided for. If a sister were to marry a man with land, and a brother a woman similarly placed, then they would not press their claims to land that could go to other, less fortunate, siblings. We shall discuss this further after dealing with the other case histories, but it comes out clearly in the McClafferty–Doohan inheritance that we have just examined.

I took this case first because the field boundaries persisted over time and were easily identified, thus making the discussion of the internal subdivisions easy. In the following cases this is less and less true, but we can still see what happened as far as inheritance is concerned, even if this is harder to pin down on the ground, as it were.

The land of the Eoins

Looking at the Eoin land takes us to Genealogy 1 and into the West Town lands. The land of Eoin was in fact at the extreme end of the West Town fields, obviously next, as we shall see, to the land of the Feilimís. Mr. Woodhouse may well have consolidated the land into vertical strips and put all the strips of each owner together, but there were soon intrusions and subdivisons. The overall pattern is clear, however. The original Eoin land was plots 1a and 2 on the 1865 map. There these are recorded as belonging to Catherine Dougan and Hugh Dougan. Catherine was the widow of Eoin's son Anton, and Hugh was of course his other son. So in 1865, Eoin being dead, half his land was held by his son Hugh and the other half by his son Anton's widow. We must look, however, at plot 3 on the 1865 map, owned by Daniel Rogers. This

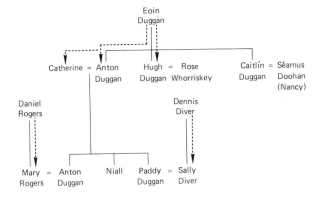

Figure 8. Eoin land, 1865

Rogers was a relative of Feilimí Rogers, and belonged to a sept that ultimately died out and left. We have already come across one of these people in the previous case: the Gránnia Rogers who married Paddy Doohan, son of Séamus Doohan, son of Donal. Similarly here, Mary Rogers, daughter of Daniel, married Anton Duggan Jr., son of Anton–Eoin. Figure 8 and Map 14 show the position at this point in time. Of the other children of Eoin, Hugh had married Rose Whorriskey, and Caitlín had married Séamus Doohan (Séamus–Nance). The latter was a land-

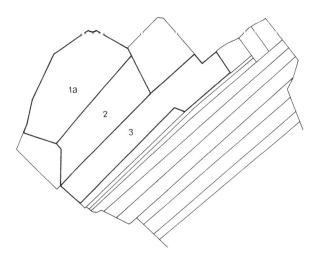

Map 14. Eoin land, 1865
Key: 1a – Catherine Dougan
     2 – Hugh Dougan
     3 – Daniel Rogers

owner, and Caitlín did not share in Eoin's land. When Hugh died, his widow, Rose, held the land for a while. When Anton died, his land went to Niall. Anton Jr., as we have seen, married Mary Rogers, whose father's land stood next to that of the Eoins. Anton acquired the use of this on his father-in-law's death. His other brother, Paddy, had married Sally Diver, daughter of Donnchadh–Shallaigh (see Genealogy 15). Through this marriage Paddy got land in the East.

The CDB records in 1911 show the owners of the plots as follows: plot 2 (1865, 1a), Neil Duggan; plot 5 (1865, 2), Rose Whorriskey (for some reason retaining her maiden name); plot 7 (1865, 3), Anton Duggan. Over in the East, plots 59, 59a, and 59b, are recorded as held by Patrick Duggan. This is shown on Map 15. The subsequent history is shown in Figure 9. Hugh died without issue and his wife held his land for a while. This is common enough on Tory, but it is firmly held that although she could hold and use it in her lifetime, unless it had "come down to" her she only had it on trust for her husband's sister's children, James and John. When she died, the land went to these two men, the children of the otherwise disinherited Caitlín. They also received land from Séamus–Nance, their father; we shall look at this below.

Meanwhile, Anton–Eoin's land went to Niall because his own brothers had found land through marriage, Anton Jr.'s being almost uncannily

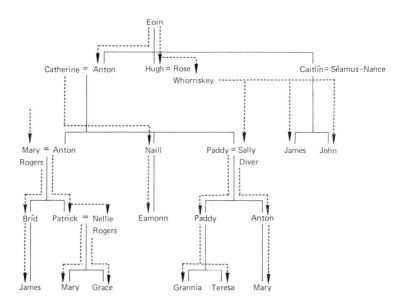

Figure 9. Eoin land, history after 1865

placed immediately next to that of his kinsfolk. It could have been pure coincidence, but one wonders. Meanwhile, Paddy was pursuing his fortune in the East. The actual plots he obtained are difficult to account for. Plot 59 is in fact next to land that was owned by the Divers in 1857. (James Diver is recorded as the owner, but informants say that it was his brother Dennis – Donnchadh–Shallaigh – who was in fact the owner.) Some deal was evidently made whereby two plots were swapped round to give plot 59 to Paddy Duggan. His other plot, 59b, may have been obtained by purchase from an emigrant.

Let us pursue Anton Jr.'s land through its vicissitudes. It was shared between half the possible claimants, daughter and son Bríd and Patrick. His other children married into land or died or emigrated. Bríd passed her land on to her son James McGinley. Patrick died, and his two daughters married and wanted shares. So Patrick's widow, Nellie, and the two daughters, Mary and Grace, divided the land three ways.

Paidí–Antoin's land was divided between two of his possible three heirs, Paddy Jr. and Anton. Anton passed on his land to his only surviving child, Mary, while the land of Paddy Jr. was divided between two of his daughters, Gránnia and Teresa. It is allowed that the claims of the other daughters (Hannah and Sarah) are open.

Map 15 shows the position in 1963 from my own notes. Plots 7 and 59b have been subdivided, but otherwise the plots have kept their shape without fragmentation since 1865 or before. We can see clearly in this case how, if all claimants had indeed pressed their claims, the fragmentation would have been excessive. Because the two sons of Anton–Eoin, Anton and Paddy, were able to get land through marriage, excessive fragmentation was prevented. We should note that Anton–Eoin's land may eventually revert in any case to the descendants of either Anton or Paddy, for Eamonn–Niaill has no children.

What of the fate of the land of the children of Caitlín? This is complicated because it involves the land of Séamus–Nance, and in the next generation land from the Neilís via the marriage of James to Caitlín Doohan, and further the land of James O'Brien (6a, 6b) and Paddy Whorriskey (8) through the marriages of Gránnia and Bríd. All this land was close to that of the Eoins and this can scarcely be coincidental. For our purposes for the moment, we have only to note that James and John kept intact as a joint holding plot 5, which was the Eoin land they received, and so far their heirs have not divided it. At the moment, it lies unused except for a small potato patch, and no one seems clear about its eventual disposition. The plot marked 5a on the CDB map came to Rose

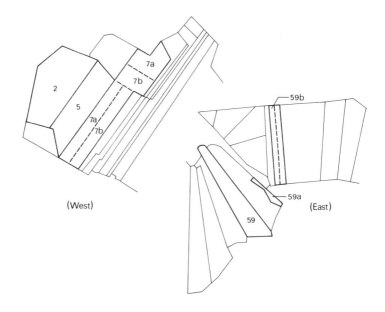

Map 15. Eoin land, 1911–63

Key: Ownership in 1911:
2 – Neil Duggan
5 – Rose Whorriskey
7 – Anton Duggan
59, a, b – Patrick Duggan
Ownership in 1963:
2 – Eamonn Duggan
5 – John and Jimmy Doohan
7a – James McGinley (from Bríd)
7b – Nellie Duggan, Mary Duggan, and Grace Duggan
59, a – Mary Rogers
59b – Grannia Duggan and Teresa McClafferty

Whorriskey through her Whorriskey connection (it is next to her brother Patrick's – number 8), and this too went to James and John and eventually to the heirs of James, ending up with Kitty. Kitty married Dan McClafferty and moved to the East, while her brother Jimmy married Dan's sister Mary McClafferty, who then moved to the West. An exchange of land took place in which Dan took over his sister's land in the East, and she took Dan's wife's land in the West – all for greater convenience. The plot that Kitty got ultimately from Rose Whorriskey (5a) thus ended up in the hands of Mary McClafferty, and hence was used by

Kitty's brother Jimmy. All very complicated, but not by Tory standards, where this kind of thing is commonplace and if nothing else helps toward the utter bafflement of anthropologists.

We must leave the children of Caitlín and Séamus–Nance for the moment. We shall return to them when we discuss the Neilís and their land. For the moment, we can absorb the continuing lessons that this example has shown us about the checks to fragmentation as a result of the nonpursuit of claims; the nature of the "reversion" of land; the general pattern of inheritance along the genealogical branches; and the idea of the "land of marriage," which again helps to stop fragmentation and ensure equitable distribution among households. Let us then proceed to the next case.

The land of the Feilimís

The Eoins, as we saw, must have held most of Páirc na roilleach, Páirc Bhrianaigh Mhóir, and parts of the adjacent "parks" under rundale, their land having been "striped" by Mr. Woodhouse but to a large extent kept together. Strip 7 (3 in 1865), which was the other half of Mullaí an Dairy, Páirc na Locha, and Páirc na Faiseanachta, was in the hands of a clann of Rogers, but, as we saw, fell into the hands of the Eoins through the marriage of Anton–Antoin–Eoin to Mary Rogers. This group of Rogers was known as the "Macken" or "Mackin" Rogers, and is so recorded in documents. They were the branch related to the Feilimís who died out and emigrated, their land passing by marriage to other clanna. Having seen what happened to 7, we shall see what happened to their other plots, 11 and 11a. But I mention them first both as an example of what can happen when a clann disappears, and because their land and that of the Feilimís was together under rundale and so represesents the same parcel in a sense, to be explained along with the Feilimí land. Some informants think that, under rundale, the ancestors of the Macken Rogers had Fál na nGearrán; those of the Feilimí Rogers, Carnán; the Doohan forerunners of the Séamus–Nances, Seán–Bhrianaighs and the Neilís, Fódacha. This may of course be a rationalization of the division of the land; on the other hand it makes sense, for the various Doohans did have land here and their descendants do still. When the land came to be striped vertically the strips got mixed up, it is maintained, with some clann lands intruding between the others. This was necessary if the various qualities of land were to be evenly shared.

But we can never be sure of whatever happened in the 1840s. What we do know is that the Macken–Feilimí land was a considerable portion of West Town land, that the strips were kept close together, and that today the descendants of the original owners are still in more or less the same place as their ancestors. Still further "intrusions" have occurred, and Mooneys, Whorriskeys, and others have intervening holdings, but the continuity is still remarkable. Again, the continuity is not exact and boundaries have changed – some quite radically. But the overall pattern is clear.

Perhaps the best way to proceed through this complicated jungle of land tenure would be to take the adjacent strips of land in West Town that include the Feilimí land and look at their recorded history in 1865, and 1911, and 1923 (see Table 8). This will involve some other owners, but they will be useful for future reference. The first column on the left shows the number and owner from the 1865 map; the second column the same for the 1911 map as nearly as possible – for example, strip 12 in 1911 is in the same place as strip 12 in 1865, but it has been reduced in size; and column three the corresponding numbers and names for 1923. The complications that follow from the changes in numbering can be quite baffling, particularly because the maps are not to the same scale. But the assessors simply chose a number for an owner and then numbered all his plots ". . . a, b, c . . ." after this number. This was repeated in 1911, sometimes on the basis of the old numbers and sometimes not, and so there is often no correspondence at all between strip "x" in 1865 and strip "x" in 1911. For 1923 we are fortunate because the Board officials merely made new notes on the old schedules and did not change the numbering, although they added "letters" for house and garden land. Also, of course, some strips were considerably changed around between 1865 and 1911, yet the same numbering system was later applied to completely altered strips.

However, with the help of Figure 10 we can follow the fortunes of the Feilimí land with side glances at the land of other owners; glances that will help when we come to the land of the Neilís. The complications of realignment, etc., make it difficult in this case to draw comparative maps for 1865 and 1911. The reader can refer forward, however, to Map 16, and glance back briefly at the 1865 field map (Map 8) if necessary. The basic strips that Feilimí left his children were, in 1865, 10a and 10b, which went to Liam (William); and 16a and b, which went to Patrick. By a series of swaps, William acquired plot 9 – next to his own – from John Doohan, in return for which John, who had married Liam's sister Bella, got plot 13 from relative William Doohan (see below); William in turn was

Table 8. *Ownership of strips 9 to 18, 1865–1923*

	1865		1911	1923
9	John Doohan	10	William Rogers	James Rogers (William)
10a	William Rogers			
10b	William Rogers	19	John Rogers	Daniel Rogers Mrs. Bridget Rogers
11a	Ed. Macken Rogers	11a	Patrick Rogers (Mackin)	James Doohan (Paddy)
12	William Doohan (Red)	12	James Doohan (Nancy)	James Doohan (Nancy)
13	William Doohan (Nelly)	13	Mary Doohan	Dennis Duggan (Paddy)
14	Owen Whorriskey	18a 36a	William Doohan James Whorriskey	William Doohan James Whorriskey
15a,b	John Doohan (Bryan)	15,a,b	Isabella Doohan	Isabella Doohan
16a,b	Patrick Rogers (Phillip)	16,a,b	Patrick Rogers	Patrick Rogers
17a	Nancy Mooney (Mick)	17	Michael Mooney	Mrs. Sarah Mooney
17b	Nancy Mooney (Nick)	17a	Michael Mooney	Mrs. Sarah Mooney
18a	Thomas Whorriskey Grace Duggan (Bryan)	18	William Doohan (Roe)	William Doohan (Roe)
18b	Thomas Whorriskey Grace Duggan (Bryan)	27,a,b	William Doohan (Grace)	William Doohan (Grace)

compensated with plot 31, which had been John's. All in the interests, one supposes, of trying to consolidate landholdings.

It is not clear that Bella got any of her father's land and certainly Mary got none; the history of her descendants belongs to the Divers. But Bella, having married Séan (John) Doohan (Bhrianaigh), came, in her widowhood, to hold strips 15 and 15b. The interest here, for the future discussion of the Neilís, stems from the island opinion that Séan and Alex Doohan (recorded as owner of 20a, b, and c) were brothers or cousins and related to the Owen Doohan who was the husband of Neilí. As we see, in 1865, the lands of Séan Doohan and those of the other Doohans – William Red (Roe, Rua) and William Nelly – were close together and separated by the land of Owen Whorriskey.

Let us pause on the Doohans for a moment because their land and that of the Feilimís are so close together. Plots 12 and 13 are recorded as

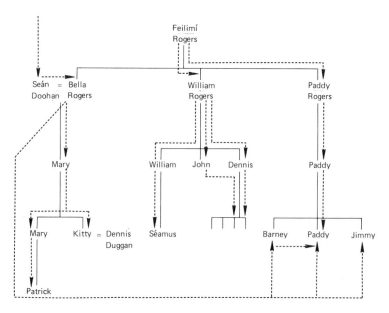

Figure 10. Feilimí land, history from 1865

belonging to two different William Doohans, but informants say that at that time they both belonged to Liam–Neilí, the William Doohan (Nelly) of strip 13. William Rua, they say, was his son – Liam–Liaim–Neilí – with whom he initially divided his land, giving the latter 12. This again was later divided when William Nelly wanted to endow his daughter Caitlín on her marriage to Jimmy–Shéamuis–Nance. Part of 12 then went to her and the rest was part of the deal with Isabella Doohan that we have mentioned, along with all of 13 (this presumably was to balance out the respective sizes of the swapped pieces). William Rua, meanwhile, got the piece of Whorriskey land that became 18a in 1911, plus 18a (1865), which became 27, 27a, and 27b, in 1911. All very complicated again, and we will come back to it when we do the Neilís. But we should note that the assessors record Caitlín Doohan's marriage land (12) as belonging to James Doohan (Nancy). This is doubly wrong in a sense, for it was Caitlín's and it was James's son who worked it. But it is common enough on Tory to refer a man back to a grandparent like this.

Of Owen Whorriskey's land, strip 14 went to William Doohan in the above-mentioned manner, and some went to James Whorriskey (36a, 1911).

So, by 1911, Séan Doohan had died and Isabella was holding his land.

Brother Alex then died, passing his land (21, 21a, b), to son Daniel, who either died or left. Isabella then took this land too, there being no more of that branch of the Doohans left for it to revert to; or even if there were (for example the Carrols, children of John's sister Máire – Genealogy 11) Isabella wasn't about to relinquish it. The connection with the Neilís, if real, was too tenuous to establish claims.

Bella then held strips 13 (which she passed to Mary on her marriage), 15a and 15b, and 21, 21a, and 21b. The latter show little physical continuity with the land of Alex, except that they are roughly in the same place, because all were realigned by the CDB.

Paddy's land went to his son Paddy, and then finally to his grandson Paddy III. William (Liam) had the two plots we have seen. One went to his son John together with Dennis, although John is recorded as the owner in 1911. John died without issue and the land now rests with the four children of Dennis, its ultimate fate still to be decided. The other plot (9 and 10a, 1865; 10, 1911) went to William Jr. and subsequently passed to his son, Séamus–Uilliaim.

Of Bella's land the history is, expectedly, more checkered. The small plot carved out of the land of Liam–Neilí (13, 1911) went to her daughter Mary as we saw, then to the joint custody of Mary's children, Mary and Kitty. Kitty's husband had no land, so she hung on to her claim, and at the moment the land is farmed by Mary's son Patrick–Bhelle, and Kitty's husband, Dennis Duggan (see 1923 list). For what reason I do not know, and it would have been impolite to pursue the matter, Bella decided to distribute the rest of her land among the children of her nephew Paidí–Phaidí–Fheilimí – Patrick, James, and Barney. Barney got 15 and 15b (1911) and James (Jimmy) got the leftover land that had once been Alex's (21, a, b, c, 1911). Barney left for America and Paddy took over the usufruct of his land, but it is still referred to as Barney's and recognized as his. Paddy also got the strip (15a, 1911) that Isabella had carved out of the McClafferty land.

We must deal briefly with 11 and 11a, which in 1865 were with Ed. Macken Rogers and in 1911 with his son Patrick. Patrick had no issue, and the only remaining Macken was his niece Gránnia Rogers, who married Paddy Doohan (see Genealogy 13). These pieces (see 1923) are now held by Paddy's sons James and Dan, and James's son Jimmy.

Map 16 shows the blocks of land now held by the descendants of the Feilimí–Mackens. With 7, which I have included, we overlap with the Eoins, of course, but this is an overlap that has no consequences because all the Mackens are gone and their land is now parcelled out among the

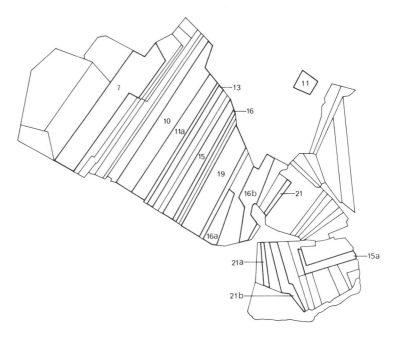

Map 16. Feilimí-Macken land, 1963
Key: 7 – John and James Doohan
            10 – James (Séamus) Rogers
            11, a – James, Dan, and Jimmy Doohan
            13 – Patrick Doohan
            15a; 16, a, b – Patrick Rogers
            15, b – Barney Rogers (Patrick Rogers)
            19 – Dennis Rogers
            21, a, b, c – James Rogers

other clanns. Let us proceed quickly, without further general discussion, to the land of the Neilís while some facts relevant to this territory are still fresh in our minds.

The land of the Neilís

We have already seen how the two Williams and John Doohan owned, in 1865, strips 12, 13, and 15a and b. We have noted that they were connected: that John himself was the son of Brian Doohan (Genealogy 11), who was a relative of the Owen Doohan who was Neilí's husband. The interest picks up when we learn also that, according to some informants, Neilí was a Rogers and "close to" the Feilimís. Certainly the Feilimís and the Neilís feel themselves to be close by blood to each other. Thus, when Isabella, the daughter of Feilimí Rogers, married John, the son of Brian Doohan, she was repeating an alliance – between Owen Doohan and Neilí Rogers – that had occurred in a previous generation. That this arrangement, like the marriage of Anton Duggan and Mary Rogers, involved people with virtually adjacent land may again have been coincidence, but again one wonders. Figure 11 shows the set of relationships involved. The Mackens, as we saw, died out, but the land of the John Doohans (the Séan–Bhrianaighs) lives on through the children of Isabella. What is of most interest, however, is the contention that Owen Doohan's land came to him from his wife and was originally Rogers land – land allied to the Feilimí land, that is. This would make Feilimí and Neilí cousins in the late eighteenth century, which fits our time scale perfectly. It also makes sense because half the land of the Neilís – that owned by William Doohan (Liam–Neilí) in 1865 – is right in amongst the land of the Feilimís and Mackens (strips 12 and 13 in 1865). That this then was Neilí's land from the ultimate ancestor of all the Rogers makes very good sense, and gains weight from the startling fact that the whole clann is called after her and not her husband.

There was, however, land from his side of the family, and it is generally agreed that plot 37 in 1865 came from this side. We must now trace the history of the plots with the help of Figure 12.

However Neilí and Owen got their land together, they proceeded to distribute it among their three children as shown. Mary got plots 23a, b, c (1865); Liam got the 1865 plots 12 and 13 (probably the Rogers land from Neilí); and Eoin got the Middle Town property of 37. As we have

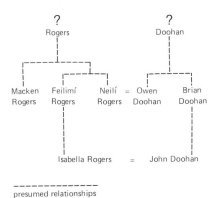

Figure 11. Doohan–Rogers relationships

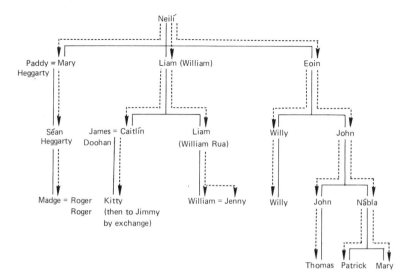

Figure 12. Neilí land, history after 1865

seen, Liam also acquired plot 31 from John Doohan. The 1865 map shows "Widow Heraghty" owning 23a, b and c. This is of course Mary–Neilí after Paddy Heggerty died. The two Williams are shown owning 12 and 13, and John (Eoin) Doohan 37. The devolution of Mary's portion then follows the Heggarty line, going first to John (Seán), who is shown owning it in 1911, and then to his daughter Madge, who married Rory Rogers, who now farms the land. This was rearranged by the CDB and comes out as plots 22 and 22a on the 1911 map. Seán still held it in 1923.

Liam–Liaim–Neilí and Eoin meanwhile – as a result of the various rearrangements of land that went on with the Whorriskeys in particular – had ended up with the plots 18a and 18b (1865). The "b" portion of this was considerably rearranged by the CDB and it became Eoin's share as plots 27, 27a, and 27b on the 1911 map. The land of the Liam–Neilís then consisted of plots 18, 18a, and 31; plot 12 had already gone to Caitlín on her marriage to James Doohan, son of Séamus Doohan Nancy. It is recorded as his in 1911 and 1923. (We will return later to the Séamus–Nance branch because they have already acquired the land of the Eoins through Rose Whorriskey.) The rest of Liam–Liaim–Neilí's land went to his son William and then to the latter's widow Jenny Doohan.

Eoin then was left with plot 37 and the rearranged 27, 27a, b, c. Plot 37 went to his son John, and in turn was divided between John's children

John and Nábla. It was Nábla who married Barney McClafferty, and we have already looked at the fracas that surrounded that division. Some of this land was sold to provide for the school and the church. It is recorded on the 1911 map as plots 34 and 38 belonging to John Doohan and Nábla Doohan. John's share has now passed to his son Tomás–John, and Nábla's children have divided her property in the manner we described, Patrick being recorded as owner in 1923. The other parcels went to Eoin's other son Willy (recorded in 1923) and then to his son Willy–Bhillí. When he died recently, it passed to his sisters and remains with them. In fact, as the islanders explain, it was always theirs; they did not inherit it from Willy; he had farmed it when he was alive and so was recorded as the owner, but he lived with his sisters and they all shared the produce of the land because it was, in effect, jointly owned.

Map 17 shows the final ownership of land by the Neilís. This includes some of the land of the Séamus–Nances, which could just as well have been dealt with under the Eoins. The overlap here is total, but we had to wait until the land of the Neilís was discussed before we could complete the inventory of Séamus–Nance land. We have already followed the history of plot 5 (1911, 7), which James and John got from Rose Whorriskey and thus from the Eoins. Plot 12 came to James–Shéamuis–Nance through his marriage to Caitín–Liaim–Neilí, and has passed on in the manner we have described to Kitty and then to Mary McClafferty and Kitty's brother Jimmy. Plots 12a, b, and c were the original land of Séamus–Nance himself and again passed to James and John and at the moment, like plot 5, hang in the balance among their descendants, claimed and largely used by Jimmy and Mary McClafferty, but not finally disposed of with certainty. O'Brien land (6, 6a, b, 30; 1911) came into this branch through the marriage of Gránnia Doohan to George O'Brien and went to Kitty O'Brien, who married Anton Rogers, who is recorded as owner in 1923. Whorriskey land (8, 36, 36a) came from the marriage of Bríd to Paddy Whorriskey. The marriage of Mary, daughter of John–Séamuis–Nance, brought in plot 49 in the East from Tom Meenan. (Similarly Séamus Bán – James Meenan – brought in land to the Neilís by his marriage to Neilí–Liaim–Neilí (plot 50).)

Continuing the acquisitive saga of the Séamus–Nances, John–Shéamuis–Nance got plots 58 and 58a in the East Town. These came from his marriage to Rose Diver (see Genealogy 3). Owen Whorriskey, from his marriage to Rose's sister Isabella (see Genealogy 3 again), also got part of the Diver land adjacent to that of John (plot 31a, 1911). This in turn is next to the land that Paddy Duggan (see Genealogy 1) got from

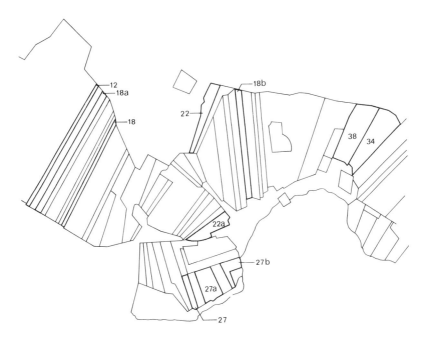

Map 17. Neilí land, 1963
Key: 12 – Kitty Doohan (to Jimmy)
        18, a, b – Jenny Doohan (from William)
        27, a, b – William Doohan (sisters of)
        22, a – Madge Heggarty (Roger Rogers)
        38 – Tomás Doohan
        34 – Patrick McClafferty

his marriage to Sally, of a different but related branch of Divers. In 1865 we can see clearly the concentration of Diver land in plots 52, 53, 55, and 56. But the various sons-in-law had made their inroads by 1911, including John–Shéamuis–Nance, who left his share to his son William (see 1923).

We could go on as we have done for the Séamus–Nances and show how many other plots were fed into the four mainstream genealogies, but we have covered the most important, and, as I pointed out above, once the principles are grasped there is no marginal return in endlessly pursuing examples. Maps 18 and 19, in any case, show the plots we have covered in this analysis to illustrate what they represent of the total. There are more in West Town than in East, because the major genealogies are represented there more heavily. The history of the rest

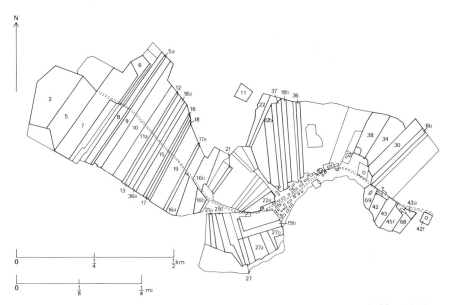

Map 18. Total number of plots discussed, East Town fields, 1911

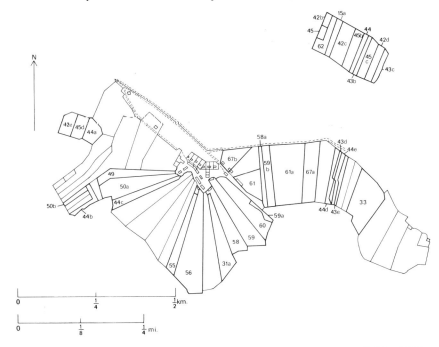

Map 19. Total number of plots discussed, West Town fields, 1911

of the land is fairly straightforward and merely reinforces the principles we have already discovered. To these we must then turn.

Principles of ownership and inheritance

The concept of "ownership" on Tory comes out clearly from this mass of detail, even if very little else does. It is certainly not the same concept as that of the officials who tried to record it. I have spoken constantly of someone "holding" a piece of land, because this seems to me a better way of describing it than speaking of ownership. That one holds a piece does not necessarily give one any absolute right to alienate it, for example, unless no person who has a claim presses it. Each plot of land is best seen as the center of a network of such claims, each claimant being a descendant of the original ancestor who held the land and who is recognized as the focal point of the descent-claim system. There have been many examples in the foregoing discussion of land "reverting" to descendants of an ancestor in the absence of any heirs, or at least heirs interested in pressing claims. Widows, we have seen, can "hold" the land of their husbands in their lifetimes, but it will revert to the husband's relatives at death.

Naturally, people will try to bend the system to their own advantage, and what is true in principle need not work out so well in practice. But what is remarkable on Tory is the consistency with which the principle is upheld. There are many interesting cases pending in which a "reversion" is expected, and it would be tragic if the island is evacuated before we can see just what happens in these instances. It will be a good test of the hypothesis to see whether or not the land consistently reverts in the manner we have examined.

This brings us to the nature and function of the clann. In Chapters 3 and 4, I said that a discussion of land inheritance would bring this out, and I think it has. A man or woman is a member of a number of clanns, and each of these represents a landholding group in which he or she has claims: groups from which land either has or could "come down to" him or her. The Séamus–Nances here are a beautiful example because they have taken in land from the Eoins and the Neilís, as well as some of the smaller groups. At numerous points the clanns overlap, and this is usually "remembered" in the older generations, if and when it has meant the fusion of land from two groups. If there was no such fusion, then the link is likely to be forgotten.

If we look at the land maps and the lists of owners we see there the familiar names from the genealogies: Feilimí Rogers, William Nelly, Séa-

mus McClafferty, Donal Doohan, "shamus Donal," "Perkin," James
Nancy, the inevitable Isabella Doohan, the Dooleys, the Sallys, the
Whorriskeys, and all the immigrants who plugged into the system. It was
a considerable thrill, after having ploughed through the genealogies
with the islanders, only half believing what I was told so rapidly, to find
in the dusty records in Dublin these same names cropping up in faded
ink and copperplate writing. They are easily identifiable even through
the anglicizations of the Valuation Office, and all our ancestors are there
in one form or another. Many also are there who are forgotten now; they
either emigrated, were removed, or simply left no immediate heirs; their
land being absorbed into a related clann.

The picture we have, then, as far as landholding groups are concerned, is the same as for the genealogies themselves. The apical ancestors, or in the case of the larger genealogies, their immediate descendants, are the original landholders from whom the clann traces descent
and from whom it got its land along these same lines and branches.
Because a branch can always die out, leaving land to be claimed, the links
are all remembered by the simple genealogical method, aided by the
naming system. Land should, in principle, always end up with someone
who is a descendant of the original owner; in the majority of cases, as the
foregoing discussion has shown, it does.

It should also in principle be subject to endless fragmentation because
all heirs have a claim. In some similar systems on the Continent (Spain,
Southern France) this indeed happens, and evidently happened under
rundale. On Tory there is fragmentation, but the principle known to the
islanders as "land of the marriage" prevents this from being excessive. I
have already described how this would work, with brothers and sisters
arranging, often with their parents, to "put land into the marriage,"
either from the patrimony, or from that of a spouse. The attitude of
parents toward many children was often described to me as: "If you can
find a partner with land then go ahead and marry, but don't expect any
from me yet." This, of course, must have influenced the marriage arrangements, and we shall look at this in Chapter 7. If a woman, for
example, were particularly anxious to marry, then she would press her
claim. I was told that brothers found it hard to refuse land to sisters who
wanted to marry, and that they would be censured for doing so. On the
other hand, it is hard for a man to demand land from his father while
the latter is still alive. It is not considered necessary to divide the land
while the parent is still living, because he will provide for his sons from
its produce. But it does happen.

Underlying all these considerations is the feeling that a principle of equal shares should operate. Thus, if a man and a woman decide to marry, and the woman has a claim to a sizable piece of property, then it is right that the land of the marriage should come from her if her husband is from a family more hard pressed. "If a man gets land through his marriage," I was told, "then he has no right to take it from his brothers and sisters." He has of course an equal claim de jure, but it is felt he has no moral right to press his claim. Because there is no land court on the island, such matters ultimately depend on pressures of family and public opinion. But, as always, it is difficult to go against the "custom of the island." We saw above in the case histories many examples of this principle in operation.

What then of rundale and associated matters? This is perhaps something best left to geographers and historians, who can make what they will of the data. I can only hazard a few guesses. We saw that the rundale system involved a "clachán," which was usually a group of "blood kin" who shared the land in common and redistributed it among themselves. No one ever discusses quite what this group of blood kin could be or ever was, but the Tory history may give us some clues. Each of the towns is a clachán, but under rundale there was more than one group of blood kin in each town. There were, however, a number of intermarrying clanns. We saw how the land of the Rogers, Doohans, and some of that of the Divers and Whorriskeys was contained in blocks in the West Town fields. Even after Mr. Woodhouse's reforms, these blocks were still fairly homogeneous, and island tradition confirms their previous existence. In ancient times (pre-1750?), it seems, the bulk of Duggan, Rogers, and Doohan land was in West Town, that of the McClaffertys and other Doohans in Middle Town, and that of the Divers and Meenans in East Town. Each group of kin probably made its own internal arrangements about the land it held, but of course each group could marry into the other groups, creating its cross-claims. The system would have been not unlike the present-day Tory system in some ways, at least as far as claims were concerned. What would have differed would have been the individual ownership on a permanent basis – although even this is not clear, because, as we have seen, "individual" or "permanent" ownership is a relatively foreign notion on Tory. If we see the modern Tory system as essentially a system of usufruct, then the tie-in with rundale becomes more obvious. A man "holds" a piece of land and uses it, but it "belongs" in an ultimate sense to the clann of the original recognized owner, the clann in which it is vested, as it were. This makes it like any piece of land under rundale, which belonged not to the individual who was recorded as owner for Tithes but to the group of blood kin he represented.

I would suggest, then, that the rundale system was much like the Tory system today, except that the land was not arranged in strips and was sometimes redistributed to prevent fragmentation and restore an even distribution of the various qualities. The clacháns must have been, on average, about the size of the towns on Tory, although West Town is perhaps unusually large, inflated by its stature as a fishing port and market. J. McParlan, in his *Statistical Survey of the County of Donegal* (Dublin, 1802), quotes a figure of twenty to thirty families per cluster. But clusters of up to ninety cottages were to be found. West Town at present has twenty-six households, Middle Town sixteen, and East Town twenty-four, so they are within the range.

I suspect that, in at least Northwest Donegal, a number of intermarrying clanns from a group of nearby clacháns made up the marriage isolate and the effective landholding community. It is noticeable that the Tory type of naming system is common in this area. The system would have had to be relatively endogamous to have worked, and could not have been very dispersed because the only inheritance was land, and this could not have been moved about on marriage. Marriages, then, usually had to be between neighbors if a division of land was involved. We have seen on Tory how marriages were often between people with neighboring land, and what trouble would be gone to to rearrange land if marriages straddled the two clacháns.

Whether this was typical of rundale elsewhere in Ireland, and what relation it had to "runrig" in Scotland, "aarkast" in Scandinavia, "gavelkind" in England, and the open-field systems of Brittany ("terres chaudes"), Spain, southern France, and the like, I will leave to the social historians. I will simply underline that it is very different from the system described for County Clare by Arensberg and Kimball, which involved the inheritance of an intact farm by the eldest son and the provision of a dowry for the outmarrying daughters. This probably reflects much of the post–land acts and postfamine situation in southern Ireland, and does not seem to have been the prefamine pattern according to K. M. Connell (see Notes). Before the famine, land was fragmented among heirs and children were provided for on marriage "from the land" – much like the Tory pattern. But always, in Ireland as elsewhere, these two systems clashed; the poorer peasantry preferring some version of rundale. I here offer the Tory data as a living example of an ancient system; a social fossil that still works and thrives. Anthropologists also will not need to be lectured on the relevance of this system to an understanding of cognatic descent groups.

But I will not labor this professional esoterica; enough to have described a remarkable system worth examining in its own right as an example of human adaptation to a difficult environment. Rationalizations such as Mr. Woodhouse's, land acts that are so beloved of bureaucrats for producing predictable systems of tenure, and notions of ownership that suit valuation officers are all foreign to the Tory soil. They do not transplant well. The system the islanders run is in fact perfectly rational and suited to their particular needs. They run it not as a clockwork machine for producing neat results, but with foresight and judgment. The rules are a set of rules to guide decisions, not inflexible formulae. The result is a rational distribution of land that is perhaps the best solution for this particular terrain and population. Once more, we learn that society knows better than planners; that custom is often wiser than science; that when it comes to adaptation, there is no substitute for centuries.

6

The boats:
recruitment of crews

Thall ar an loch tá na bádaí ar fósgadh,
Ag snámh mar a bheadh ealaí ar bharra na dtonn.

The two lines above, from a popular song, express the solicitude the islanders feel for their boats:

> Over there on the lake the boats are at shelter
> Sleeping as swans would on top of the waves.

If the Tory people seem excessively poetic about their means of transport, they are not to be blamed. Without the boats, they say, they are nothing. This is not simply a matter of such mundane things as communications and supplies: It is a matter of life and death, literally. Every time a boat puts out there is a potential loss of life. It has happened often enough for the memory of it to haunt all the older people. The Tory men are certainly brave sailors, but they have a great respect for, and fear of, the sea. They do not believe in taking foolish risks. A boat from Inishboffin once came into Tory at the height of a storm and delivered some visitors. The Tory sailors were amazed and angry to learn that it was a price of twenty pounds that had prompted this madness. To risk lives for money was considered highly immoral. If the Inishboffin boat had run into trouble, they argued, it would have expected Tory boats to come to its aid. They would surely have gone, but it would have been grossly unfair to put them at risk for such a reason. Had the boat been out fishing and gotten into difficulties, that would have been another matter.

Boats are everyone's concern, even if they are individually owned. When any bona fide islander wants to leave the island or return to it, he simply gets into whatever boat is going or coming. Nonislanders are charged, of course – as much as the traffic will bear. But young people, bird-watchers, and those obviously with small means are rarely overcharged – and when this once happened it was pointed out that the overcharger was not a native Tory man at all or he would not have tried

Young men loading the new-style cylindrical lobster pots into a yawl, in preparation for a drop.

to cheat the "bird men." These bird-watchers – like myself – came regularly, spent money on the island, and were regarded as quasinative. Thus they were not expected to pay more than a nominal ten shillings for the trip. Mainlanders who had relatives on the island or people from Inishboffin or Mín Lárach were not usually required to pay either.

All this is important for an understanding of the Tory attitude to boats and the responsibilities of the boatmen. However the boatmen might secretly grumble, in the manner, perhaps, of entrepreneurs everywhere, their boats were very much regarded as public property as far as coming and going were concerned. Any suggestion that islanders might be charged would have been regarded as scandalous; indeed it would have been incomprehensible.

In return, the islanders felt responsible for the boats. One stormy day on Tory, after several of the larger boats had come in, the rush of men and boys to the slipway to help haul them up was a spectacular scene. This was a laborious business, which required several of the boys and older men to hold up the boats with their backs while the younger men wound on the winch. It often took as much as an hour to get a boat high enough up the slip, and then another had to be hauled after it. All this in driving rain and often high winds, and certainly without material rewards. As many as thirty men and boys might be engaged at a time in boat hauling. Insofar as riding in the boats was everyone's privilege, hauling them up whatever the conditions was everyone's responsibility. As far as I could see, there was no relationship between the haulers and the boat owners other than that of fellow islanders. It was true collective responsibility.

There was another custom whereby men who traveled over in a boat – for example from the mainland – would help unload any stores the boat owners might have aboard. This was another way of giving some return, but it was not required – it was simply done.

Among all the Tory songs that aroused emotion, none aroused more than the songs of shipwreck. There were many of these that celebrated local events such as when, for example, a whole boatload of young people went down off Arranmore while returning all gaily dressed from a dance. Their parents had heard their cries in the night but had not been able to get to them to help. The next day all that was found, brought in by the then calm waves, was "caipín lása agus ribín bán" – a lace cap and a white ribbon. Tales of shipwreck are common, and particularly of events in island history where men – and women too – were lost in storms.

It is perhaps foolish to try to make such judgments as "boats are more important to the islanders than land," for in the days when land meant sheer survival it is unlikely that this was true. The islanders can also become quite emotional about their land. But somehow it does not have the same emotional quality as do the boats. No one ever died digging potatoes; there is no danger in planting barley. The land is not the magical bridge between the island and the world; it is not the stuff that songs and heroes are made of. Boats are of a different order, and over and above their mundane economic uses they have a meaning for the islanders that only song and poetry can express.

It is, however, to these mundane uses that we address ourselves in this chapter; in particular to the question of the recruitment of boat crews. The inheritance of land is very much a matter of position in a genealogy. To what extent is the same true of this other arm of the Tory economy, fishing? Did one's place in a boat depend on the same kind of genealogical considerations as one's share in the land? Or was there another principle at work? First, we must ask what these boats were, how the islanders came by them, and what they did with them.

I have rather hesitantly used the past tense so far because I want to start in the past, in the heyday of Tory fishing times. The islanders still have boats and still fish, but this is no longer the mainstay of their economy. Nor was it before the advent of big sailboats, which was probably in the latter part of the nineteenth century. Before this, the typical boat was the *curragh* (coracle). These still exist but are very rarely used. One of the last was the subject of a dispute when someone wanted to buy it for a museum. The boat had belonged to an old man who died, and finally his children decided that he would not like to have it in a museum despite the money, which was tempting. He was rotting in the clay, they said, and it could do the same. So it did.

This attachment to the curraghs was very strong. A man built his own, and it was half his means of livelihood; the other half was his land. There were two kinds: the one-man curragh and the two-man curragh. Both were made in the same way with a framework of light wood covered with canvas. The latter was about eight feet long, with the ends of the gunwale projecting from the stern so that the canvas would not be damaged when the boat was dragged up the beach. Tory never evolved the four-man "racing curragh" famous from the Aran Islands, and some authorities consider the two-man paddling version an intermediary in the evolution of this type: between, that is, the rowing curragh developed farther south and the round coracle of the River Boyne, the most ancient type.

The Tory curragh was propelled by two paddles: one paddler kneeling in the prow providing the power, a second in the stern doing the steering. These boats had the great advantage of being light to handle and carry and easy to construct. There being no wood on the island, it was difficult to make larger boats. The curragh required only light boughs, canvas, and tar, with some harder wood for the gunwale. Getty reports that Tory men were discovered in the 1840s near the monastery at Ards looking for suitable branches of a particular kind from which to make their curraghs.

But these small and fragile craft were only really good for inshore fishing, could not take the big nets, and were dangerous on rough days. Their use thus was limited. The next size of boat was the yawl, which could be rowed by two to four men and could take a small sail. Sixteen feet long and of shallow draft, these boats were better for large-scale net fishing in open waters. With the help of landmarks on the island (still in existence today), from which sightings could be taken, these boats could get in good hauls of fish that shoaled up to about a mile out to sea. Watchers on the island would call out and signal with special signs to the fishermen to direct them to shoals that showed up dark in the water. The cairns or the land provided sight lines for placing the boats directly over the spots where certain fish regularly shoaled. Thus the yawls were able to do well. But fish evidently change their habits, and the vagaries of the markets and the difficulties of selling the catch meant that there was never much market for the yawls and most of their catch was for island use. The main point about this type of boat (and about a later version of the curragh adapted to oars that was used in the same way as the yawls), however, is that it required very small crews of two or four men. It presented, therefore, little problem of recruitment as far as crews were concerned. It was with the advent of the larger boats toward the end of the nineteenth century that crewing became a problem.

It is with this problem that we shall be concerned. But first let us consider the boats. The small yawls needed at most four men. One old man recalled the hard work involved with them. They would sometimes be rowed from Tory to Downings (thirty miles) with two men rowing and one steering, taking turn and turn about. This could only be done in good weather and, of course, the weather was always better then. The journey took four hours each way, I was told, and it was too hot to row in the middle of the day, so one left early in the morning and came back in the evening. The sea was so calm that if you threw out an eggshell on the way you would find it floating in the same place when you came back. But despite this idyllic weather, the rowing was back-breaking and few men wanted to do it very often. It was often, however, the only way to sell a catch of fish.

The bigger boats began to be built toward the end of the century, when profits from lobster and kelp enabled groups of men to club together and buy the timber to build them. But they suffered the disadvantage of being difficult to haul up the beach – there being neither slipway, winch, nor pier then. This was rectified when the Congested Districts Board built a pier – between 1903 and 1911. The CDB also made loans to the islanders to help them develop the fishing industry and built them a curing station, which made the problem of marketing easier. All this led to the growth of a considerable herring- and mackerel-fishing industry, and at its height some eleven large herring boats requiring crews of up to ten men were in use. This presented a new problem to the islanders, because previously there was no real precedent for the recruitment of large work teams for such relatively complicated risk-sharing ventures.

The problem lay, then, in funding, building, and crewing the boats. Those that were not built from CDB loans were financed, whether by a single man or a group, from the profits of other enterprises. Some boats were bought from boat builders in Derry and Moville, some from private owners – and often continued to bear the name of the original owner. But, encouraged by the Board, and drawing on their own skills nurtured over centuries through the construction of curraghs, agricultural implements, furniture, and houses, the Tory men soon developed considerable expertise as boat builders. This skill and its reputation live on. A "Tory boat" is always something to be admired.

Success breeds success, and as more profits came in and more capital was available, the islanders took more and more to building their own boats. Requiring larger and larger versions – up to forty feet and deeper in draught – they used an ingenious method of construction. Around the bones of an old boat that had been holed or damaged enough to render it unseaworthy, they constructed a new version, plank by plank, adding here and lengthening there until the phoenix was complete. There was always then the problem of the philosopher's shoe – was it the old boat rebuilt or a new boat? It generally took the old name. This method was still in use when I was on the island; one man had been five years constructing, in his garden, such a boat, single-handed – or with the intermittent help of a migrating son.

Once, when a group of men wanted a boat for the summer fishing and were desperate to get it built over the winter, they took over the church hall and built it there. When they had finished, they had to knock down one end wall of the hall to get it out, and then rebuild the wall again.

But who are these "groups of men"? We have seen that the larger boats that carried sail (bádaí seoil) required perhaps as many as ten men to handle them, as opposed to the curraghs and rowing boats (bádaí rámhaíochta), which required never more than four, usually less. Sometimes the men who formed a crew also owned the boat in shares. If they had indeed put up the money for the boat together, then the usual method of sharing proceeds was "one share for each and one for the boat"; the share for the boat going toward its upkeep. The capital costs of course included the nets, which were often as valuable as the boat itself and were passed from boat to boat much repaired. One boat was called *Bád an Chlub* because it was built by just such a club. There are stories of the folding of such clubs where the division was so meticulous that the boat was sawn up into as many sections as there were shares, and the timber thus divided.

Otherwise the boat was the enterprise of one or two men who put up the capital, built it, or bought it, and then set about recruiting a crew. There were no set rules about how profits (or for that matter losses) should be shared. The only rule was that an agreement must be reached at the beginning of the season and strictly kept. Various arrangements included "one for each member and one for the boat"; half for the boat and the rest divided equally among the crew; two shares for the owner, one for the boat, and one for each member; and so on. The merits of the various arrangements were often discussed, but there seemed to be no agreement on the best. It depended on the exact circumstances of the boat, and the nature of the fishing, etc.

At this point it is worth noting that, in mackerel and herring fishing, two boats (at least) were used: There was the main, large boat, "bád na h-angaí" (boat of the nets), and the smaller rowing boat, "bád fhreastala" (serving boat). The "net boat" and the "servant boat" between them required eight to ten men. The smaller boat was used for putting out the nets and for bringing some of the fish in to shore if the fishing was close to land and particularly good. Today, a motorboat (bád innill) will often team up with a sailboat to do this job. The advent of these motorboats – about the time of the First World War – is very important, as we shall see, for they reduced the need for large crews. The engines replaced oar power and thus reduced the need for muscle power.

Meanwhile, however, the larger crews had to be recruited, and it is to this process that we must turn for the rest of the chapter. I was able to record the crews for eleven of the big herring boats as follows:

1.	*Bád Dubh*	West Town
2.	*Bád Bán*	West Town
3.	*Bád Uilliaim*	West Town
4.	*Bád an Churing*	West Town
5.	*Bád Bhlackie*	West Town
6.	*Bád na Stócach*	East Town
7.	*Bád an Cháirnealaigh*	East Town
8.	*Bád MhacDaibhéid*	East Town
9.	*Bád Chonchubhair*	East Town
10.	*Bád John Bhig*	East Town
11.	*Bád an Chlub*	West Town

The allocation to a town is with respect to the base of the boat – where its owners came from and where it was regularly kept; although after the advent of the pier and the slipway, West Town became the permanent harbor of boats in use. When beached for the winter, however, they tended to separate according to town, with the East Town boats being beached at Port Doon. In any case, as far as the islanders are concerned, the boats "belonged" to one town or another.

We can quickly run through the names. It is of course more or less de rigeur to have, on the one hand, the black boat (dubh) and, on the other, the white (bán). It would somehow offend against Gaelic canons of classification to be otherwise, as in the classification of individuals, cousins, strangers, rocks, cows, or anything else. It is perhaps also significant that these two were always given first by anyone willing to talk about the boats. They were the "first" to be built, I was told, but this was disputed; in any case, the fact that something was told first was often rationalized by saying that it had chronological precedence. *Bád Uilliaim* was named after its builder, William Rogers, who appears in Genealogy 3 and was Uilliam–Liaim–Fheilimí. However, it was largely fished by his son, Séamus–Uilliam, who is still alive. The fourth boat was built by Phillip Doohan (Genealogy 3) at the same time as the CDB built the curing station, and to take advantage of same. It was therefore called after the mother that necessitated its invention – the Curing Boat. *Bád Bhlackie* (or, as some purists would have it *Bád Bhlagai*) was connected with a Mr. Blackham, well known to the islanders as "Blackie," and something of a local worthy. It was evidently not purchased from him but built on the island, but perhaps he had used it at one time to take trips in, or to take cattle from the island or something such. *Bád na Stócach* – "the Lads' Boat" – was exactly that: a boat that a group of lads built and went shares with. Number 7 was called "the Cardinal's Boat" with special pride. It had been used, shortly after being built and because it was the newest and the fastest, to bring the great John, Cardinal O'Donnell, to the island to conduct a service and to visit in his capacity as Bishop of Raphoe. This was a great event for the islanders, and is still spoken of. O'Donnell was a strong supporter of the work of the Board, as well as perhaps one of the finest-looking princes of the Church ever. So important is this name (and the O'Donnells were, of course, the old kings of Tír Chonaill) that, when the original boat went out of commission, the boat that took over the nets also took over the name. The nets are, amazingly, still in use, and custom is that whichever boat is using the nets is *Bád an Cháirnealaigh* while it uses them.

Number 8 was built by a Mr. McDaid in Moville and bore its builder's name. I was surprised to find this boat still in commission, but was told that it was in fact a successor boat built from the skeleton of the old in the manner described above. Informants seemed unsure of the original owner of number 9, but he was called "O'Connor." Ten is simply named after its builder, "Little John." The last boat we have already come across: It is the "Club" boat built by Owen (Eoghan) Whorriskey (Genealogy 3) and financed by the club members. It was, several maintain, the second to be built (*Bád Uilliaim* the first), but it didn't last long because of disputes among the crew.

So to the crews. In the illustrations of recruitment to follow, I have, as with the genealogies, not interposed any interpretation of my own. The links between crew members that are shown, for example, are the links as informants gave them to me, not links I discovered for myself. There are links of kinship between everyone on the island, and it would not have been difficult to show these for the boat crews in great detail. But unless they themselves specified such links as the operative ones, I have not included them, although often they merit a passing comment.

I first obtained a list of all the crew members. Then, starting with the originators of the boat – owners, builders, or "club secretaries" – I asked how the crew got together. It was generally agreed that no one just asked anyone. Sometimes an outsider to an already established network was brought in to make up a crew, and even men from Inishboffin and the mainland, if there was a labor shortage. But it was agreed that this was not favored. Crew members were better if they were "related." Well, then, what about relationship on the genealogical pattern? Should not a clann provide a crew? This was commonly agreed to be unlikely, although the core of a crew was likely to be a group of related brothers, fathers and sons, or cousins. But the clann was not a suitable unit. It was largely a conceptual unit that could be activated as a "group" in the case of a land inheritance problem, and might be a recruiting ground for family feuds, etc. But it in no way constituted a working group. Any particular branch, for example, just might not have in it the right number of skilled fishermen. Also, because of the overlapping problem, a man might have conflicting loyalties. Which clann would he choose? No. The islanders were definite: Descent as a principle for the recruitment of crews was usually no more than a basis – it could not be the whole story. The core of crew members would be likely to call on, for example, affines as much as consanguines (although in many cases there would be a dual relationship). "If a man asked his wife's brother, then this brother would ask his uncle, and if he wanted he would come in, certainly, and he would ask his daughter's husband, and they would make a crew like that until they had enough." So said one very articulate informant who fully understood my problem.

Therefore, in what follows I will try to indicate the order in which the crews were built up and the reasons advanced by the islanders for their composition, following exactly their own descriptions. If these sometimes seem tortuous, remember that each islander knows every other and all his connections and is always referring to these. Remember also that there was, and this is acknowledged, always a keen competition for good crew members. This meant that every string had to be pulled, every connection exploited to fill the places with good men – connected men.

And also remember that, for most of the islanders who were not genealogists, the kinds of affinal links we are describing were the real ongoing links that they knew about from their own knowledge of current and recent marriages. Most of them who could not give their ancestors back to Neilí or Feilimí could tell you quite easily how they were linked affinally to everyone else on the island, and genealogies given by the nonexperts would often look more like these than the finely tuned versions of Chapters 3. People might know they were Clann Fheilimí or Clann Neilí, for example, but not be able to recite the genealogy at all. But everyone could about follow with ease the relationships traced in this chapter.

In some cases, however, I suspected an ex post facto explanation. Some of the marriages cited as links in the recruitment process could not have taken place until after the boats in question were built! It may be that these were rationalizations, but in some cases the boats were in use over a long period and members were added as time went on, whereas original members may have been forgotten if they did not last long. Also, it does not matter too much if there are the odd rationalizations, because these at least help to illustrate the way the islanders conceptualize the *ideal* method of recruitment.

I should also emphasize that many of the men who worked these boats were still very much alive and had very lively memories, even if most of the boats had long since been laid up. Many nights were spent in tales and memories of the herring boats and the great days of Tory fishing and the nature of the different crews, their relative merits, etc. So this is not really "historical" material at all. For an anthropologist, I suppose, history begins from the birthdate of his oldest informant. Let us take the boats in turn.

1. *Bád Dubh.* All the boats are in fact painted white. *Bád Dubh* had a black line painted on it, which was enough for classification purposes. It was built by Patrick Rogers – Paidí-Phaidí-Fheilimí of Genealogy 3. It is a good one to start with because it uses most nearly the principle of descent in simply linking genealogies 2 and 3 (see Figure 13). But, as subsequent examples will show, there are many other members of those two genealogies in other boats as well. As is shown in Figure 13, Paddy called in his two cousins, Phillip and Paddy Doohan, sons of the redoubtable Bella. Now they are said to be "connected" through their father to the Doohan's of Clann Neilí – though no one knows how. It was "way back." Anyway, for whatever reason, they called on Sean Heggarty, who in turn called on his cousins. Because this was given to me first I was convinced that boat-crew recruitment and genealogy were going to be connected very closely. But this turned out to be a false start. The other two members are Edward Rogers from Genealogy 16, who married Grace McGinley from the mainland, who was related somehow to Patrick McGinley, also from the mainland, who came and married on Tory partly because there was a promise of a place in a boat. No "connection" was cited between these two and the rest of the crew.

2. *Bád Bán. Bád Bán* was initiated by the two Willy Doohans, senior and junior (see Figure 14). Séamus Doohan (Nancy) was an associate of Willy, and he brought his daughter's husband, the outsider James O'Brien. Willy's brother John (Eoin–Neilí) was "close" to his wife's nephew Hugh Doohan, who in turn brought in his brother's wife's brother, Patrick Diver. Patrick had a cousin Madge who married an outsider, Dennis Dixon, and he was roped in too, being an excellent boatman. Here we see how two outsiders, James O'Brien and Dennis

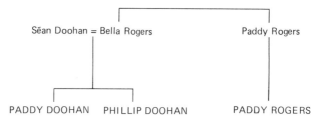

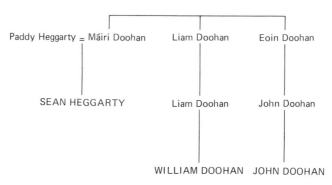

Figure 13. *Bád Dubh. Crew, with genealogy reference:* Paddy Rogers, 3; Paddy Doohan, 3; Phillip Doohan, 3; Seán Heggarty, 2; William Doohan, 2; John Doohan, 2; Paddy McGinley, 5; Edward Rogers, 16.

Dixon, were brought in. At the height of Tory fishing prosperity and at the height of the season, there were always too many boats chasing too few crews. But even so, if affinal and other links could be exploited, they would be; it was better than asking outsiders.

The order of preference seemed to be (1) consanguines, (2) affines, (3) islanders who were associated in some way, (4) other islanders, (5) Inishboffin men, (6) men from Mín Lárach and Bloody Foreland, (7) others as a last extremity.

If a man married in who was a good boatman, there would be competition to claim him as "close" in order to get him into a boat. Dennis Dixon was evidently such a catch in this case.

It is perhaps too much that although *Bád Dubh* showed up strongly with principles of descent, *Bád Bán* should be heavy on alliance; but there are stranger things in nature, which, as we know, follows art and not the other way round.

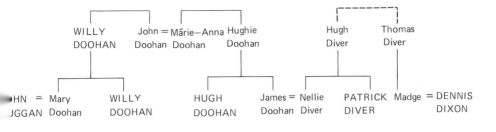

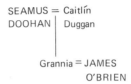

Figure 14. *Bád Bán. Crew, with genealogy reference:* John Duggan, 18; Willy Doohan, Sr., 2; Willy Doohan, Jr., 2; Hugh Doohan, 12; Patrick Diver, 5; Dennis Dixon, from outside; Séamus Doohan, 1; James O'Brien, 1.

Again I must stress that the connections given are those narrated by old crew members, who knew how the boat came into being and exactly how the crew was put together. The formation of a crew was evidently argued about for hours and even days or weeks, and its recruitment was not at all a haphazard or chance affair.

3. *Bád Uilliaim.* William's boat is in some ways more like the first than the second of our examples, and calls into play two major genealogies: that of Eoin (1) and that of the McClaffertys (4); see Figure 15. But they are linked by two cousins who never married and so had no affines: William's son Séamus–Uilliaim, and his cousin John. Séamus and his father went into business with the boat, along with John. John's sister had married Paddy McClafferty and this pulled in that clan together with the offspring of two of its marriages with incomers – Mooneys and O'Donnells. It is not clear that there was any affinal link of consequence with the Eoin branch of Anton that pulled them and their affinal Whorriskey into the net. These can be found, but were not cited. William and Anton Duggan were close, had fished together before, and this was enough. This boat had a reputation for daring and enterprise. Séamus–Uilliaim is still alive and his exploits are spoken of often, as are those of Micí Mooney. It was "one of the great boats."

4. *Bád an Churing. Bád an Churing,* an enterprise intended to take advantage of the CDB curing station, was initiated by Phillip Doohan –

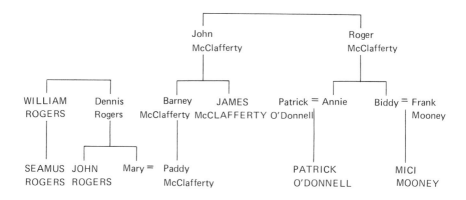

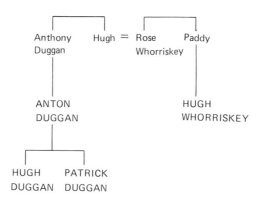

Figure 15. *Bád Uilliaim. Crew, with genealogy reference:* William Rogers, 3; Séamus Rogers, 3; John Rogers, 3; James McClafferty, 4; Patrick O'Donnell, 4, 7; Mící Mooney, 4; Hugh Duggan, 1; Patrick Duggan, 1; Anton Duggan, 1; Hugh Whorriskey, 1.

branching out from *Bád Dubh* – and his brother Paddy. These two brothers had connections with the McClaffertys by two marriages: that of their cousin Sally to Ned McClafferty and that of their sister Mary to James McClafferty. This brought in neither of these two direct affines, but their father and brother, John and Mící, who appear as crew members in Figure 16. As the narrative goes, then, the other brother Patrick, although not in the boat himself, asked his brother-in-law Dennis McGinley, while the brother of John McClafferty, Roger, asked a grand-nephew of his wife's, James Doohan Paddy. This was a big boat and they were anxious to get it working because of the station, so the immigrant

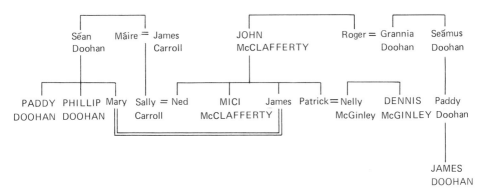

Figure 16. *Bád an Churing. Crew, with genealogy reference:* Paddy Doohan, 3, 11; Phillip Doohan, 3, 11; John McClafferty, 4; Micí McClafferty, 4; Dennis McGinley, 5; James Doohan, 13; Patrick Rogers, 16; Barney Rogers, 16; Hugh Dixon, from outside; James Dixon, from outside; Patrick Whorriskey, 9.

Dixons – all excellent seamen – were called in: Hugh and James, brothers of Dennis. A Whorriskey and a Rogers made up the full compliment, and again, although connections can be found, they were not cited; so one presumes that seamanship and the fact that they were not outsiders counted here.

5. *Bád Bhlackie.* Paddy Rogers, who built *Bád Dubh* and was one of the island's great boat builders, also built *Bád Bhlackie* and pulled in some of the same people, as we see in Figure 17. Along with his brother Barney and his cousin Dan, he recruited his other cousin, Owen Whorriskey, and the two Doohans from his original boat. To these he added Eamonn Duggan of the Eoins, who had connections with the McGinleys by the marriages of two of his cousins, Anton and Bríd. These brought in Hugh McGinley. Another Doohan makes up the crew, but I have no information on his connections, if any.

6. *Bád na Stócach.* At first *Bád na Stócach* was laughingly described as the lads' venture, but it turned out not to be so simple. For a start, two generations were involved, but the initiative came from the younger in the shape of the two Meenan cousins, William and John, who form the core of the network we see in Figure 18. John, through the marriage of his sister Sarah, brought in her husband's uncle, Anton Rogers; William, through the marriages of two sisters, Hannah and Kitty, brought in Edward Duggan and Ned Doherty. Through William's brother Ned another chain of affines was started. Ned's wife Biddy brought in her maternal uncle, Patrick Diver, and Biddy's brother Michael brought in

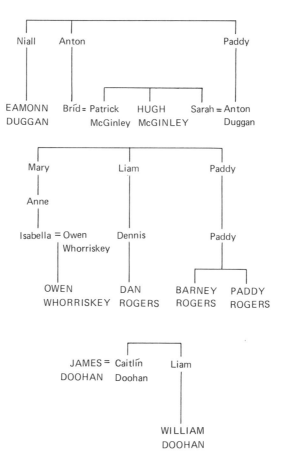

Figure 17. *Bád Bhlackie. Crew, with genealogy reference:* Eamonn Duggan 1; Hugh McGinley 5; Owen Whorriskey 3; Dan Rogers 3; Barney Rogers 3; Paddy Rogers 3; James Doohan 2; William Doohan 2; Dan Doohan 13.

his wife's uncle John Diver, who in turn brought in Jimmy and Eamonn Rogers, who were connected through both kinship and marriage. This is probably one of the most exhaustive and exhausting examples of how these chains of affinality work. And, as we can see, it is not just a random collection of lads who did it for a lark. The network was as ruthlessly exploited, and as skillfully, by the lads as by their elders. Sisters' marriages continue to be very important, and maternal uncles also figure prominently.

7. *Bád an Cháirnealaigh. Bád an Cháirnealaigh* is the "immortal boat," which will live as long as its nets live – and, I suspect, longer by symbolic

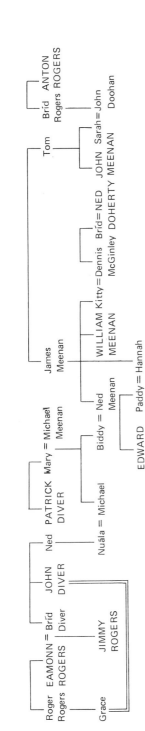

Figure 18. *Bád Na Stócach. Crew, with genealogy reference:* Anton Rogers, 16; John Meenan, 10; William Meenan, 2; Ned Doherty, 6; Edward Duggan, 1; Patrick Diver, 3; John Diver, 15; Eamonn Rogers, 17; Jimmy Rogers, 15, 17.

subterfuge: A cardinal is, after all, a cardinal, and his name long lasting. The three sons of Séamus Bán, Pat, John, and Ned Meenan, were at the heart of this boat (see Figure 19). They brought in their friend Patrick Rogers, who brought in his uncle. The McClafferty clan then entered the picture through Dan Sr. and Dan Jr. and the in-law John Doherty. Through another chain of associations from Dan Sr.'s Uncle Roger, Ed Diver was recruited. As has been the case in a number of these boats, there is sometimes no obvious connection between the various "blocks" of relatives involved – here the Rogers, Meenans, and McClaffertys, plus connections. But it is rare for there to be a lone person. Even if there is no cited affinal relationship between the blocks, once a contact has been made with an "unrelated" person, that person then "brings in" relatives of one kind or another.

8. *Bád MhacDaibheid. Bád MhacDaibheid* (Figure 20) presents us, however, with another good example of a total and recognized network encompassing a whole crew. At the heart of it are a pair of paternal

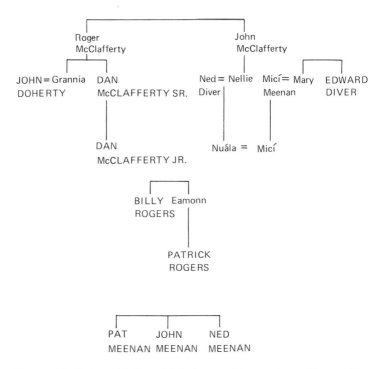

Figure 19. *Bád an Cháirnealaigh. Crew, with genealogy reference:* Dan McClafferty, Sr., 4; Dan McClafferty, Jr., 4; John Doherty, 4; Edward Diver, 3; Billy Rogers 17; Patrick Rogers, 15, 17; Pat Meenan, 2; John Meenan, 2; Ned Meenan, 2.

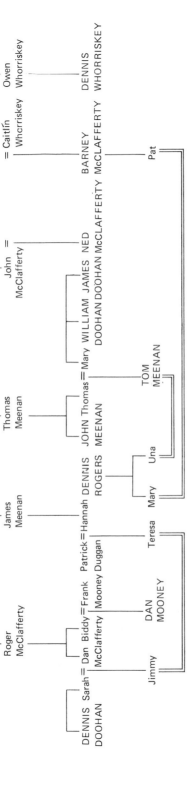

Figure 20. *Bád MhacDaibheid. Crew, with genealogy reference:* Dennis Whorriskey, 9; Barney McClafferty, 4; Ned McClafferty, 4; James Doohan, 1; William Doohan, 1; Tom Meenan, 1, 10; John Meenan, 1, 10; Dennis Rogers, 3; Dan Mooney, 4; Dennis Doohan, 14.

half-brothers, Ned and Barney McClafferty, and Dan Mooney, who is a McClafferty by descent as we saw in the genealogies. Dan McClafferty's brother-in-law, Dennis Doohan, joined in. Then a chain of connections brought in John Meenan and his affines the two Doohan brothers, William and James. His nephew Tom Meenan also joined bringing his affine Dennis Rogers. This only leaves Ned to call on his stepmother's brother's son, Dennis Whorriskey, to complete the crew.

9. *Bád Chonchubhair.* Figure 21 shows us two blocks of relatives again, the original group being the Diver–Duggan connection. James and Ed Diver brought in their affine John Meenan and, through their half-sister Sally, her husband Paddy Duggan and his two sons Paddy and Anton and their affine Roger Rogers. The other group is that of Paddy Doohan, his two sons, and their connection, Barney Doohan.

10. *Bád John Bhig.* For the *Bád John Bhig* crew we have a core of relatives – or rather another chain of affinal connections and one out-

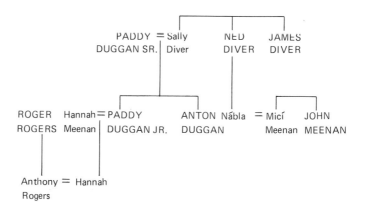

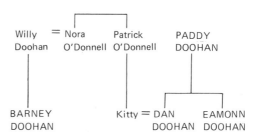

Figure 21. *Bád Chonchubhair. Crew, with genealogy reference:* John Meenan, 3; James Diver, 15; Ned Diver, 15; Paddy Duggan, Sr., 1; Paddy Duggan, Jr., 1; Anton Duggan, 1; Roger Rogers, 18; Paddy Doohan, 13; Eamonn Doohan, 13; Dan Doohan, 13; Barney Doohan, 2.

sider. John Duggan – "Little John" – and his brother-in-law, John Rogers, started the boat. Through the connections shown in Figure 22 they brought in Dennis Duggan (not otherwise related) and his affines Eddie Doohan, Michael Meenan, and the two Carrols (see Genealogy 8). The mainlander John Gallagher made up the crew.

11. *Bád an Chlub. Bád an Chlub,* the second boat to be built by some accounts (but not by others) and relatively short lived, was started by Owen Whorriskey, who formed a club to run it. Figure 23 shows how he started by pulling in relative Dan Whorriskey and affine Dan Mooney. Owen probably invoked his kinship with the other Feilimís (Johhny and Paddy Rogers) through his mother (see Genealogy 3). Even so, it was affinal connections again that pulled in James Doohan and Patrick Rogers. John Gallagher completed the crew.

In general, then, we have seen how very important affines were in the recruitment of boat crews. There would often be little cores of people related by descent, but these were never enough to make up a crew with the right distribution of skills, capital, or whatever else was needed – even sheer muscle power. One had to go farther afield. Preferably, this was to fairly closely connected in-laws, but often it was necessary to bring in an unrelated person who was known, for example, to have good connections. Thus it was rare, except as a last resort to make up a complete crew, that any of the initiators picked out someone at random once they had exhausted their own connections; they would go rather to a friend, or someone with whom they had sailed before, who was known to have some attached people of his own. Even better, they would go to another "core" group of relatives who had good affinal connections. Note, also, how often a relative on the mother's side is appealed to; the "mother's brother–sister's son" connection being very important. "A man would turn to his brother-in-law or his uncle," I was often told. Sometimes the connections were not quite so definite or close, but if we turn this formula – and it is a formula – into anthropological jargon and render it "A man would often turn to an affine or to a matrilateral relative," then it becomes quite accurate. And the reason for this strategy of recruitment, so different from the principle of land inheritance, lies simply in the need to complete a crew and to compete for members. It was often a question of sheer manpower and a limited supply. We see from the illustrations that men changed crews, but of course sometimes this was to successor boats. However, as we saw, a new agreement had to be negotiated at each season's start, and it was necessary to have "connections" to keep the crews.

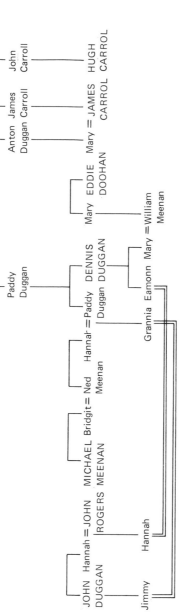

Figure 22. *Bád John Bhig. Crew, with genealogy reference:* James Carrol, 8; Hugh Carrol, 8; Dennis Duggan, 1; Eddie Doohan, 1; Michael Meenan, 3; Owen Doherty, 4; John Rogers, 16; John Dugan, 18; John Gallagher, from outside.

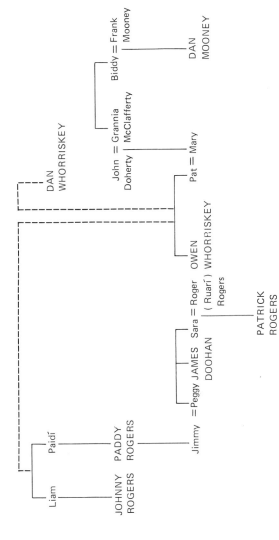

Figure 23. *Bád an Chlub. Crew, with genealogy reference:* Owen Whorriskey, 3, 9; Dan Whorriskey, 9; Johnny Rogers, 3; Paddy Rogers, 3; James Doohan, 13; Patrick Rogers, 17; Dan Mooney, 4; John Gallagher, from outside.

About the time of the First World War or shortly thereafter, a change came over the whole pattern of Tory fishing. One enterprising islander acquired a car motor and adapted it as a marine engine with typical Tory ingenuity. After this, motors became the thing, and although the sail-boats continued to operate, the motorboats made the running. This trend was aided by the presentation to the islanders of two "Bollanders" – motor-powered fishing boats – by the newly formed Irish Fisheries Board in 1934 (Bord Iascaigh Mhara). The first of these, *Pride of Tory,* was given up in 1937 and the second, *Pride of Moville,* in 1940. The islanders are not well up on cooperative enterprises of this kind, but these boats encouraged the trend toward motor power.

I will list the motorboats with their owners or managers.

1. *Réalt na Maidhne* ("Morning Star"). Dan and Mickey Mooney (Genealogy 4). This was built in 1917 and adapted later to motor power. It was originally used to transport fish for *Bád Bhlackie* on a cooperative, profit-sharing basis.
2. *Ave Maria.* Johnny and Jimmy Dixon. Built originally by Hugh Dixon around 1920 and quickly adapted to motor power.
3. *Pride of Tory.* Owen Doherty (Genealogy 4). The sea fisheries boat already described.
4. *Pride of Moville.* William Doohan (William–Liaim–Neilí). Also a Sea Fisheries boat as described above.
5. *Saint Maria Goretti.* John and William Rogers (Genealogy 3). This boat drew its crew from the two Bollanders when they were given up. It was later sold to Inishboffin and is still in service.
6. *Little Flower.* Paddy McGinty (Genealogy 4).
7. *Naomh Columcille.* ("Saint Columba"). Roger Rogers (Genealogy 18).
8. *Saint Pius and Saint Jude.* William Rogers (Dennis) (Genealogy 3). This boat now fishes away from Tory with a hired crew, but originally it had a Tory crew.
9. *Noamh Proinnsias* ("Saint Francis"). Owen Boyle (Genealogy 1).
10. *Naomh Peadar.* ("Saint Peter"). Cormac Rogers (Genealogy 16).
11. *Naomh Anton.* ("Saint Anthony"). Dennis Duggan (Genealogy 1). No longer in use.

It is immediately obvious that the whole naming system changed with the coming of motor power. The Bollanders were christened by the Sea Fisheries Board, so we cannot count them, but the islanders turned almost entirely to saints: Maria Goretti, Pius, Jude, Francis, Columba, Peter, and Anthony – and of course Saint Mary. *Little Flower* is named after Saint Thérèse of Lisieux. Motorboats being more cosmopolitan

than their sail- and oar-powered cousins, the names also were broadened
to have a more catholic and less anecdotal and homespun flavor. This
being noted, however, we must look at the crews. It will not be necessary
to draw out the connections of kinship and affinity here, for such as they
are they can be easily ascertained from the genealogies and the foregoing diagrams. But for a start I should note that the crews are of necessity
much smaller than for the sail/oar boats. The engine does the work of
five or more men, it is reckoned. In consequence, the crew of the motorboat is never more than four or five men, and the owners therefore do
not have to look too far afield to find a crew.

Réalt na Maidhne. The "Morning Star" was owned, as we have seen, by
the two Mooneys, who brought in their relatives Owen and Dan Doherty
(Genealogy 4) – related to them through the McClaffertys. For a while
John McClafferty also joined in, as did the two McGinleys, Patrick and
Hugh (5), but these were intermittent.

Ave Maria. The original *Ave Maria* crew was the Dixon brothers –
Hugh, Dennis, Jimmy, and Johnny. Jimmy and Johnny have, ever since
Hugh and Dennis died, brought in various people to make up the
number, including their affine Hugh Doohan, who married into the
island; the Meenan brothers, John and Edward (Genealogy 2); Eamonn
Duggan (1); Patrick Doohan (3); William Meenan (1); Willy Diver (15);
and Paddy McGinty (4). There are never any connections cited here,
because the boat has been for a number of years the official mail boat for
the island, and the crew is recruited more on a "paid" than a sharing
basis. This means that "connections" lessen in importance and even an
element of bureaucracy enters with the open employment of wage ear-
ners rather than the cooperative venture of relatives.

Pride of Tory. The two Bollanders drew their crews from men left over
when some of the older sailboats went out of commission. Again, the
crews were somewhat motley. *Pride of Tory* was managed by Owen Doherty (Genealogy 4), who brought in relative James McClafferty (4), and
then topped up with Dan Rogers (3), Johnny Doohan (1), and John
Meenan (10).

Pride of Moville. The *Pride of Moville,* managed by William Doohan,
included Dan Mooney (for a while), Ned Meenan (Genealogy 2), James
Doohan (1), and Dennis McGinley (5). Again, the semiofficial status of
the boats reduced the chances of the crew being built up on "connections" because men could apply for positions on the boats and there was
some overseeing by the Sea Fisheries Board.

Saint Maria Goretti. The *Saint Maria Goretti,* built just after the war,
picked up the crews of the Bollanders much as they had picked up the
men unemployed through the decline of sail.

Little Flower. The *Little Flower* uses the "maternal uncle" principle we have come across above, combined with the "in-law" principle. Paddy McGinty (Genealogy 4) married Betty Sheils, the adopted daughter of Dan McClafferty (4). Paddy therefore called in Dan, who in turn called in his maternal cousin, Anton Doohan Mór (14). James McClafferty was also an intermittent member. This is a classic "sailboat" type of recruitment and, of course, the boat here is not semiofficial, but run on the old "shares" principle.

Naomh Columcille. Owned by Roger Rogers (Genealogy 18), the crew of *Naomh Columcille* is his sons, Sean, Anthony, Jimmy, and Patrick (Genealogy 2). Sean owns a shop and the boat is used mainly for ferrying goods. But it also fishes extensively.

Saint Pius and Saint Jude. William Rogers (Genealogy 3) recruited uncle and nephew Cormac and Eamonn Rogers (16) for *Saint Pius and Saint Jude*. Otherwise, there were only intermittent members, including Hughie Doohan (2) and Paddy Whorriskey (1).

Naomh Proinnsias. The "Saint Francis" is owned by Owen Boyle, who being an outsider went the in-law route for a crew. He and his wife's mother's brother, Ned Meenan (Genealogy 2), own the boat together, and he brought in, occasionally, his wife's sister's husband, Jimmy Duggan (2). Otherwise, he recruits as best he can; even non-Tory men.

Naomh Peadar. Cormac Rogers (Genealogy 16) forms the "Saint Peter" crew entirely from the paternal cousins Eamonn–Ghrainne (16), Eamonn–Chormaic, (2), Jimmy–Chormaic (2), and Eamonn–Antoin (1).

Naomh Anton. Dennis Duggan formed the crew entirely from his sons listed in Genealogy 1. But the boat is not now used.

Thus we see that *Little Flower* and *Naomh Proinnsias* use a very close circle of affines and relatives; *Naomh Columcille, Naomh Peadar,* and *Naomh Anton* use an even closer circle of fathers and sons or patrilateral first cousins. McGinty and Boyle, being "outsiders," of course could not do this. But whether the crews in these cases are "patrilateral," "matrilateral," or "affinal" in their recruitment, it is always immediate relatives that are concerned, with none of the elaborate chains employed in the recruitment of the sailboat crews. The other boats have fairly motley crews for the reasons cited, but where relatives are involved, again they are close.

What motor power did, in effect, was to cut out the need for any extended network of relatives. The crews were therefore reduced to the "core" of the boat's "compliment," the owner and his immediate kin. Most strikingly, in at least three cases it is his immediate patrilateral kin:

Two men pulling a rowing curragh up to the head of the old slip. Another, upturned curragh, two yawls, and two large fishing boats are already there. A "tau" cross has been set into the concrete of a projected new slipway (Tau is the Gaelic pronunciation of the letter "t".)

brothers or paternal cousins. This more than halved the number of men required for fishing and ferrying enterprises, of course, and those who could find nothing else and were not willing to live on the dole left either permanently or temporarily for work abroad. Motor power increased the prosperity of some, but cannot be said to have contributed much to the commonwealth.

The other types of boats constantly in use are the yawls – primarily for inshore lobster fishing and some ferrying. These need a crew of three men, perhaps four if there is a heavy load. They can be quickly dealt with without the necessity of giving details. In every case, the men involved are paternal relatives: fathers and sons, brothers, or paternal cousins. It is that simple. About ten of these are in use. Some still-smaller boats are occasionally used by groups of young men on a "friendship" basis, but only intermittently.

It is easy to see, then, that the principle of recruitment to the sailboats, although heavily dependent on kinship and affinity, was different from the principle of recruitment to land-claiming groups. The latter was "genealogical" in the Tory sense; the former was based on networks of kin and affines using "in-laws" and "maternal uncles" rather heavily. Motor power, by reducing the need for large crews, more or less destroyed this principle of recruitment, and recruitment has tended to move more and more in the direction of a strict patrilateral basis, which has little in common with either of the other two principles.

Boats are still the life of Tory. Everyone is still involved; there is still a sense of reciprocal responsibility between the people and the boats, the owners and the islanders. A young woman with a sick child was once taken out by boat to a doctor on the mainland. The boat she went in had an unreliable engine. That day another boat, more reliable, also left for the mainalnd and returned, in very bad weather, before the "ambulance" boat. It was laboriously hauled up by the usual thirty men and boys, who then went home for a well-earned rest and meal along with the exhausted crew. The news then came in that the boat with the poorly child had broken down out in Tory Sound. Because the second boat was on the slipway and therefore the only feasible one to launch, the crew turned out again, still in their wet clothes, and all the able bodied men on the island came to launch it. The stranded vessel was successfully towed in and the whole process of hauling had to be gone through again, with the two boats this time. It was after midnight, fiercely cold, and blowing a gale before the operation was completed. But it was done; it was everyone's responsibility; it was taken for granted.

If boats are still in this sense the life of the island, in another sense they can never be what they were in the heyday, when all the adult men of Tory were involved in the great fishing enterprise. Ten or more herring boats with their attendant serving boats would put out from An Camus Mór and Port an Dúin with brown sails hoisted and oars swinging, and with the crews singing "Song of the Herring" (Amhrán na Scadán), which comes over but poorly in my English rendering:

> Isn't it a nice thing for the herring
> To be leaping around the boat;
> And all my lads with the baskets,
> Grabbing them while they're afloat?

7
Family, marriage, and household

An cheist – "Do chara, do namhaid, agus ceann urraí an tí?"
An freagra – "Do mhadra, do bhean, 's do bheithíoch!

The above quotation is a well-known island riddle. It asks the question: "What are the following: your friend, your enemy, and the head of the house?" It gives as its answer: "Your dog, your wife, and your beast!" Although the first and last might be taken as universally recognized – at least among country people – the middle term of this equation would only be thought a universal judgment by the most cynical. But it expresses, for the Tory islanders, a value both real and paradoxical, and to the explication of it I must devote this chapter.

The ideal family unit on Tory island is the conjugal family of father, mother, and children, living under one roof. This is enshrined in the ideal of the Holy Family. It is also universally agreed that old people should be cared for by their children, indigent relatives helped, etc. But this family ideal is not often realized, for the very reason that the islanders consider it treasonable to break up this ideal unit. This is the paradox: Marriage, which is needed to found the unit in the first place, is destructive of the unit once formed. If the children of the family marry and leave their parents, then the ideal unit is destroyed; but unless they do this, ideal units cannot be formed. The "extended household," so beloved of anthropologists, is not popular with the islanders. They tend to regard it as somewhat overextended, and so do not favor "two women in the kitchen" – at least if those two women are affines and not mother and daughter or two sisters.

One solution to the paradox – although an incomplete one – is for the children *not* to marry and leave. If all did this there would be no more families, of course – but the Irish have not only never heard of cognitive dissonance, they positively thrive on it. In many parts of Ireland, investigators have found a considerable number of households consisting of unmarried siblings. When these die, a nephew or niece usually comes in to take over the farm. Arensberg and Kimball have elegantly shown how

Elderly islander and the house he is refurbishing for the wife who will never move in.

this is related to the inheritance of family farms and the attendant difficulties (see Notes). And, of course, if the daughter of the house is unwilling to move, she has no alternative but to stay unmarried, for these people live in scattered farms. But on Tory the situation is different, and must have been different in the clacháns of Donegal and Ireland generally before they were broken up. In the "towns," people are not very far from each other, and as long as marriage is locally endogamous – as it usually was at least on an isolated island – then even if spouses did not live together, they would still be close to each other. This was the Tory solution.

At one time, I was told, at least half the married couples on the island would not be living with each other, but would be in their natal homes with parents or siblings. This was considered normal, and is defended by various arguments. When, in 1963, I was trying to reconcile my census of households with my records of marriages, I found that of fifty-one marriages ten conformed to this pattern. Thus, twenty married people were not living with their husbands or wives, but were still in their natal homes.

It may seem odd to devote a chapter to the explication of ten marriages – and when we have finished there will still be unsolved mysteries – but it is necessary if we are to understand the Tory pattern of relationship between family, household, and marriage. It might also add something to the discussion of marriage generally, because, as far as I can tell, the Tory situation is in some aspects unique and hence a test case.

Let me first present the picture painted by the islanders themsleves when talking about the general principles or particular cases. Often they would phrase it from the point of view of the women: That is, they would say – men and women alike – that a woman's first duty was to her "own" people (a muintir féin), or her "own household" (a teaghlach féin). If she had, for example, brothers or old parents who needed her, she should stay where she was born, even if she married; she should only move when these obligations were fulfilled. The cases cited to illustrate this principle, however, contained an oddity. In one household of an elderly brother and sister, both were in fact married. I asked how the principle applied here, for each could have moved into the spouse's house, or one could have moved and the remaining one brought in his or her spouse, etc. There were obviously several possibilities.

Then a subsidiary principle would be cited: If people married late, it was unnecessary, and even bad, to disturb long-standing household arrangements just to accommodate one couple. It was perhaps different when people were young, but for older people, who had less need for a common bed, it almost verged on the indecent.

Again, if there were more than one sibling in the household – say it was a household with a brother and two sisters – the sisters, for example, might not want a "strange" woman to move in with them. Equally, the woman's parents or siblings might not want a new man moving in with *them*. All this would disturb existing household arrangements and make for quarrels and bad blood. It was positively better, therefore, for this to be avoided by the simple expedient of staying put.

All agreed that if a separate house existed, and if there were no overwhelming obligations to the natal family to be fulfilled, it would be better for young people to move into a new house and set up a separate establishment. But in the past this was rarely possible. The number of houses was fixed, the number of people relatively large, and the possibilities of neolocal residence (to use the jargon) consequently reduced. The solution of staying in the natal home on marriage was therefore preferred to the alternative of creating extended households. It was also commonly agreed that it was better to marry than to "go against nature." This value again does not jibe with the assumption that it is treason for children to marry. But evidently marriage was considered a marginally lesser evil than illegitimacy – although no great fuss is made about illegitimate children and as far as I can tell they suffer absolutely no disadvantages. The contrast with the rest of Ireland could not be more marked, and this tolerance of illegitimacy was one of the main reasons given by mainlanders for being ashamed of Tory. In this day and age we rather take it as an example of the islanders' humanity, and plain good sense.

It is obvious from the foregoing that peace in the home is a value that overrides that of the holy family. Unless the holy family can have a house of its own, it is sometimes better for it to remain a conjugal unit without being a commensal one.

The way such marriages work will depend a lot on the actual household circumstances of the partners. If they are split between the West and the East, there might be problems of sheer communication. If the other members of the two households are hostile to each other, relations might be difficult. But under ideal circumstances, the woman would stay with her relatives and work and cook for them. Her husband likewise would remain with his. He would, however, be a privileged "visitor" (cuairteoir) in his wife's household, taking some meals there and, in the early days at least, staying overnight for some nights.

One might ask: If he is taking meals there and sleeping there is he not "living" there? I did indeed ask this and was roundly told that he was not. He was a visitor. His "things," that is, his personal possessions, were in his own house, and that was what counted. He did not regularly sleep or eat – with rare exceptions – at his wife's house, and indeed that would have strained relations too much. Nor did he, for example, ever have anything to do with the repair and upkeep of her house – although he might help out her male relatives on a friendly basis. No. The islanders were adamant: He could in no way be construed as living in his wife's house.

For economic support, he is supposed to give her half his dole (unemployment pay) or pension, and most men evidently do. In the predole days, he was expected to give her payment in kind – fish or meal or the like, or a small cash contribution. If she has land he might farm it for her, but there is no rule about this. Her brothers are equally likely to do it, and very often, in the land records, the land was registered as theirs. If there are children of the marriage, they stay with the mother, thus making their relations with her family very close. But as they grow older, they might spend as much time in their father's house as in their mother's. They sleep at "home," however.

The islanders agree that these arrangements, oddly, have become easier in modern times – since the Congested Districts Board built the new houses with several bedrooms. In the old cabins where everyone slept around the main living room and where only the old couple would have either a small bedroom or the built-in curtained bed, it was often difficult and embarrassing. If the marriage were to be consummated, I was told, it had often to be in the fields at night. My inquiries as to the exact mechanics of the arrangements were always countered by "there's always the fields, surely." It was considered a curiously urban type of inquiry, as was my obvious puzzlement about what happened in the inclement winters. There were the byres, and who would want to be spending a long time at it, anyway? Intercourse on Tory is clothed and brief, nor is a horizontal position deemed essential. Keen anticipation of the act is reckoned to create excitement, and immediate orgasm is the goal and the boast of sophisticates. This may be changing, but it was certainly the ideal of the older generation. In consequence, the not-sleeping-together of the separated partners, or at least their not-sleeping-together-very-often, was not considered a hindrance either to the production of children or a satisfactory sex life.

It is noticeable that sex as such was not considered treason. It was acknowledged formally to be sinful, but on the other hand it was seen to be natural and unavoidable. Sex did not break up the family; neither did an illegitimate child. In any case, I was told, better an illegitimate child than an unsuitable marriage. This is not, and was not, a common attitude in Ireland – which almost goes without saying (see reference to Connell in Notes). A child was always to be welcomed; a son- or daughter-in-law spelled trouble. Nor was illegitimacy a bar to marriage or desirability either for the mother or the child. Women with illegitimate children often married, as did the children themselves. At the time I was there, two of the marriageable youngsters generally considered the best matches were, boy and girl respectively, illegitimate. Marriage, however, was often urged "to please the priest"; it prevented unpleasantness. This is yet another example of the paradoxical attitude to marriage. It is fully accepted that if two people have sexual relations they should marry – the church requires it, apart from anything else. However, although this is the overt valuation and the islanders would be shocked by any suggestion to the contrary, when it comes to particular cases they will often agree wholeheartedly that the mother of an illegitimate child should not marry, what one of them charmingly referred to, in his acquired business English, as "the putative father of the child."

It was pointed out to me that in the "old days" it was often difficult to get married – but then again this was no reason to go against nature. The difficulty stemmed from the absence of a permanent priest on the island. Either a priest had to come out in a boat – which he was usually unwilling to do – or the islanders had to travel to the mainland. This, I was told, they were usually too "shy" to do, because they were regarded as objects of curiosity by the people on Tír Mhór (the mainland). Sometimes a mainland priest would agree to conduct a strange long-distance marriage ceremony at night. A fire would be lit on Bloody Foreland and one on the cliffs of Tory. On a clear, calm night these could easily be seen. The priest on the mainland would read a portion of the marriage service and then his assistant would put a blanket in front of the fire, cutting off its light. This was the signal for the couple on the island to make their response, after which they would in turn cover their fire, and so on. If, under these circumstances, the old Tory people decided to start their liaisons without benefit of church, they can scarcely be censured.

Two factors, then – the strong attachment to parents and siblings on the one hand, and the possessiveness of parents toward children on the other – seem to be at work in the pull against marriage. Even if the marriage is achieved, these factors again militate against the setting up of a common household by the conjugal pair. The extremes of both these attitudes can be gauged by two examples. An extreme expression of grief on the death of a parent is quite common; grief that goes beyond anything considered "normal" even by the islanders afflicts some young people. One young man went to the graveyard gate and wept every day for several years after the death of his mother. If the idea of "marriage as treason" seems bizarre, consider the custom whereby a couple who had agreed to marry and, being of full age, did not need parental consent nevertheless arranged to meet after dark and be married by the priest in secret. In one case – and these were people alive in 1965 who told me their own story – the couple crept around the island in different directions, meeting up at the church and marrying there without benefit even of oil lamps or candles. Even though the parents knew that the marriage had taken place, there was a tacit silence by all concerned, and it was only after the old couple died that the marriage was openly acknowledged.

To my question, why bother marrying at all, came the quick answer, "to avoid sin." This often meant that a child was on the way, but not always. The priest, knowing there was a liaison in effect, would often talk a couple into marrying. But sometimes this would be late in the day. Better risk illegitimacy than the wrath, and even the curse, of an old mother. I might add that marriages do not seem to be celebrated on Tory. One that occurred when I was there was more or less fitted into the working day, and after the brief service the couple went back to their natal homes, where they continued to live. Marriage may be a religious necessity, but it is not a matter for celebration. It is deaths that are celebrated with high jinks and practical jokes and late-night card parties with snuff and whiskey. It is the assumption of immortality that is a cause for joy, not the achievement of conjugal bliss. Marriage is a compromise between the lusts of the flesh, the laws of the Church, and the demands of the parents. But a common household is something else. That can be going too far. At least at first.

Thus, I was told, in the past (and in the past people were as likely to marry young as old – although the average was about twenty-nine) most marriages started like this: the couple living apart and often secretly married. Even if openly married (which was more likely) they would still live apart. Often, I was told, they would not bother to get married until quite late because there was no chance to live together and it didn't seem worth upsetting the parents. They might, afterward, move in together when the parents of one or the other had died, and when various brothers and sisters had either died or emigrated or found homes for themselves. Often, however, once they had started living apart, the habit was not easily broken and they continued apart for the rest of their lives.

It did seem, then, that this might be a fluid arrangement rather than a fixed "custom of residence at marriage." It could be in some cases a stage in a cycle of domestic development (see Notes). It was very difficult to get histories to back this up, because the islanders were most unwilling to talk too much about actual cases. This would have been a breach of confidence, and if anything appeared in print they would get people into trouble with the church, and themselves into worse trouble for informing. The few cases that were described to me were told in confidence, and I must respect that confidence, merely discussing the generalities as above. Also, there have been many changes in residence because of emigration and particularly because of the CDB housing project, which changed the face of residence on Tory and caused many shifts.

Consequently, I must use what data there are on the extant marriages that follow this pattern and try to extrapolate, adding such historical information as I have where relevant. A great deal can be achieved this way, as we shall see, and we may go some way toward understanding the dynamics of the marriage system and its relation to family and household. I cannot here name names for the obvious reasons, which is a pity because it would be interesting to refer the cases to the appropriate genealogies. The islanders themselves will of course know of whom I am speaking, but there is no reason to reveal this to the rest of the world. No confidentiality is breached here, for what I do write about is common knowledge and could not be hidden from outsiders. Again, this analysis is going to involve a few technicalities of definition and numeration. But if the reader who is neither anthropologist nor statistician will be patient with a few details, the general picture should emerge from the descriptive material alone.

As I said above, there were ten marriages in which the couples were living apart in 1963. We must examine these in the wider context of Tory marriages generally to see what makes them unique; to see, that is, why in some cases the couples do not move on marriage but stay in the natal home. A few technical words concerning residence at marriage are introduced here simply for the sake of shorthand – to avoid cumbersome descriptive phrases. The first is the term *natolocal:* where, at marriage, the spouses continue to live in their natal homes (see Notes). We can contrast natolocal with *virilocal* (wife goes to live with husband) and *uxorilocal* (husband goes to live with wife). These are all the terms needed to describe the mode of residence at marriage, because they exhaust the Tory possibilities.

Noting that these are the forms of residence at marriage, we can leave them aside for the moment and look at the composition of Tory households. Certain types of households can be distinguished, largely in terms of the islanders' own notions of what constiutes a different "type." These are not abstract definitions of household types, but simply the islanders' own partitioning of their universe of households. There may be other types that have existed or will exist; what we are concerned with here are those that do exist. Each household was discussed in detail and compared with others. Excepting the households with only a single person, it was agreed that there were five types. The basic criterion was the "core" of the household – variously described. To whom did the house belong? Who were the original members? Thus two households might look alike in composition, but be considered different. Each, for example, might consist of a man, his wife, and the wife's sisters; but the first would be considered a "sibling" household because the sisters owned the house and the man moved in there when he married one of them, and the second a "conjugal" household because the man owned the house and the sisters came to live there after one of their number married him. In most cases, however, the types were quite distinct and were made up as follows.

1. *Sibling households.* More properly, this might be "joint-sibling households," but the shorter form will do. In Gaelic it would be called something descriptive like "household of two brothers" or "household of a brother and sister." The core here would be a group of two or more siblings who owned the house, and whatever accretions occurred in the form of spouses, children, and other dependents.

2. *Widow/widower households.* These would be households where the house was owned by a widow, usually, or perhaps a widower, with married or unmarried children. Widow households were quite common, because women tended to live longer than men, and men were often lost at sea.

3. *Nepotal households.* I have invented a jargon word here as a shorthand for "households consisting of an uncle/aunt with his/her married/unmarried nephew/niece" – for that is what these are. They are not at all uncommon. A nephew or niece will often stay with an old uncle to "take care of him." Also this is sometimes a way of setting up a household away from the natal home. A young nephew can move in with an old uncle and bring his bride to this relatively uncrowded house. The uncle or aunt, of course, owns the house, but should either lack immediate heirs, the nephew or niece can inherit it.

4. *Extended households.* Despite their dislike of these, they sometimes occur and are recognized by the islanders. Again they would be variously described, but essentially they consist of two related families under one roof. In all the known cases they consisted of a father and mother with several unmarried children, but also at least one married child and the spouse and children of that child.

5. *Conjugal households.* The core of these – and usually the full complement of members – is a man and his wife and their dependent children. There may of course not be children, and other dependent relatives may accrue – but the core is what counts, and this is the conjugal pair. This, as we have seen, is the ideal, but by no means most numerous, kind of household.

I had some difficulty in a couple of cases in distinguishing nepotal and sibling households. If a couple of old brothers, for example, owned a house and a niece came in to care for them, was this not basically a sibling household? The answer was that it was in a way – more so than a house owned by a single old man, for example – but that the "niece coming in" transformed in into something else because she was a potential heir. It was thus more like the sibling household than like any of the others (because the essential tie was between consanguines other than parents and children), but it was distinct. I have respected this opinion in the classifications.

Table 9 shows the distribution of these types of household between East Town and West Town. The figures in parentheses show the number of each type having married members, for it is with these that we will have to deal below. Conjugal and extended households have married members by definition. We can see that of the total, conjugal households represent only 40 percent (twenty-five out of sixty-one). Sibling and widow households account for the same (twenty-four out of sixty-one). Not much more emerges except that proportionately more East Town households have married members than West Town; there is a preponderance of conjugal households in West Town; only half the widow households have married members; and East Town monopolizes extended households. Of the total of sixty-one households, forty-seven have married members; it is to these that we must now turn.

If the patterns of residence that we have defined – natolocal, uxorilocal, and virilocal – were not in some way connected with household composition, we would expect them to be randomly distributed among the household types. Tables 10 and 11 show the distribution for East and West Towns, respectively, and Table 12 shows the totals for the island.

The tables show the distribution of married *persons* rather than marriages per se, to accommodate the natolocal phenomenon. Given the latter, it is impossible to show the distribution of marriages by house-

Table 9. *Total household types: East and West towns*

| Household type | Town | | |
	East	West	Total
Sibling	4 (2)	9 (6)	13 (8)
Widow	6 (4)	5 (1)	11 (5)
Nepotal	3 (2)	5 (3)	8 (5)
Extended	4 (4)	0 (0)	4 (4)
Conjugal	7 (7)	18 (18)	25 (25)
Total	24 (19)	37 (28)	61 (47)

Note: Figures in brackets indicate number of households with married members.

Table 10. *Number of persons in each household type by type of marital residence: East Town*

| Household type | Type of marital residence | | | |
	Natolocal	Uxorilocal	Virilocal	Total
Sibling	2	0	0	2
Widow	5	0	0	5
Nepotal	1	4	0	5
Extended	1	6	10	17
Conjugal	0	6	8	14
Total	9	16	18	43

Table 11. *Number of persons in each household type by type of marital residence: West Town*

| Household type | Type of marital residence | | | |
	Natolocal	Uxorilocal	Virilocal	Total
Sibling	8	2	2	12
Widow	1	2	0	3
Nepotal	1	0	6	7
Extended	0	0	0	0
Conjugal	1	10	26	37
Total	11	14	34	59

Table 12. *Number of persons in each household type by type of marital residence: totals*

| Household type | Type of marital residence | | | |
	Natolocal	Uxorilocal	Virilocal	Total
Sibling	10	2	2	14
Widow	6	2	0	8
Nepotal	2	4	6	12
Extended	1	6	10	17
Conjugal	1	16	34	51
Total	20	30	52	102

holds because partners in these marriages are, of course, in different households by definition.

For each town taken separately, there is the same overall pattern, but we see that East Town has most of the widow–natolocal cases and West Town has most of the sibling–natolocal. There is also a considerable preponderance of conjugal–virilocal persons in West Town. The table showing the combined totals for the island is, however, the one on which to concentrate (Table 12). No sophisticated statistics are required to see that there is not a random distribution of types of marital residence among the various household types. We have seen how, according to the islanders' own arguments, we would expect that couples would be more likely to live natolocally if they had old, widowed parents, or siblings to care for. The table bears this out. Natolocal residence is more strongly associated with sibling and widow households than the others, whereas virilocal residence is most strongly associated with extended and conjugal households. To some extent, for present purposes we can lump virilocal and uxorilocal residence together, for the only difference is the movement of the man or wife. They contrast equally with natolocal, where *neither* man *nor* wife moves. Thus we can see in Table 13 that the association is strong and clear, 90 percent of the cases being in the expected direction. (I have not used measures of association or significance, since they would be overexact and not add much to what can be seen from inspection, but the relation in Table 13 is significant at the .05 level.)

Because the figures on the table are from a total of 102, they can be read more or less as percentages, which is helpful. Thirty-four percent of the cases are conjugal–virilocal, and if we add the conjugal–uxorilocal, then the figure rises to 50 percent. This is the largest category, but it still leaves half the cases as something other than the ideal. I have given the benefit of the doubt here to the nepotal cases and counted them as "other," although in some sense they should be classed with the "consanguineous households," the sibling and widow. Even if they are, the distribution is not much affected, 84 percent of the cases still being in the

Table 13. *Type of residence by household type: grouped figures*

	Natolocal	Other	Total
Sibling/widow	16	6	22
Other	4	76	80
Total	20	82	102

predicted direction. But I feel that the nepotal cases are truly ambiguous, for it is often the case as we have seen that a couple will move into an uncle's house – this being in some sense the opposite of the natolocal principle. We do, however, have two people living natolocally in nepotal households. This again requires brief discussion, for in these cases "natolocal" might not be strictly accurate; that is, there may have been a move from the natal home to the home of the uncle. We shall here just have to take "natolocal" as a synonym for "separate." But this underlines the rather odd quality of the nepotal case.

Again, according to our argument, there is no particular reason why natolocal residence should *not* be associated with conjugal households. A son or daughter could stay with old parents, and indeed this happens. But it is agreed that it is more likely to happen if there is an "incomplete" family; that is, a family where someone lacks a spouse or parent. If the two parents are still alive, the children can claim that they can look after each other. If only one is alive, it would be considered heartless to leave home and leave the survivor alone. Thus we see that it is the incomplete and consanguineous households that hold onto their married members and resist the intrusion of outsiders.

The conjugal households range from those of young newly married couples, to those of old people with no children left, to various stages in between. It is in some ways surprising that there are not more natolocal cases among them. It may be that their preponderance in this form – straight virilocal or uxorilocal – reflects not an aspect of the domestic cycle at all, but an absolute historical trend. With relative depopulation and the easier availability of houses, there is less and less of a tendency to form extended households and to live natolocally, and more to set up independent households either in the wife's or the husband's house. The relatively large number of couples living uxorilocally – 30 percent – again may reflect an increasing tendency of women to insist on their own households at marriage.

The above considerations must lead us to look at the dynamics of household composition and residence at marriage, for the tables present only a static picture of the state of affairs in 1963. We have seen in a couple of cases how one state of marital residence could lead to another. Obviously, for example, if a child married and stayed at home with two parents, one of whom then died, a "conjugal–natolocal" case would be converted into a "widow–natolocal" one. What we have in the tables may simply reflect not absolute choices that are adhered to for life – the "rules of residence at marriage" to which anthropologists are so addicted – but rather stages in the cycles of domestic development like the simple one just cited. The "rules" that we should look for are then rules of decision making, not laws. On what basis are decisions made regarding where to live at marriage and subsequently? The tables merely suggest that there is a basis for decision in the composition of the household. We must now look at the ten natolocal marriages in more detail to try to see how they reflect this.

It must be remembered that it only takes one partner to a natolocal arrangement to make the decision: The other is affected, however unwillingly. We may then only be looking at ten initial decisions, but of course as household composition changes over time further decisions may be needed. What we must examine is not simply whether sibling and widow households are indeed associated with natolocal residence, but how they are so associated, and how they are associated with each other.

Figure 24 shows the composition of the seventeen households involved; we can conveniently refer to them by number. I have classified each and also put in, for future reference, the age and age of marriage of each of the partners. The horizontal lines show what is in fact a division of generations, the married members of households 10 through 17 being of the same generation as the parents of the married members of households 1 through 90. (The exception here is the marriage linking households 14 and 15, but the generalization is otherwise correct.) We can see immediately that households 10 through 17 are the total sibling–natolocal cases and that they belong to the older generation. But before we discuss this, let us run through the households in turn and discuss them as case histories.

Household 1 is a widower household where two sons stay with their widowed father (East Town). One of them is married to a woman who lives with her father's brother, her father and mother having died (West Town). This is her natal home, but owned by her father's brother. This uncle has a sister, but the sister is herself married and the uncle wishes to keep his niece with him. During the lifetime of the girl's father, this was a sibling household that added two spouses: the girl's mother and her father's sister's husband. The girl's attachment to the household is strong, and she does not want to move in with her husband and the husband's brother and old father. It is agreed among the islanders that she probably should move because there is a woman in the one household and not the other. But there is also sympathy for her not wanting to disturb a situation she has known for thirty-one years. The men in the other house obviously look after themselves quite well, and she sometimes goes along and helps out. On the other hand, it is universally

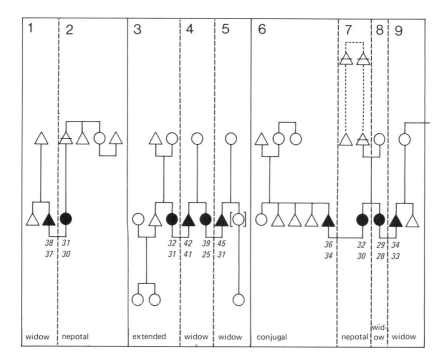

Figure 24. Natolocal households in 1963. *Note:* Upper italic figure gives age in 1963; lower italic figure gives age at marriage.

agreed that it would be quite wrong for the husband to move in with her ménage. This would create a dreaded extended family, and the present situation is both preferable and the best compromise. The distance between the towns is also a factor: The girl feels she would be "too far" from her uncle.

Household 3 is one of the villains – a true extended family with all the attendant difficulties. The two families try to be as separate as they can, and the house has been partially divided in some way to try to make this possible. But it is not a great success. The son's wife has been pregnant or bringing up children since the marriage, and it is reckoned that in consequence she either cannot or will not manage the old couple as well as her own family. What is more, the old couple don't want her to. They prefer their daughter. This is how the husband sees it (household 4). He is supporting a widowed mother, and his sister, also married, is still living at home to keep house and look after the old lady while he works. He would like his wife to move.

No one disputed the wife's position in household 3. It was considered reasonable for the old couple to demand her services and for her to stay.

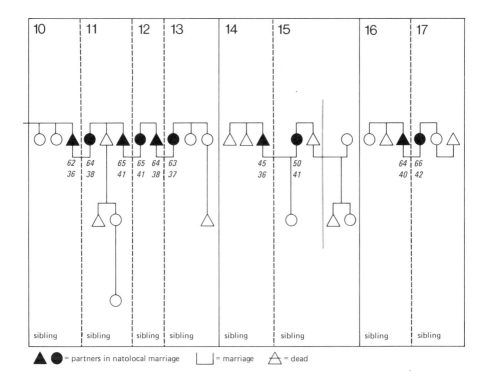

It was hard on the husband, but then he had his sister and it was agreed that *she* was not in a hurry to move, in any case. It is usual, in these cases, for the husband to farm the girl's land, especially if he is in the same village. But in this case he did not, probably indicating somewhat strained relations.

This takes us on to household 5 – the last of this "chain." The husband here was "taken care of" by his mother and his niece – whose own mother was away in Scotland. There was also another "relative." The old lady had been married twice, and had recently taken in the sister of her first husband. So there was plenty of female help in the house, and the husband seemed in no hurry to change the situation.

Households 6, 7, 8, and 9 form another chain of natolocal establishments. Households 6 and 7 are complicated. In 6, we have a core of the old man and his wife, with the wife's sister having moved in. Of the many children, only one is married, and he is living at home. He is away a good deal in Scotland working, and his wife does not particularly want to move into an already crowded household. It is agreed in this case that there would be no point in her doing so. She, in turn, lives with her father's father's brother's son (household 7), who counts as her uncle for our purposes, and indeed is called such by her and the other islanders; although the more correct will point out the exact degree of cousinship when prompted. The old man, who has no children, has to be taken care of, and this is taken as a very clear case where the rules of natolocal residence apply. It is here, however, that we have to note the slight weakness of the term when used for nepotal cases, for this is not the girl's natal home.

Her natal home is in fact household 8, where her sister lives with the widowed mother of the two girls. This is in the East Town, and one reason for the universal approval of the arrangement between households 6 and 7 is that it brings the spouses nearer to each other by placing the girl in West Town. The sister in household 8, however, although herself married, has to stay to look after the widowed mother, and this brings us to the last link in this chain, household 9. Here the two brothers stay with their widowed mother, but it is agreed that there is no real barrier to the married brother's moving in with his wife in household 8. The girl and her mother are willing, and the boy farms his wife's land. Relations are amicable. But the boy's mother and brother object. Both cried bitterly when he suggested it. Although the islanders agree that he could move in this case, it is again agreed that "for the time being" – that is, for the lifetime of the mother – he had better stay where he is. Even after the mother dies, it is agreed that it would be hard for him to leave the other brother alone, and it would be better for the latter to marry and bring in a girl. But he is not "the marrying kind," it seems.

We might pause at the end of this generation to note that, as we saw above, although there is no real reason why more conjugal households should not be involved, this does not seem to happen. If, for example, people from widow households married people from conjugal ones but refused to move, then as many conjugal as widow households would be involved. The overall distribution would still reflect the connection of consanguineous households with natolocal residence, however. But this does not seem to be the case. What we get are chains of more or less incomplete households engaged in natolocal residence. This emerges still more clearly in the next set of households, 10 through 17, which as we saw are the sibling–natolocal cases.

The first of these, household 10, is linked to household 9. The widowed mother of that household is the sister of the siblings in household 10. This immediately lifts us up into the senior generation. Households 10, 11, 12, and 13 are again all linked in a chain. The marriage that links 10 and 11 is long standing, and the couple are very fond of each other. The man in number 10 is cared for by two sisters; neither is married. He would like his wife to move in with him and has converted his house to give her some privacy. For twenty-six years of marriage he has tried to persuade her to move, but she will not. She has two brothers to care for. One of these is himself without a wife and has in turn two dependent children and a grandchild. All these need to be taken care of. The judgment here again is that she is right. Her brother and his children need her, whereas her husband has two sisters to look after him. The husband takes meals regularly at his wife's house and gives her half his dole. The pace of his meal taking has evidently slackened recently, but he continues to visit every night for a chat.

The other member of household 11 is another married brother, who shows no inclination to move in with his wife. She is in household 12 looking after her brother, who in turn is married to one of the three sisters in household 13, who live together and look after each other and the child of one of them. It is not considered possible for the wife in 12 to move into her husband's household, and he does not want to move in with her and her brother. The brother in 12 in his turn does not want to move in with the three sisters, and his wife does not want to join his sister – and so it goes.

These are all marriages of long standing, and they are the ones referred to when the "custom" (béas) of separate living is cited. As we have seen, "she has her brothers to care for" is the norm. The couples in two other marriages, involving households 14, 15, 16, and 17, are of much the same generation, and share with the ones just discussed the fact of not having any parents alive. In the case of 14 and 15, there is again an East–West separation. Household 15 was an instance of a married woman and her child living with her married brother. Originally, the brother and sister had lived together; both had married and continued to stay where they were apart from their spouses. The man then opened a shop and needed his wife's help because his sister was pregnant. The wife moved in and the man converted his house so that the sister and her child had a more or less private establishment. Her husband continued to live in East Town with his brothers.

The last case is again one of two sibling households, 16 having a woman looking after two brothers and 17 a woman and her sister with the sister's husband. An East–West split again makes the separation more absolute, and again this is a long-standing marriage. It was another case where the principle of "it's too much trouble to move so late" was cited. There was evidently a relative estrangement between the couple.

Having looked at the individual cases, we must now discuss the pattern. As we saw above, the "sibling" cases are all of an older generation, and this may reflect something about the life cycle of the domestic group. Thus, most cases may start like those in households 1 through 9, and end like those in households 10 through 17. This would be more plausible if it were not that the average age of marriage in the sibling households is somewhat older than in the others. Table 14 shows the differences.

The difference between the men is not so great, but there is a ten-year difference in the case of the women. This may not reflect something about the life cycle of the family, but rather something about an absolute historical change. The women in the sibling households are much older than the others and tended to marry much later. This may well reflect the fact that resistance to marriage is not so vigorous today.

However, it is still obvious that logically there is a cycle involved. Once the parents and widows of households 1 through 9 die off, there will be a string of sibling households. Alternatively, if any of the husbands who now will not, or cannot, move do eventually do so, they will produce more widow–uxorilocal cases, or even, once the widows have died, more conjugal–uxorilocal cases. It is easy to see what some of the possible cycles are. Thus a conjugal–natolocal case could become a widow–natolocal case, then a widow–uxorilocal one, then a conjugal–uxorilocal one, then, in the next generation, a conjugal–natolocal one again, and so on. I have obtained such histories in a few cases, but these simply illustrate the logical possibilities, which the reader can work out. It would be interesting to have complete histories for all the households but, as I explained above, this is virtually impossible.

To see for our seventeen households whether or not there is a similar cycle or whether the sibling households represent something totally different, let us look at the situation of all our households at the actual time of the marriage in each case. Figure 25 shows the composition of the households at the date of marriage. I have reclassified them, and what we see is the preponderance of widow households, and incomplete and consanguineous households generally. But strikingly, at marriage, most

Table 14. *Average age and age at marriage of men and women in natolocal marriages*

	Sibling households		Other households	
	Age	Age married	Age	Age married
Men	56.3	38.2	39.2	34.7
Women	61.6	39.8	32.6	28.8

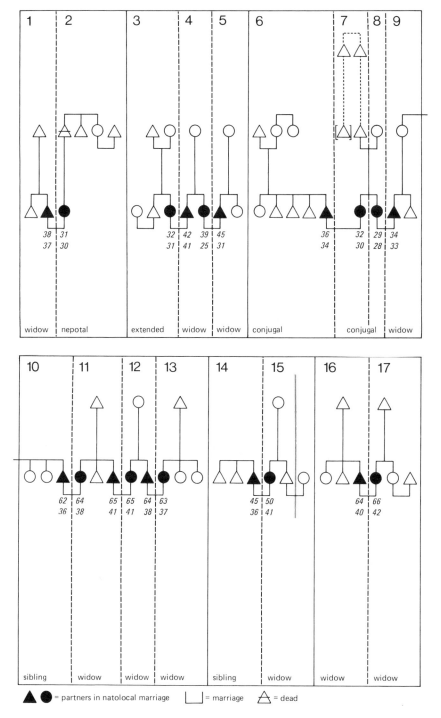

Figure 25. Composition of natolocal households at marriage. *Note:*
Upper italic figure gives age in 1963; lower italic figure gives age at
marriage.

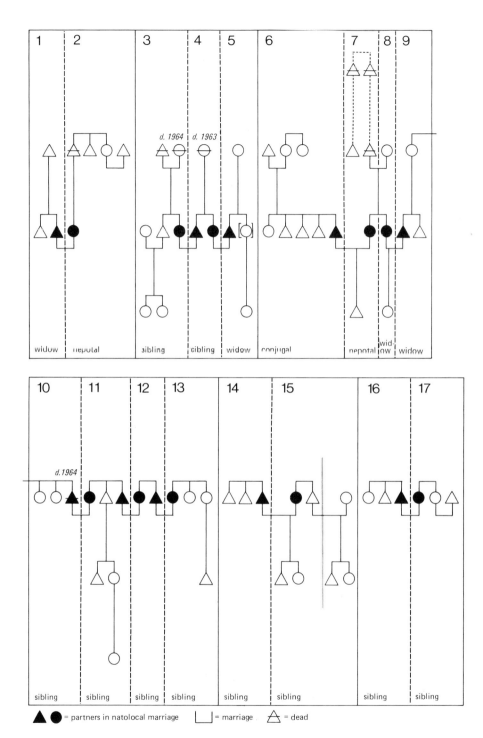

Figure 26. Natolocal households in 1965.

of the partners were faced with a widowed parent. Exceptionally, households 10, 11, and 14 were already sibling households, and in 13 we have the odd phenomenon, if the records are to be trusted, of the father dying on the day of the marriage. I was never able to get the full story, but I suspect the marriage was arranged and the father died inconveniently (or conveniently as the case may be) shortly after it was celebrated. The case of 7 and 8 is awkward, but it is enough to note that the parents were alive and living together at the time of the marriage. The girl later moved in with her uncle.

It is possible to take this a stage further, for I know what the state of affairs was in 1965. Figure 26 shows the household composition in that year. Apart from the addition of some children, we see most noticeably the deaths of some parents, increasing the number of sibling households. In the case of households 3 and 4, we might have expected the girl to move after the raison d'être of the separation had been removed, but as of 1965 this had not happened. Sadly, the old man in household 10 had died, and all his efforts to get his wife to move in died with him.

Because this latter situation had not changed, we can count him as alive in 1965, thus giving the results shown in Table 15, which shows the changes over time in the household composition of our natolocal couples. The table shows that the number of sibling households has increased and the number of widows and others declined markedly. We have seen how this is the most logical outcome of the cycle, and the table bears it out. Thus our proposition that the cycle is most likely to originate in an incomplete household – one parent dead – and end in a sibling household seems to be true for most cases. The logical extension of it, if there are children, is a system of consanguineous households – nepotal in fact, on the model of the Nayar of southwest India or the Ashanti of

Table 15. *Changes in household composition over time of twenty people in natolocal residence*

Household type	Time		
	At marriage	1963	1965
Sibling	2	10	13
Widow	13	6	4
Nepotal	1	2	2
Extended	1	1	0
Conjugal	3	1	1

Ghana. But this never seems to have crystallized into a total pattern on Tory, and the reasons are clear. There is a strain toward conjugal households, and most people live in them. Other forms of household are a compromise and are recognized as such. A sibling–natolocal household, for example, is definitely a second-best household, but it is preferable to other arrangements. Thus, it will not usually be continued into another generation if the young people can find some way to set up a household of their own. As I have said, we are not dealing here with "rules of residence," but with factors affecting decisions. There are "rules" here, but not regulations.

Our 1963 sibling–natolocal cases, therefore, represent one version of this compromise. Some of them had started as widow households, but in others, the partners had waited for the death of the remaining parent before marrying; which probably explains the seemingly very late age of marriage of the women. In turn, this reflects the strength of parental opposition.

For the situation after 1965 I have only a few details from letters. Households, 6, 7, 8, and 9 have ceased to be natolocal. The couple in 7 and 8 have rented a house from an islander who is away, while the man in 9 has finally moved in with his wife despite the continuing weeping and protestations of his brother and mother. He continues, however, to spend most of his time in the natal home. The old lady in 5 had died, giving us yet another sibling household. Although we have lost a couple of natolocal households, of the new marriages on the island, at least two are natolocal – for the moment.

Because the data are available, a couple of points can be cleared up before we move on to a final discussion. We have agreed that it appears likely that natolocal residence is more likely to start with an incomplete household than with one that contains two parents. Because there is a cycle involved, it is hard to use the extant marriages alone to look at this without household histories. But let us, as they say, ask the data about it and see what they say. Table 16 shows, for all married couples (1963), the number of parents who were alive at marriage out of the number it was possible to get data on. Thus for our sibling–natolocal group there were twenty possible parents, and we have data on sixteen. Of these, six were alive at the time of the marriage (if we count the rather odd case of the father who died on the same day). At the other end of the table, the conjugal–virilocal cases, we have fifty parents, of whom twenty-six were alive at the time of the marriage.

These rather crude figures can, by inspection, give us some leads.

Table 16. *Numbers and percentages of parents alive at marriage by household type and mode of residence*

Household type	Mode of residence							
	Natolocal		Uxorilocal		Virilocal		Total	
Sibling	6/16	37%	0/0	—	1/3	—	7/19	36%
Widow	6/10	60%	0/0	—	0/0	—	9/14	65%
Nepotal	2/4	—	2/2	—	6/10	60%	10/16	62%
Extended	2/2	—	12/12	100%	14/19	74%	28/33	84%
Conjugal	2/2	—	12/25	64%	26/50	52%	44/77	57%
Total	18/34	52%	33/43	77%	47/82	57%	98/159	61%

Outstanding is the high total of parents alive at marriage in the extended cases, whatever the form of residence. On average, 84 percent of the parents were alive. This makes sense, because with the younger couple in an extended household by definition there is an older couple alive. It does indicate, however, that there is no trend in the perpetuation of extended households, because for the older couples at least, some of their parents were dead when they married. The sibling–natolocal cases show what we know anyway: Only 37 percent of the parents were alive at marriage. But in the marriages where we now have widow–natolocal households, 60 percent were alive when the couple married.

The interesting figure, however, is that for the conjugal households, which we might have expected to be the opposite of the sibling–natolocal and widow–natolocal ones. True, there are more parents alive at marriage here – 64 percent and 52 percent – but the latter figure is lower than for widow households and not much higher than the sibling ones. If we take our average figure from the totals column – 61 percent – we can compare the others with it to give an idea of relative strengths. Figure 27 shows the relative positioning. The categories "extended" and "uxorilocal" are consistently above the average, whereas "conjugal," "sibling," and "natolocal" are below. "Widow" and "nepotal" hover around the average mark.

The low number of parents alive at marriage in the natolocal case was related, as we saw, to the relatively late age of marriage of the partners, especially the women. What are the facts in the other cases? Table 17 shows the average age at marriage for men and women in each household type. (Where there were only data on one case, or where the cell only contained one case, I have not given an "average" because it would obviously be meaningless. But where there are several cases in a cell the

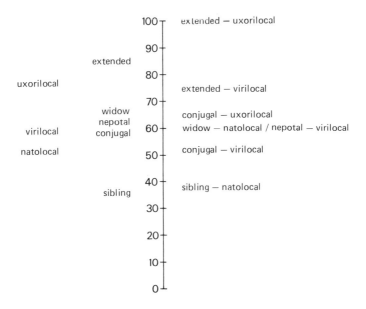

Figure 27. Relative positions of household types and modes of marital residence with respect to percentage of parents alive at time of marriage.

figures are revealing.) The average age for all marriages is 35.1 for males and 31.2 for females, so we can see again the relative positions. Sibling–natolocal, as we know, comes out very high, but so does extended–virilocal for both males and females, while extended–uxorilocal and conjugal–uxorilocal come out very low. This is because the extended–virilocal cases are from the older generation of the extended households, who married later and had fewer parents alive than the younger generation, which in turn is predominantly uxorilocal, and which married very young by island standards and had all its parents alive. Again, this may represent an absolute historical change, but it at least reinforces the fact that there is a cycle involved here and not a perpetuation of household residence types over time.

Our conjugal–virilocal cases, both male and female, hover exactly around the average, the female being exactly average. They share this position with the nepotal–virilocal cases. Equally, as we saw, there is little to distinguish the sibling–natolocal and extended–virilocal cases on this dimension. Putting together the two dimensions, however, we get some clear differences. Figure 28 shows these, with the two axes of "average age at marriage" and "percentage of parents alive at marriage." The

Table 17. *Average age at marriage of males and females by household type and mode of residence*

| Household type | Mode of residence | | | | | |
| | Natolocal | | Uxorilocal | | Virilocal | |
	Male	Female	Male	Female	Male	Female
Sibling	38.2	39.8	—	—	—	—
Widow	35.5	26.5	—	—	—	—
Nepotal	—	—	--	—	35.0	30.6
Extended	—	—	26.6	22.5	38.5	34.5
Conjugal	—	—	33.3	26.7	34.9	31.2

Average for Males = 35.1
Average for Females = 31.2

dotted lines cross at about the average of each (roughly 33 years for marriage and 60 percent for parents alive). (It is interesting that in Leyton's description of a County Down village, he found 82 percent of marriages there took place after the death of the parents; see Notes). I have given, for convenience, a combined score for the ages of men and women, because they are not, except in the widow–natolocal case, very different. We are interested in relative positioning, which comes out just as well with the combined score. (In the one exceptional case, we have only two examples giving the aberrant female score, so we cannot be too certain of it in any event).

We can see at a glance, then, that the really big difference is between extended–uxorilocal and sibling–natolocal. These are the two extremes. And, strangely, they are also the two extremes in island ideology. We can perhaps best sum up the positions in between by labeling each as follows:

extended–uxorilocal:	marry very young, all parents alive
extended–virilocal:	marry old, three-quarters of parents alive
conjugal–uxorilocal:	marry average, more than half of parents alive
widow–natolocal:	men marry old (women young?) at least half of parents alive
nepotal–virilocal:	marry average, at least half of parents alive
conjugal–virilocal:	marry average, about half of parents alive
sibling–natolocal:	marry very old, three-quarters of parents dead

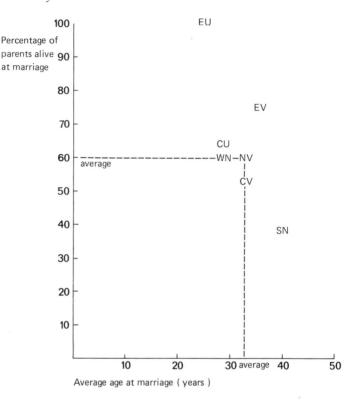

Figure 28. Household type and mode of residence by average age at marriage and percentage of parents alive at marriage.
Key: EU = extended–uxorilocal
         EV = extended–virilocal
         CU = conjugal–uxorilocal
         WN = widow–natolocal
         NV = nepotal–virilocal
         CV = conjugal–virilocal
         SN = sibling–natolocal

(I have not distinguished between males and females on the "number of parents alive" dimension simply because there was not any great difference.)

In all cases after the first two, then, the tendency to later and later marriage (in absolute, not island, terms) will mean that the cycle is in about half of the cases bound to start with a "widow" household. We saw this clearly when looking at the natolocal cases and their development over time. What these figures and tables show, even in the absence of specific histories, is that it is just as likely to be true in, for example, the conjugal–virilocal cases, where marriage takes place after thirty, and 48 percent of the parents are dead at the time of the marriage. Again, we must remember that the category "conjugal–virilocal" includes both the new households of newlyweds who actually started that way as well as the old households that might have achieved this status after a couple of stages of the cycle. Thus I know of four cases in this category of older couples (a quarter of the total) who started life in widow–natolocal households, moving later to form, in one case, a widow–uxorilocal household and then a conjugal–virilocal one (the man moved back into his own house when his brothers emigrated), and in another changing to sibling–natolocal then to conjugal–virilocal. In the other two cases, the move was straight from widow–natolocal to conjugal–virilocal on the death of the old parent.

Thus it becomes clearer and clearer that the fifty-two marriages, as currently distributed between household types, represent stages in a domestic cycle that is likely to start late in life with an incomplete household, and end, most typically, as a conjugal or sibling household. Extended and nepotal households seem to represent unstable stages in this cycle and not end products. Some that I know of went as follows:

1. Conjugal–natolocal → widow–natolocal → sibling–natolocal → sibling–uxorilocal → conjugal–uxorilocal . . .
2. Sibling–natolocal → sibling–virilocal → conjugal–virilocal . . .
3. Conjugal–virilocal → extended–uxorilocal → widow–uxorilocal → conjugal–uxorilocal . . .
4. Sibling–virilocal → nepotal–natolocal → conjugal–virilocal . . .
5. Widow–natolocal → sibling–natolocal . . .

(all can be continued)

These are rather simple, and greater complexity can be introduced because, of course, several kinds of marital residence can coexist in the same household – a virilocal couple with a daughter living natolocally, and one with an uxorilocal husband, for example, and many more similar possibilities. But once the idea of the cycle is established, all the variations become easy to place, and even other possibilities than the types listed here can be envisaged and probably have existed: Some cycles, though, for the reasons we have examined, will be more likely to occur than others.

We saw above how nonmarriage was, in many parts of Ireland, a solution to the problem of unwanted in-laws moving in or siblings moving out. This solution also exists on Tory in a number of cases. Of the thirteen sibling households, five did not have married members. In two cases these were a brother and two sisters, in the others, respectively, three brothers and one sister, three brothers and two sisters, and two brothers and one sister. One of the first two cases involved a brother with two widowed sisters, so this we must exclude, but in the other cases all were unmarried. They do, however, as is easily seen, constiute only a small proportion of the total households, and clearly this is not a favored solution. We must add to these, however, some of the nepotal households where the "uncles" are literally that: several old unmarried brothers with a niece to look after them. The "married" member, of the nepotal households that have married members, is usually the niece and not the uncles. If we take all the nepotal cases and the four nonmarrying sibling cases, we have twelve out of the sixty-one households where "nonmarriage" has been tried (widows, by definition, have tried marriage). This is twenty-one percent of the total – respectable but low. If we take the better measure of the percentage of unmarried adults of marriageable age (who are no longer "dependent," that is, and have households of their own with or without other adults) as a percentage of all such adults, it works out as 24 out of 126, or 11 percent. Not even respectable, and very low. Clearly, natolocality and attendant solutions – uxorilocality, extended families – are preferred to nonmarriage on Tory.

Arensberg and Kimball related the phenomenon of late marriage and the large number of nonmarriages in the rest of Ireland (or at least in County Clare) to the problems of farm inheritance and the custom of not handing over the farm until late in the owner's life, when the heir could marry, and the girls be provided with dowries. This does not seem to be much of a factor influencing Tory marriage, which can be either quite late or quite early, depending on the solution chosen. On the whole, it is late. Dowries do not exist on Tory. Even so, in some cases, I was told, there was resistance to a sister marrying; for example, because her husband might demand that she take her share of the family land. Her brothers might not want this to happen. Land, as we saw in Chapter 4, is very important, but joint ownership and the joint provision for all members of households from the land attached to them meant that every household ended up with much the same share. It may, however, have been a more important consideration in the old days with a larger population and more pressure on the land. The natolocal solution may again have been preferred because if the sister stayed with the house there would have been less likelihood of her wanting to subdivide the land to the benefit of the household to which she moved. This is not often cited as a reason today. Much more popular are the "she must look after her own people" or the "it's too much trouble to move" reasons. These, plus the obvious and genuine sadness that the loss of a member provokes in a tightly knit family, especially if it lacks one of the parents or even both, is currently more important to the islanders than the land considerations. Add yet again the dislike of extended households – of in-laws "coming in," plus the hostility to the idea of marriage from both parents and siblings, and one has the mix that provokes the household cycle with all its peculiarities. A dog and a beast a man can depend on, and even parents and siblings, but a wife is a different matter: If not exactly an enemy, she is never, in the significant Irish terminology, a "friend" – a true relative. Nor is a husband for that matter; the proverb works both ways. But the overall result on Tory is a complexity of patterns of marital residence, household type, family composition, and age at marriage that are probably a unique mixture of common Irish trends and peculiar island characteristics. These patterns are another example of the charming ingenuity of the Tory social system in its constant rhythm of adjustment and adaptation. This rhythm manifests an almost breathtaking subtlety, reaching into something I can only characterize as the wisdom of ages or some such cliché. But it is, truly, the distillation of a profound collective experience, woven into a social fabric at once strong and flexible, and thus totally responsive to the exigencies of the environment in the fullest sense. This, rather than towers, crosses, and crumbling shrines, will be perhaps the real memorial to the people of Tory Island.

8

Epilogue:
structures and strangers

Ní bhfuil scím ar mhínleach maolchnoc;
Ní bhfuil tartha ar thalamh aolbhaigh;
Ní bhfuil ceol i mbeolaibh éanlaith;
Do bhalbuigh cláirseach bhláithgheal Eireann.

Aodhagán O Rathaille

The full gamut of social processes is run on Tory Island: There is absolute, cumulative change through time (or history if you prefer); there is abrupt social transformation; there is nice, balanced equilibrium; there is rhythm, ebb, and flow; there are cycles; there is acculturation; there is progressive adaptation; there is continuity; there is dissolution and decay. Above all, there is survival: The islanders are masters of it. They will change the rules, change the strategies, change the game; but they will survive. The strategies they cling to are indeed long term; they are not interested in maximizing profits over a short period, but in maximizing survival over centuries. If, to the exasperation of planners, they, like so many "ignorant peasants," stick to their superstitions, we can be sure it is because these superstitions have maximized survival – good years and bad – over many generations of experience. The quaint customs turn out so often on close inspection to be the minimax plays par excellence in the game of survival.

To the landlord – well-meaning enough as he was – neat strips, a smaller population, and primogeniture were sensible reforms. The islanders obligingly striped the land and kept their customs, which, as we have seen ad nauseam, worked well enough in any case. They kept the balance between household need and available soil, without either agricultural surveys or sociological inquiries.

But the social structure is flexible. It realizes (if we dare anthropomorphize it) that what will work for inheritance of land will not work as well for the new problem of recruiting large boat crews, or for the composition of viable households. Yet if we must look somewhere for some central principle, some relationship around which all the various substructures and cycles seem to revolve, it has to be the sibling bond. (There is no need to be afraid to use the word: It is not an invention of psychologists – who quite erroneously have taken to using "sib" anyway. We have no other word in English meaning "brothers and/or sisters," but the Anglo-Saxons in their wisdom endowed us with this one.)

The bond between siblings, as we saw dramatically, provides the pivot on which the household cycle turns, the fulcrum on which the inheritance of land balances, and the root from which the boat crews grow. It overrides the weaker conjugal bond in cases where there is a clash, although it can itself be said to be derived from the bond between mother and children.

Thus, when a boat crew was recruited, if it were small it could consist of brothers alone, plus, perhaps, a patrilateral cousin or two: the children of brothers. If it had to be larger, then sisters' husbands and mothers' brothers were likely to be approached. The result would be a series of chains of siblings variously linked through alliance and kinship to the original core. With the household it was more obvious still. The siblings – originally probably clinging to a widowed mother – continued to live together despite marriage to outsiders for at least a portion, and often for the whole, of their married lives. The unique features of the Tory household cycle tended to rest on this ever-present probability, despite changes over time.

Even if disrupted by separate household residence, the sibling bond remained, expressed in the naming structure. Formal names aside (and they were rarely if ever used), two siblings were readily identified by their sharing of a string of ancestral names, which they retained after marriage and which would be unique to them. For dealing with the outside world, a woman might be "wife of" someone or other; but to the island she was still "offspring of" her ancestors, in common with her siblings.

Again, even if the siblings separated at some point (insofar as anyone can be considered to separate as long as they live on the island) they were united in the scheme of land inheritance – in the clann. Truly the "land of the marriage" would have gone to some, whereas others would have inherited the rest, and yet others gotten the house or nothing at all. But we must recall that this is, in essence, a system of usufruct: Someone "holds" the land; he or she does not really own it. The title, to use the legalism, rests with the corporation – and the effective executive of the corporation (the clann) is usually a group of siblings.

Dying without heirs – or with heirs abroad and uninterested – although not common, occurred often enough for the claims on land to be remembered and kept alive through the memory of genealogy. A sibling of a holder and his/her children always had this claim, even if they were abroad or had waived it. It is even hard to see how, except by default, one can ever really waive a claim: It is only a claim to use the land that is effectively waived. If, for example, a sister marries a man with land, what she does not claim from her other siblings is the *produce* of the patrimony, which they may use.

Some readers of this analysis have suggested that there must be a connection between sibling households and land ownership. I have stressed other factors, such as sentiment and the pressure on housing (when there was a much larger population). But this is not literally earthy enough for some, or "structural" enough for others. It is hard, however, to see the exact connection. Let us look at Figure 29. Here we have a household of a brother and a sister (1), both of whom are married. The brother will usually farm the jointly owned land, providing from it, and from his catch (in predole days), a small contribution to his wife's household (2). But this would be usually no more, it was told to me, than would "make up for the meals he took there." His sister's husband (in 3) likewise would provide for her. But say the sister's husband had no land. Then the sibling pair in 1 might well have divided theirs, and the husband would work it and provide for the sister out of it, as well as contributing a little to his own natal household (3). In the meantime, of course, the brother's wife's brother (in 2) would be farming "her" land and performing likewise.

The outcome is that *all households* concerned end up with about as much land and produce as the others. Some of the produce of each household flows into other households. It would be different, of course, if there were children, or if there were a household of two sisters married but living alone, etc. This is just one possible schematic alternative. But it serves to illustrate the kind of relationships that could spring up among a string of related households.

The point is that division of the land as such, as opposed to the disposition of its produce, is contingent on marriage, *not* residence. The land in household 2 was divided because the husband's brother (or brothers) perhaps married earlier and got the land of the marriage. So the husband farmed the land of his wife in household 1. The "flow" of produce can be seen at work. The only way that either nondivision of the land, or retention of all its produce, would ensue would be *if the siblings did not marry at all;* although this happened, it was rare. As we saw in Chapter 7, there might have been resistance to sisters marrying for just this reason, but if they did then a division of land was likely whether or not they moved.

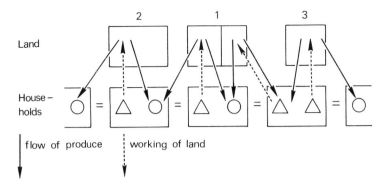

Figure 29. Land, produce, and sibling households.

By and large, in any case, the majority of the produce from land attached to a household returned to it, whoever farmed the land. The islanders were always flexible about this, and "flows" could be adjusted to meet needs. Ecologists and students of exchange might even see in the system a hidden hedge against the failure of crops or the like in some areas and not others. Because produce was flowing in this way, somebody would always get something, whatever happened.

But we should not get carried away with the importance of the products of the land: They were hardly spectacular. They were certainly necessary, but we are talking of subsistence farming at its most subsistent here. The non-living-in husband's contribution over a year might be a few sacks of potatoes, some barley for the chickens, and a few pounds of oats – and that would be substantial. The major contribution, before cash in the form of wages, profits, the dole, and pensions became important and rendered produce even less decisive, would have been fish, and that had nothing to do with land.

I am sure that considerations of "keeping the land in the family" occurred and might well have been important in decisions about moving in some cases. But I cannot see how they could have been a "structural" feature, or anything such, for the reasons advanced.

In the inheritance of land, then, we get flux and change over time resulting in a long-term equilibrium – not perfect but very near, in which the division of the land and the needs of the users stay in balance. This takes generations to work out and contrasts with the seasonal need to recruit boat crews. That the former (land) depends on descent as a principle whereas the latter leans on kin networks and alliances shows both the importance of kinship in each case and the strikingly different use of it in the two different spheres. Social usages that are going to capitalize on descent must be those that unfold over many generations. The network, by contrast, is there to be used immediately for immediate purposes.

There is another kind of "cycle" that might be noted, in addition to that of the domestic group. It is not unique to Tory, but must be true of any small community that is largely endogamous and where marriage is prohibited within the range of first and/or second cousins, as in Catholic peasant Europe (the prohibition has been extended to fifth cousins and beyond). Again we can take our sibling pair as the focus of this cycle. Figure 30 shows how it would work over two stages of the cycle. The siblings and children of siblings cannot marry (first cousins). These have to look elsewhere than their closest kin. However, the children of first cousins can marry and, what is more, in a small community probably must. It is going to be hard indeed to find anyone in the community available for marriage who, not being a first cousin, is not a second. Every third generation, then, we should see a "turning in" of marriage on second cousins. This will not be 100 percent, but it will be there. It will

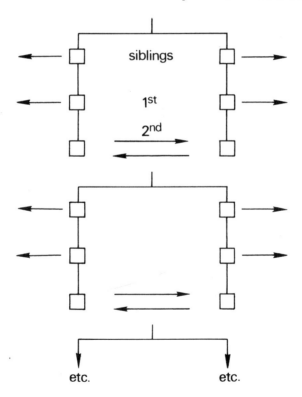

Figure 30. Cycles of cousin marriage.

be more effective – and the cycles one generation longer – with a second-cousin prohibition. Thus, although there is no rule of marriage with a second cousin, there is a de facto cycling effect that will produce one. Depending on how marriages have gone in previous generations, there may even be a shortage of second cousins, and dispensations will be needed to marry first cousins (about 12 percent officially on Tory – probably higher).

We are used to looking at such cycling in systems that *prescribe* cousin marriage. What we see here is that in a small community (up to 400 souls) such marriage cycles are inevitable with only a negative rule. Of course, they lack specificity – any second or third cousin will do; it does not have to be a mother's mother's brother's daughter's daughter or anything so exact. But several of the effects might be similar. Thus, land which has been dispersed from the clann core during two generations of outmarriage could easily recombine in the third generation. It would flow outward, as it were, and then flow back in again, thus providing a rhythm, over successive three-generation cycles, of dispersal and reintegration that would itself work against fragmentation over time. It would again, like the flows of produce between households, but over much longer periods of course, work to redistribute land among households with similar ecological "hedging" consequences. Land, like produce, could thus be seen as constantly flowing between units; combining, dividing, dispersing, and recombing over time.

The ideal system is never exactly realized because of historical changes in tenure systems, outmarriage, adoption, and emigration. The faint outlines of it can be seen in the genealogies where second- and third-cousin marriages abound – and where in the higher generations many are said to have been such (between fair and dark grandchildren for example) even though the genealogical evidence for them no longer exists in the already overstocked memories of the old ones. We would need more data in greater detail over six to ten generations to get any idea of how closely the actual pattern resembled the theoretical possibilities.

Absolute change, cyclical fluctuations, long-term equilibrium, abrupt adaptive strategies – and survival overall. Every "rule" has its modifier. The holy family is modified by the sibling household; the partible inheritance by the land of the marriage. Imposed solutions of externally perceived problems are molded to fit the wisdom of long-tried structures. But, in the end, the money economy, the dependence on subsidies, emigration, the aging population, and the decline of land use will all cause the absolutes of historical change to predominate over the cycles and balances of traditional continuity. A vibrant, demographically balanced society could cope with the cash-crop intrusion of large-scale fishing, for example; but can an older, subsidized, dependent population in a money economy cope with inflation?

In the end it is the strangers – not just the British now but all of nonpeasant Ireland and the Europe of which it is an enthusiastic part – that call the tune. After years of subtle resistance based on isolation, the very isolation has turned against them. When they could be left to their subsistence and ignored, they could survive. Now, along with the crofters of Scotland and the outporters of Newfoundland, they are being sucked into the welfare state which, paradoxically, cannot let them live in their culture of relative poverty but must, because it cannot tolerate their poverty, destroy their culture. With the very best of intentions. The game of hide and seek, dodge and dissemble, talk slowly and think fast, stay low and speak quietly, and just occasionally stand up and hit back is almost over. Even so, I should be delighted to be proved wrong. But we shall see, as they say – tchifimid; that's how it goes – sin a' dóigh. After all, the strangers have come and gone before. There was that time of the wreck of the *W*_____. hadn't it been brought onto the rocks by the ever-present and sometimes helpful ghosts? Not that the ghosts are always so helpful. As it was told to me (and the translation is very very free):

"Wasn't it Paddy up on the hill saw his brother Anton working away over in the field and waved to him and he waved back and went on working at the turf there, and when Paddy got home what did he find but all there sobbing and wailing and his brother lying out on the bed, dead as a board. It was a 'dead-alive man' he'd seen – fear marbh-bheo – already judged and working out his time in purgatory. And didn't Paddy have the great shock in his heart and drop down like he was dead himself when he knew what he'd seen; and wasn't it only when the priest came with the holy water, and his granny with a drop of poteen, that he came back to life again?

"But when the *W*_____ was wrecked, the captain himself – for they were all saved, praised be the saints, by our prayers – told us, and crossing himself twice as he told it, that someone had taken the wheel from his hands as they rounded the point, someone who just appeared on the bridge from nowhere. The crew saw him: a big fellow with black hair and two front teeth missing. They all froze in a heap with fright and this fellow pulls the ship around onto the rocks gently like and then disappears. Well, now, and wasn't that the ghost of Anton himself, God rest his soul, and him not dead these three weeks but out there working for us like the good fellow he was.

"Well – we had the stuff off the ship and into the caves before the sun came up, but the damned revenue man was already on his way – his soul to the devil. What a prancer and a mincer he was, and a bully too. Always dressed like he was off to a wedding with the starched cuffs and the pretty white shirt. He was there by midmorning, and it was the devil of a hot day and a drought on all the island. 'I'll have it all back,' he shouts at us, 'ye thieving rogues' – and we saying nothing and grinning a lot the while. 'I'll wipe them smirks off your silly faces in short order,' says he. Now, hadn't Willy D.____ just the week before buried an old sheep that fell and broke its leg and rotted in a gully before he found it? He'd buried this rotten sheep in some soft earth, and he begins acting funny round the spot – darting up, then running away as if he hadn't meant to look there. 'Ah ha ha!' says Mr. Fancysuit, 'you'll not fool me.' He runs over all aquivering with eagerness and excitement when he sees the loose sods. He peels off his coat and shoves both arms up to the armpits down into the rotting, stinking belly of the poor old sheep and comes out covered with dung and carcass.

"Well, you should have heard the laughing and the screeching. We could scarcely stand up for laughing, and him running around like a mad thing looking for water and vomiting and screaming, 'Give me some water now ye heathen, for the love of God give me some water.' And it was Mary D.____ who says to him, all full of sorrow and sympathy, 'Oh, sir,' says she, 'isn't it the pity now, there's scarcely a drop at all for drinking even on the whole island. Oh, and this such a wonderful hot day, too.' And he has to run down the slip and slop about in the water to get it all off, and spoil his lovely suit in the doing of it.

"Well, they bring round the boat and off he goes cursing and weeping and shaking his little fists. And he never did come back, no matter what was wrecked, from that time out – though he vowed he'd have us all in hell or worse for shitting up his new shirt. Ah, 'twas a fine time we had then. There are no wrecks now. Sin a' dóigh."

Let us hope we may not, after all, have to mourn with the great O Rathaille, whose words in Gaelic began, and in English shall end, this chapter, and this book:

> There is no fortune from rough-hill pastures;
> There is no produce from the lime-light land;
> There is no music in the mouths of birds;
> Silent the bright-flowering harp of Eire.

Appendix 1. List of landowners from Tithe Applotment Rolls (1830s)

1. James Diver
2. Hugh Dougan
3. Patrick Horisky
4. James Dougan
5. Philip Rodgers
6. Owen Dougan
7. Sarah Heraghty
8. James Bawn Dougan
9. James Dougan (blind)
10. Edward Heraghty
11. Owen Doughan jnr.
12. Dennis Doughan
13. Mary Doughan (widow)
14. Hugh Dougan Beg
15. Hugh McLafferty
16. Owen Rodgers
17. William Doughan (Bryan's Son)
18. James Doughan
19. Charles Doughan
20. Dennis Diver
21. Peter Rodgers
22. James Heraghty
23. Hugh Diver
24. Shaun Diver
25. Patrick McElroy
26. Alexander Doughan
27. Patrick Doughan
28. James Horisky
29. Shaun Dougan
30. Thomas Horisky
31. Dennis McGinley
32. Catherine McGinley
33. Dennis Corran
34. Owen Doughan
35. Simidin Doughan
36. Catherine Meenan (widow)
37. William Roe Doughan
38. Bryan M'Cafferty
39. William Doughan jnr.
40. Old Mary Doughan
41. Shaun Doughan
42. Shaun More Doughan
43. Sarah Coyle
44. Michael Meenan
45. Patrick Bawn Rodgers
46. Daniel Doughan
47. Edward Dougan
48. Hugh Doughan
49. Nail Herraghty

Appendix 2.
Woodhouse's list
supplied to Getty (1845)

Mr. Woodhouse, the proprietor of the island, has furnished the following list of his present tenants' names, which is preserved, as showing those of most common occurrence on the island: –

1. Patrick Dugan
2. James Doohan, Senr.
2. Edward Doohan, (Shane)
3. Owen Dugan
3. Shane Doohan, (Mackan)
4. Roger Doohan
5. Shane Doohan, Senr.
5. Widow Grace Doohan
6. Widow B. Doohan
6. Pat Doohan, (Daniel)
7. Owen Doohan, (Nelly)
7. Edward Doohan, (Margt.)
8. Widow W. Doohan
8. William Doohan, (Roe)
9. James Doogan, (Roe)
9. John Duugan
10. Owen Doohan, (Oge)
10. Hugh Doohan
11. Denis Doohan
11. Edward Doohan, (Roe)
12. Bryan Doohan, (Shane)
12. John Dugan
13. Widow Mage Doohan
13. Bryan Doohan, (More)
14. Owen and Teague Doohan
14. Alexander Doohan
15. Pat Curran
15. Pat Rogers, Junr.
16. Owen Diver
16. Anthony Rogers
17. Daniel Rogers
17. Phelim Rogers
18. Daniel Whoriskey
19. Denis McGinley, Senr.
19. John Whoriskey
20. James M'Clafferty
20. Michael Meenan
21. Denis Diver, (late Pat Carrohy)
22. James Diver, (Hugh)
22. John Meenan
23. Daniel Whoriskey, Junr.
23. Bryan Curran
24. Edward Diver
24. Neal Heraghty
25. Denis Diver, Senr.
25. Owen Whoriskey
26. Mary or Pat Diver
26. Pat Rodgers, Senr.
27. James Diver, (Sally)
27. Owen M'Carroll
28. James Herraghty
29. Thomas Meenan
30. Shane Diver
30. Edward Herraghty
31. Shane Diver, Junr.
32. Denis Curran
33. Owen Doohan, (King)
33. William Doohan, (Oge)
34. William Doohan, (Nelly)
34. William Mackan, (or Anthony Rogers)

Appendix 3. List of landowners from Griffith's valuation (1857)

West Town

1. Philimy Rogers
2. Daniel Rogers
3. James Doohin (Ned)
4. Denis Doohin
5. William Rogers
6. Jack Devir (Hugh)
7. Edward Herarty
8. Sally Doohin
9. John Doogan (Left)
10. Edward Rogers
11. Bryan Doohin (More)
12. Grace Doohin (Shane)
13. Alexander Doohin
14. John Doogan
15. Teague Doohin
16. Daniel Whiriskey
17. William Doogan
18. John Martin
19. Hugh Doogan
20. Ed. Doogan (Rowe)
21. Edw. Doohin (Shane)
22. Roger Doohin (Big)
23. Jas. Doohin (Nancy)
24. Wm. Doohin (Rowe)
25. Hugh Devir
26. Michael Mooney
28. James Doohan (Hugh)

Middle Town

29. Jno. Doohin (Mackin)
30. Bryan Curran
31. Ptk. Doohin (Danl.)
32. Jno. Doohin (Nelly)

33. Denis Diver (Grace)
34. John Whiriskey
35. Roger Doohin (Shane More)
36. Denis McGinley
37. Wm. Doohin (Rowe)
38. Jas. Doohin (Nancy)
39. Jas. Doohin (James)
40. Owen Shiriskey
41. Patrick Shiriskey (Owen)
42. James M'Cafferty
43. Charles Rogers
44. Jas. Doohin (Danl.)
45. Roger Doohin (Big)
46. Jack Devir (Hugh)

East Town

47. Neal Herarty
48. Edward Devir
49. James Devir
50. John Devir (James)
51. Patrick Devir
52. Grace Devir
53. Thomas Minnion
54. Patrick Rogers (sen.)
55. Mackin Rogers (sen.)
56. Patrick Rogers
57. Patrick Doogan
58. John Minnion
59. Denis Devir (James)
60. Catherine Minnion
61. Anthy. Rogers (Patt.)
62. Patrick Currin

63. James Devir (Hugh)
64. Margaret Doohin
65. James Herarty
66. Bryan Doohin
67. John Doogan (Ned)

68. Patrick Rogers, jun.
69. Owen Doohin (King)
70. Maggy Rogers
71. Patk. Herarty (King)

Notes

1. Prologue: myths and masters

The basic piece of historical writing on Tory, which includes an account of its history and legends, is Edmund Getty's "The Island of Tory; Its History and Antiquities," *Ulster Journal of Archaeology*, vol. 1, 1853, pp. 27–37, 106–16, and 140–58. This, in turn, leans heavily on John O'Donovan (ed.), *Annala Rioghachta Eireann* (Annals of the Kingdom of Ireland by the Four Masters) (Dublin: 1851). Although Getty also relied on earlier translations, these lacked the informative notes so valuable in O'Donovan's version. Further scattered accounts of early Tory history can be found in the standard lives of Columba and in the various annals, e.g., W. A. Hennessey (ed.), *The Annals of Ulster* (Dublin, 1887).

The various "high" versions of the Tory legends concerning Balor, etc., can be found in T. P. Cross and D. H. Slover, *Ancient Irish Tales* (Dublin: Allen Figgis, 1969). The account of the lady archaeologist referred to is J. M. Sidebotham, "The Promontory Fort on Tory Island," *Ulster Journal of Archaeology*, vol. 12, 1949. Sir William Petty's *Civil Survey of Ireland* is edited by Robert C. Simmington (Dublin: Irish Manuscripts Commission, 1931). The material on Tory is in vol. 3. The "Ulster Plantation" is described by the Rev. George Hill, *An Historical Account of the Plantation in Ulster at the Commencement of the Seventeenth Century: 1608–1620* (Belfast, 1877).

The purchase of Tory by Joule is on record at the Registry of Deeds in Dublin (15 Feb. 1861). The extraordinary pamphlet, *Tory Island Letters*, by the Reverend James J. O'Donnell, C. C., resident priest of Tory, "the Torroneans," and B. St. J. B. Joule, J. P. for the County of Lancaster, etc. (Rothesay, n.d.), is very rare. The only copy I know of is in the British Library of Political and Economic Science, London School of Economics. There is no date, but it is clearly 1883, and although no publisher is given, it would appear to be Joule himself, who added footnotes favorable to his position. The admiralty kindly supplied me with its version of the *Wasp* disaster – the rest is common knowledge! The records of the Congested Districts Board were made available by the Land Commission, Dublin. The work of the Board is discussed in Chapter 2, and appropriate references are given there. There are numerous stray references to Tory in travel books of the nineteenth century, and some interesting brief accounts of social conditions from time to time. I have not cited them all here, but of particular interest are W. R. Le Fanu, *Seventy Years of Irish Life* (1893); W. Harkin, *The Scenery and Antiquity of North-west Donegal* (1893); Stephen Gwynn, *Highways and Byways in Donegal and Antrim* (London, 1899); A. McFarland, *Hours in Vacation* (1849). Also see E. Maguire, *History of the Diocese of Raphoe* (1920).

2. *The island and the people*

The best geological description of Tory is H. G. Williams, "Tory Island, County Donegal," *Irish Geography,* vol. 2, no. 4, 1952. A brief account is also available in James Andrew Hunter, "An Interpretation of the Land-scape of Tory Island," B.A. honors thesis, Queen's University, Belfast, 1960. The earliest account is C. L. Gieseche, *Account of a Mineralogical Excursion to the County of Donegal* (1826). The work of the CDB is admirably described in W. L. Micks, *History of the Congested Districts Board,* Dublin, 1925. The various "baseline" and "confidential" reports of the Board (now with the Land Commission) also provide valuable material. "Kings" and shore divisions, as well as a wealth of general detail, can be found in E. Estyn Evans, *Irish Heritage* (Dundalk: Dundalgan Press, 1942). My own article, "Tory Island," in B. Benedict (ed.), *Problems of Smaller Territories* (London: Athlone Press, University of London, 1967), gives a general background from which some of this chapter (the demography in particular) is derived. For those who read Gaelic, there is a delightful book by a former parish priest of Tory, An t-Athair Eoghan O Colm, *Toraigh na dTonn* (Dublin: Foilseacháin Náisiúnta Tta., 1971). Mici Mac-Gabhan's *Rotha Mór an tSaoil,* first published in 1958, was translated as *The Hard Road to Klondike* by Valentin Iremonger, (London: Routledge, 1962).

3. *Genealogy: principles and practice;* and
4. *Kinship and naming*

The Reverand Patrick Dineen's *Foclóir Gaedhilge agus Béarla* was first published in 1904. The plates were destroyed during the Easter rebellion, 1916, and a subsequent edition was published by the Irish Texts Society, Dublin, 1927. This is the edition referred to throughout.

The "standard method" for collecting genealogical material was developed by W. H. R. Rivers, "A genealogical method of collecting social and vital statistics," *Journal of the Royal Anthropological Institute,* vol. 30, 1900, pp. 74–82.

"Cognatic" or "bilateral" descent groups did not receive much attention in anthropology until taken up by Firth and Goodenough. See, for example, Ward H. Goodenough, "A Problem in Malayo-Polynesian Social Organization," *American Anthropoligst,* vol. 57, 1955, pp. 71–83; for a summary of his views: R. Firth, "Bilateral Descent Groups: an Operational Viewpoint," in I. Schapera, (ed.), *Studies in Kinship and Marriage* (Occasional Paper of the Royal Anthropological Institute no. 16, London, 1963). These groups are now much discussed and some good descriptive monographs exist (for example H. Scheffler, *Choiseul Island Social Structure,* 1965).

A concentrated discussion of their features appears in my *Kinship and Marriage* (New York: Penguin, 1967), chap. 6.

The quote by Synge is from *The Works of John M. Synge: Volume Three, The Aran Islands* (Dublin: Maunsel, 1910), pp. 160–2.

The whole discussion of personal names here continues and supersedes those that appeared in my "Structure of personal names on Tory Island," *Man,* vol. 63, 1963, pp. 153–5; and the chapter "Personal Names" (chap. 8) in *Encounter with Anthropology* (New York: Harcourt Brace Jovanovich, 1973; Harmondsworth, Eng.: Penguin, 1975). For example, there I recorded Neilí's son as "Eoghan" and not "Eoin." In compounds, the two names sound much alike to the untrained ear. I do not claim the versions here as final, but they are more nearly correct. For the spelling of Gaelic Christian names I have usually followed Patrick Woulfe, *Irish Names for Children* (Dublin: Gill and Macmillan, 1923), except where the islanders were firm in their own preferences.

5. *The land: use, ownership, and inheritance*

A list of place-names from Tory (in Gaelic only) appears in Nollaig O hUrmoltaigh, "Logainmneacha as Toraí, Tír Chonaill," *Dinnseanchas* (Dublin), vol. 2, no. 4, 1967, pp. 99–106.

The "open-field" system is discussed by E. Estyn Evans, "Some survivals of the Irish open-field system," *Geography,* vol. 24, 1939, pp. 24–36. See also his *Irish Heritage.*

The Gweedore reforms are fascinatingly described in Lord George Hill, *Facts from Gweedore: compiled from notes by Lord George Hill, with additions up to the present time,* 4th ed. (Dublin, 1868).

"Rundale" is dealt with generally by D. McCourt, "The Rundale System," Ph.D. thesis, Queen's University, Belfast, 1953; in "The Rundale System in Donegal: its Distribution and Decline," *Donegal Annual,* vol. 3, 1955, pp. 47–60; and in "Traditions of rundale in and around the Sperin Mountains," *Ulster Journal of Archaeology,* vol. 16, 1953, pp. 69–84. See also the Very Rev. P. MacLoinsigh, "Rural villages and the rundale system," *Journal of the County Donegal Historical Society,* vol. 1, 1948, pp. 115–17. There are many other references; I have picked those most relevant to Donegal.

The Griffith survey, available from the Valuation Office, should be referred to for reference purposes as D. Griffith, *General Valuation of Rateable Property in Ireland,* (Dublin: H.M.S.O., 1857). The Tory data are in the volume "The Union of Dunfanaghy."

Again, this discussion supersedes my previous one, "Kinship and Land Tenure on Tory Island," *Ulster Folklife,* vol. 12, 1967, pp. 1–17. There, for example, in discussing the Eoin land, I showed it *all* as coming from Eoin himself, which is not the case. It is interesting, however, that that is how it was *told* to me by one informant. Jogged memories, checking the records, and further cross-checking with other heirs gave the correct picture. The informant in question had, in fact, good reasons for *not* wanting to remember the correct details.

Prefamine landholding is discussed by K. H. Connell, in *The Population of Ireland* (London: Oxford University Press, 1950), and in "Peasant Marriage in Ireland: its Structure and Development since the Famine," *Economic History Review,* vol. 14, 1962, pp. 502–23. See also his "Peasant Marriage in Ireland after the Great Famine," *Past and Present,* vol. 12, 1957, pp. 76–91. Also, Michael Drake "Marriage and Population Growth in Ireland, 1750–1845," *Economic History Review,* vol. 14, 1963, pp. 307–13.

6. The boats: recruitment of crews

The data here are entirely from fieldnotes, and thus there are no references. Micks (see notes for chap. 2) describes the CDB fishing enterprises, whereas those interested in curraghs will find delightful J. Hornell, *British Coracles and Irish Curraghs* (1938). Other such details can be found in T. H. Mason, *The Islands of Ireland* (1930). On the general history of Tory fishing, I was instructed by Dr. Seán O Siadhail, parish priest of Gortahork, who, being interested in the general topic, had kept press cuttings relating to fishing in the area for many years. I have used "curragh" as the anglicized version of what should properly be *curach* in Gaelic.

The Gaelic text of "Amhrán na Scadán" can be found in Father O Colm's book, pp. 192–3. The lines I have mangled are as follows:

> Nach deas an rud na scadáin,
> Ag léimnigh fríd an bhád,
> 'S mo chuíd stócaigh leis na bascaeidí,
> A dtógáil as an snamh.

7. Family, marriage, and household

The discussion of nonmarriage and inheritance referred to in the text is in C. M. Arensberg and S. T. Kimball, *Family and Community in Ireland,* 2d ed. (Cambridge, Mass.: Harvard University Press, 1968).

On illegitimacy and attitudes to it in the rest of Ireland, see K. H. Connell, *Irish Peasant Society,* London: Oxford University Press, 1968, chap. 2.

The idea of "developmental cycles" rather than fixed "rules of residence at marriage" originated in Meyer Fortes, "Time and Social Structure: an Ashanti Case Study," in M. Fortes (ed.), *Social Structure,* London: Oxford University Press, 1949. It was carried on in Jack Goody (ed.), *The Developmental Cycle in Domestic Groups,* Cambridge: Cambridge University Press, 1962, and has now become a standard part of ethnographic analysis.

"Natolocal" was, I believe, originally coined by Professor John Barnes of Cambridge, and I gladly yield precedence to him, even if this was a case of independent invention!

Leyton's description of County Down marriage is: Elliott Leyton, *The One Blood: Kinship and Class in an Irish Village,* Saint Johns: Institute of Social and Economic Research, Memorial University of Newfoundland, 1975.

The residence patterns of the Ashanti are described in Fortes, op. cit. The latest and most complete description of the Nayar is: C. J. Fuller, *The Nayars Today,* Cambridge: Cambridge University Press, 1976.

8. Epilogue: structures and strangers

The quotation is from O Rathaille's "Ar bhás Ghearailt mac Ridere an Ghleanna", (On the death of Gerald, son of the Knight of Glin), verse twenty-four. See Rev. Patrick S. Dinneen and Tadgh O'Donoghue (eds.), *Dánta Aodhgáin Uí Rathaille* (The Poems of Egan O'Rahilly), 2nd Ed., Dublin: Irish Texts Society, 1965. The translation is my own.

Index